Three Language-Arts
Curriculum Models

Three Language-Arts Curriculum Models

Pre-Kindergarten through College

Edited by

Barrett J. Mandel
Douglass College, Rutgers University

National Council of Teachers of English
1111 Kenyon Road, Urbana, Illinois 61801

It is the policy of NCTE in its journals and other publications to provide a forum for the open discussion of ideas concerning the content and the teaching of English and the language arts. Publicity accorded to any particular point of view does not imply endorsement by the Executive Committee, the Board of Directors, or the membership at large, except in announcements of policy, where such endorsement is clearly specified.

Library of Congress Cataloging in Publication Data

Main entry under title:

Three language-arts curriculum models.

    Includes bibliographies.
    1. Language arts. I. Mandel, Barrett John,
1937–   II. National Council of Teachers of English.
LB1576.T527   372.6   80-22889
ISBN 0-8141-5458-1

Contents

III. High School

IV. Community College

V. The Four-Year College

1 Introduction

Barrett J. Mandel
Rutgers College

I. History

At the 1977 Business Meeting of the National Council of Teachers of English in New York City, Maree Blackwell, president of the Alabama Council of Teachers of English, introduced a sense-of-the-house motion calling for national "guidelines for curricula in English similar to the Bullock Report of England." The motion was carried, and the charge to implement it was given to the Commission on the English Curriculum. Since this publication may seem rather a far cry from the intention of the motion, a few words on the development of the project are in order.

Having spent three years focusing on questions of competency-based education and minimal competencies, the Commission on the English Curriculum felt it appropriate to turn its attention more directly toward questions of curriculum per se: What is it? What is being taught and how? To whom? What ought to be taught? How? To whom? Blackwell's sense-of-the-house motion gave focus and direction for the Commission's new emphasis. But it did not take long for us to discover that the charge would have to be radically interpreted if any book was to ensue.

During the early stages of planning, it became clear that the Council did not have the resources or the desire to follow the lead of *A Language for Life* (the so-called Bullock Report), which had, after all, been a 600-page, blue-ribbon project of the British government's Department of Education and Science, not the work of any professional organization. Furthermore, it soon became evident that those involved with the planning of this publication could not see themselves defining national guidelines in a prescriptive manner. The state of the art in curriculum (for which I use the working definition of the Commission: "goals, contents, and

1

teaching-learning procedures") is uncertain and evolving. We all felt that where curriculum is concerned, the times were not right for a document comparable in scope and tone to the *Statement on the Preparation of Teachers of English and the Language Arts* brought out in 1976 by the NCTE Standing Committee on Teacher Preparation and Certification. No one on the Commission or the NCTE Executive Committee seemed disposed to interpret the sense-of-the-house motion as a call for one set of national curricular mandates covering all levels of language-arts instruction. If we were to address ourselves to the issue of a national curriculum for the eighties, the focus would have to be on a catholic collection of curriculum models that had been found effective in various regional and educational contexts. "National guidelines" was therefore loosely interpreted to mean "the best of what is happening" rather than "what ought to happen." It was also decided that what we wanted were real human voices, not necessarily in agreement, rather than statistics or a policy statement.

What we decided to do is harness the liberation of diversity rather than bow to the domination of conformity. The following story (called to my attention by Lewis Epstein) is taken from Leo Luscaglia's book *Love* and represents the point of view of the planners of this book, not only about curriculum, but also about the choices of curriculum designers who need to be trusted to develop their own strengths, following their own intuition while keeping open to new influences.

> The animals got together in the forest one day and decided to start a school. There was a rabbit, a bird, a squirrel, a fish and an eel, and they formed a Board of Education. The rabbit insisted that running be in the curriculum. The bird insisted that flying be in the curriculum. The fish insisted that swimming be in the curriculum, and the squirrel insisted that perpendicular tree climbing be in the curriculum. They put all of these things together and wrote a Curriculum Guide. Then they insisted that *all* of the animals take *all* of the subjects. Although the rabbit was getting an A in running, perpendicular tree climbing was a real problem for him; he kept falling over backwards. Pretty soon . . . he couldn't run any more. He found that instead of making an A in running, he was making a C and, of course, he always made an F in perpendicular climbing. The bird was really beautiful at flying, but when it came to burrowing in the ground, he couldn't do so well. He kept breaking his beak and wings. Pretty soon he was making a C in flying as well as an F in burrowing, and he had a hellava time with perpendicular tree climbing. The moral of the story is that the person who was valedictorian of the class was . . . an eel who did everything in a half-way fashion. But the educators were all happy because everybody was taking all of the subjects, and it was called a broad-based education. (pp. 22-23)

Allan Glatthorn, my predecessor as director of the Commission on the English Curriculum, similarly argues that we do not live in a time when we can reasonably expect to put together an "ideal" English learning environment. "In fact," Glatthorn writes, "the diversity among individual pupils and the complexity of the task of developing language competency suggest that we should forever abandon such a notion. Instead, it seems more fruitful now to ask how we can provide multiple options in the learning environment so that we can perhaps achieve a better fit among environment, task, and learner" ("Creating Learning Environments," in *The Teaching of English: The Seventy-fifth Yearbook of the National Society for the Study of Education* [Chicago, 1977], p. 219). I certainly share this sentiment, and it is this point of view that is the premise of this publication.

On a flight from Chicago to Urbana, Marlene Caroselli (associate director of the Commission) and I struck upon the idea of three curricular paradigms, with the implications of each one traced from pre-kindergarten language-arts activities through college English. Our idea was that in lieu of one curricular model for all, we could present three curricular models, each viewed as powerful and resourceful by its adherents, each used with varying degrees of success at the different instructional levels. In Urbana the executive planning committee accepted the idea of paradigms and after considering the many curricular strategies in use in the schools, agreed on the three: the process or student-centered model, the heritage or traditional model, and the competencies model. The task then was to select outstanding teachers and researchers to write essays for each of the paradigms. This collection represents the fruit of their labors.

II. Design of the Book

The three paradigms developed in this publication represent especially fertile areas for curriculum development. This book should assist those professional educators who wish to see the implications of each type of curriculum spelled out in practical detail at every grade level. The book also is meant to serve as a resource for those working within one of the paradigms as well as a practical introduction to the paradigms for those who have not had much exposure to them.

Despite disclaimers by those with opposing points of view and despite excesses by some who espouse one or another of these teaching models, each of the approaches here is a deeply rooted, compassionate point of view on teaching. And despite the various accusations occasionally hurled between what may seem like armed camps, there is no reason to doubt that each of these groups of teachers is deeply committed to the well-being of children. In faculty lounges and NCTE meetings where voices are raised, it may occasionally appear that a teacher interested in competency-based education is more interested in hardware than in children, that the process teacher is more committed to proving the validity of a Rogerian theory than to preparing a child for the arduousness of life, that a traditional teacher blindly values the past more than the present, thereby sacrificing the actual or the imminent for some dead ideal. When a teacher polarizes and becomes strident—how well I know this from my own experience!—in defense of a particular theoretical point of view, it becomes difficult for others to keep in mind that the lounge or NCTE forum is not the classroom, that the debater-proponent is not the teacher.

Teachers as teachers are overwhelmingly committed to serving the educational needs of their students. The teacher in the classroom is always occupied with fellow human beings first—and only secondarily with hardware, theories, or tradition. Of course, some teachers reach their students more powerfully than others do, but the difference in pedagogical effectiveness is, in my view, probably only tangentially related to the pedagogical theory that underpins the teacher's classroom choices. Teacher effectiveness has always and will continue to be produced by the teacher's vivacity, willingness to share while acknowledging the separate realities of the students, and an ability to communicate a basic support and compassion for others. I am humanist enough to believe that it has always been and will always be who the teacher is, more than what the teacher does, that truly counts.

It must also be said, however, that while compassion is indispensable, it is not sufficient. Compassion is the human context in which learning can occur, and yet teachers certainly need to do something in order to manifest and give form to their willingness to serve their students. Teachers engage in constant pedagogical decision making, deciding minute by minute to teach in one way rather than another. It is the point of view of this book that the compassionate teacher can guide students through their education in many different ways—for instance, in one of the three curricular ways suggested here. But whatever the pedagogical choice might be, all pedagogical paradigms, if understood correctly, are devoted to process, competencies, and heritage. No one becomes educated without undergoing personal growth (process), becoming adroit in the manipulation of the symbols of society (competencies), and thereby perpetuating and indeed fulfilling the implications of the past and the promise of the future (heritage). And yet a teacher teaching makes choices constantly, selects materials, emphasizes certain values, creates goals, develops programs. The more consciously the teacher makes these choices, the more likely the students will be assisted along their paths.

I have chosen three metaphors—mastery, discovery, and surrender—as keys to the curricular models set forth in this book. They are all metaphors for "learning," but each one points to a particular mode in which learning may occur. One is not better than another; each one opens learning from a distinct angle of perception. Mastery suggests the mode of learning in which one becomes skilled or proficient in some activity; it brings to mind a sense of dominance and control: one takes charge, subdues, exercises self-discipline. Only a master masters. Discovery is the mode of learning in which one brings into visibility some knowledge or insight hitherto unseen; it also allows for the solving of problems through sudden illumination. There is a wide-eyed wonderment in this metaphor; it suggests surprise and the seizing of opportunity. Surrender is the mode in which one learns by giving oneself over to an influence, going where the river goes, rather than attempting to control it. There is no passivity or weakness implied by this metaphor; it is the voluntary surrender of ego to something larger than one's own immediate needs or concerns. Each of these metaphors, it seems to me, points to a genuine and by no means mutually exclusive way of learning. And each one, I think, may open our understanding to a particular teaching paradigm.

III. Mastery—The Competencies Model

The competencies approach, based on behavioral studies, holds that a child matures in predictable and recognizable stages. The informed competency teacher introduces pupils to new knowledge and skills at the appropriate developmental moment and in amounts that are easily learned, or "mastered." *Mastery* is an important term in the competencies approach: it usually points to the segmenting of teachable skills and processes into levels and amounts deemed appropriate to the individual child. The assumption underlying this approach is that learning is incremental, that children learn what they can learn only when they are ready; the mastery of one skill readies a student for the next one. It is a heads-up, no-nonsense approach that serves the students by not only providing mastery, but also the sense of well-being that comes along with mastery. The master knows what skills have been brought under control. The ultimate accomplishment is to be found in the symphony produced by the mastery of many interim skills, like so many ensembles within an orchestra.

Karl Taylor, in his chapter on competencies at the two-year college level, argues that writing is mastered in stages: that fluency must precede an ability to specify, that control of specificity must precede organization, and so forth. (One need only hold this idea up to the approach, say, of Strunk and White's *Elements of Style*, a heritage approach, in order to see at a glance that Taylor's whole pedagogical grounding is essentially different from that of Strunk.) In the competencies paradigm, the student is expected to master A before moving on to B. Rewards are given for mastery, while no punishment is given for failure to master. Ideally, students stay at their developmental level and are provided with feedback and rein-forcement until they have successfully learned the skill or technique on which they are working and without which no real progress into more rarified areas is possible.

There is such a wave of support for and hostility against competency-based educational *testing* (CBE), often occurring at the state level, that a beleaguered teacher or curriculum specialist may, by being caught up in the emotionalism about this related issue, overlook the values inherent in a *pedagogy* that stresses mastery of communication skills and competency in language arts. It is often difficult to separate testing from the teaching and learning prior to testing. Yet the spokespersons for the competencies para-digm in this publication resolutely make this distinction, focusing on the sequencing of skills to the point of mastery rather than on evaluation. They are advocates of a learning theory, one meeting with considerable success if we can trust the accounts of Bloom and others. They are perhaps more influenced by the procedures of science than the other paradigm writers are. And while they all stress the mastery of skills, each one also speaks for the cultivation of the cognitive and affective domains. Mastery of competencies, for the authors in this volume, can occur only in a context of human understanding and support.

IV. Discovery—The Process Model

Process as a term used to label a pedagogical strategy may be said to be the "inside out" of competencies. Whereas the competencies approach advocates the introduction of concepts and skills at the appropriate time so that students can master them, the process approach advocates the creation of an environment in which students can "discover" what has heretofore been unknown to them. Because of the energy released in the delight of discovery, the student is emotionally receptive to seeing new associations and relationships. Many "process" instructors will argue that a person learns only what is already known at a preconscious level, that one discovers at the conscious level what one has, in a sense, already known unknowingly.

For process-oriented teachers, insight can be triggered by the teacher consciously designing a learning field or matrix within which a student will be able to discover or intuit the knowledge and skill that has been already appropriated at a preconscious level. There is less effort put into deciding what the student needs to learn at a given moment and more into noticing or observing what is transpiring for the student. For the teacher of process education, the paradigm means the natural, inevitable flowering of an individual's skills and concepts under the guidance of teachers who pose questions that are open-ended and provocative. Needless to say, the "nonteaching" done by process teachers requires great sensitivity, knowledge of cognitive levels, and patience.

There is a striking difference between this approach and the competencies model, though certainly they both stress developmental potential in learners. As I see it, the difference is this: the competency approach asserts that an individual may predictably be expected to master a particular skill at a certain stage in the development of the conscious mind (although the stage may occur at varying ages). The process motivation, on the other hand, stresses the student's own power to uncover intuitively what is true or what will work in each given situation and maintains that this discovery is usually accompanied by a shock of recognition since one has known the truth all along. Using a heuristic, such as Young, Becker, and Pike's in *Rhetoric: Discover and Change*, the competencies model could be said to highlight the stages of "preparation" and "incubation," while the process approach could be said to emphasize "illumination." (Ultimately, of course, both paradigms would have to fulfill all the heuristic terms, so I am speaking only of degree of emphasis.) Thus, the process approach is more descriptive than prescriptive. Whereas a competencies model can fairly clearly state behaviors expected to occur (in this volume, for instance, Sara Lundsteen, Betty Mason, and Paula Martinez are able to write of "appropriate objectives" with predictive precision), a process approach focuses more on watchfulness, the observation of what is developing at a given moment of instruction and then the harnessing of its energy. For example, the Stanfords do not, in their process paradigm, speak of expecting a particular competency to be mastered at a specific time; instead, their assertions typically involve "students' natural interests" and the "opportunity to show students more possibilities."

V. Surrender—The Heritage Model

The heritage model of instruction cuts across the other two from an entirely different angle. If competency calls for mastery and the process of growth calls for discovery, then the word for heritage, with its emphasis on time, is *surrender*. Even though *surrender* may sound unnecessarily harsh, I mean it, of course, in a purely positive sense and do not by any means intend to imply defeatism or passivity. What I have in mind is rather the Zen consciousness of joyful acceptance of the forces that operate in our lives. By *surrender* I mean something like *recognize, acknowledge*, and *endorse*. But these other verbs do not fully capture the paradox of "freedom in discipline" that, to me, *surrender* connotes when understood in its active sense. The way I use *surrender* here is the way Pirsig's protagonist in *Zen and the Art of Motorcycle Maintenance* acknowledges his need to gain power over the machine by submitting to learning its every calibration. Heritage learning acknowledges that there is *something* to be learned and that the something demands consciousness, ethicalness, care, and discipline.

In the heritage model, the underlying assumption is that the way to acquire skills and knowledge is to submit to something larger than oneself, that is, to the culture. By culture I mean traditions, history, the time-honored values of civilized thought and feeling (including the time-honored resistance to these values) and the skills that make it possible to share in one's culture and to pass it on. For the heritage teacher, there is value in surrendering one's ego-bound sense of relevance to a more informed or enlightened sense of what truly endures. That is why the heritage teacher worries more about writing standard, edited English than about the students' right to their own language.

Let me expand this last point without, I hope, oversimplifying. It is easy to imagine a process teacher's subscribing to the position of the Conference on College Composition and Communication that the individual student has a right to the oral language of his or her home and language group. The process teacher could be expected to emphasize dialect awareness in class. On the other hand, a heritage teacher, while never disregarding or maligning the student's dialect, would emphasize the written dialect—standard, edited American English.

For the heritage teacher, meaning in life comes from knowing who one is in relation to the societal, religious, moral, ethical, and esthetic forces that characterize civilization at its best. Our culture certainly has its quirks, biases, and blindnesses (the written dialect, for instance, certainly reflects the sexist, racist, and class biases of the people in power over the centuries); but when all is said and done, nothing will nurture us better, even with all its imperfections, than our culture. For the heritage teacher, the culture that is being passed on inspires through its literature. Its strength lies in its endurance and pliability: it is an oak and a reed.

The heritage teacher argues that it is pointless to elevate the present moment, the literary fads of the day or transitory oral parlances when there are larger forces operating through time that shape us though we be blind to them. By moving with these forces instead of against them, one increases the chances of maximizing personal fulfillment. George Bernard Shaw was an enlightened exemplar of this approach. And in this book, Ronald LaConte, a futurist, is as much a heritage teacher as Eldonna Evertts, with her emphasis on the myths and stories of the past. Both are saying to us that the student will prosper to the degree that the student surrenders to forces operating in time.

VI. Why Paradigms at All?

The selection of three paradigms may seem to suggest a somewhat simplistic notion of the teaching of language-arts. I would like, if possible, to dispel that notion. Indeed, no such simplistic idea is intended. Neither I nor any of the authors in this volume believe that good teaching occurs in one form exclusively. From what I can tell from my correspondence with the more than twenty authors, not one of them feels that one preferred paradigm can or should be viewed as *the* approach to the Temple of Pedagogical Truth. These paradigm teachers take a soft line and for good reason. These three classifications, like all human constructs, are, at least to some degree, grids placed *over* the experience of teaching; they are a way of seeing at least as much as a way of doing. In actuality these categories shade off into each other, especially at the two extremes of the educational spectrum: the elementary and the college years. The reader will surely observe that the ways of teaching are more noticeably different from each other in the middle years of schooling, giving rise to the questions: Are the paradigms less useful indicators and guides for elementary and advanced work? Is renewed investigation of the worth of these paradigms called for in elementary and collegiate education? Readers may advance their own answers to these questions.

Readers will also have to decide for themselves the meaning behind various authors' decisions to emphasize one aspect of language arts over another. At the university level, "competencies" seem to point to reading skills, while at the two-year college level, "competencies" focus on writing skills. While each essay is written from the point of view of a particular author's interests at the moment of composing, the reader is left with the question: Do these paradigms mean the same thing at each level of instruction? In this volume, for example, Elizabeth Cowan clearly does not mean by *process* what the Stanfords mean—or even what I mean, for that matter.

These observations and questions notwithstanding, it seems clear to me that most teachers tend to gather their intellectual and emotional resources together in one kind of teaching more than another, that schools and districts usually favor one kind of curricular emphasis over another, and that students profit from learning in an environment which, while richly heterogeneous, is conscious of its dominant curricular style, goals, and values. Indeed, since many teachers actually gravitate towards one of these approaches without perhaps even realizing it, this book, while not advocating a particular paradigm or suggesting that the paradigms are mutually exclusive, is nonetheless designed to serve readers by disclosing where the roots of their own best teaching lie, how to strengthen and deepen their understanding of their own dominant approach, how to develop new teaching strategies within the same model, and how to branch out into the use of other models in ways that might not have seemed feasible or even apparent before.

From the outset, Commission members were eager to turn this volume into an aid for real teachers in real classrooms, not into ammunition for a war among ideologies. Commission member Jayne DeLawter urged that the book be a charge to individual teachers to use their own gifts; Barbara Lieb-Brilhart saw the paradigms as pedagogical emphases, not as purist models. And all the Commission members were in agreement that it is time to turn the present curricular tensions experienced by teachers at all levels into an opportunity for professional growth rather than internecine war.

To take advantage of this opportunity, we need to look closely at the curricular models of our colleagues, with a willingness to explore the implications in our own teaching and an openness to change when, in fact, someone has clearly discovered and can demonstrate a strategy that produces the results it claims for itself. We are teaching at a moment in history when, despite our stridency, there are no fixed answers to the questions that beset us all. It is in our best interest to listen to all points of view with an ear cocked to the sound of common sense. We can continue to turn the welter of curricular approaches into an acrimonious marketplace. Or we can, as I say, recognize the present moment as a period of creativity by altering our way of apprehending it. Any serious teacher of good will and experience has a contribution to make, and we can each be the beneficiary of others' contributions. There is a wealth of ideas—theoretical and practical—in this volume. The reader is invited to use it wisely as a supplement to teaching as well as a resource book for new ideas.

An objection may be raised that a particular paradigm may not be as useful for a certain skill as another paradigm. What does the competency teacher at the college level do about *King Lear*? What does the process teacher in sixth grade do about transitive verbs? What does the heritage teacher in second grade do about the students' different dialects? These are certainly crucial questions, and what the various practitioners have to say about such matters cannot help but be of interest. The authors of this volume provide a few surprises, making inroads into our preconceived ideas and prejudices. (I certainly had this experience during the work of editing the chapters.) Indeed, many a teacher enamored of a particular approach and yet stymied by problems that arise when using it may find that an author in this volume has an idea that untangles the knot.

And if not? What if it becomes clear that a certain paradigm has great strengths in most areas and some limitations in others? In that event I would ask, what better place to discover the reality than in a book on curriculum that has been designed to be as useful and as unpolemical as possible? Some of the authors have actually assisted us by suggesting some of the limitations of the approach they are describing. It is reasonable to assume that particular paradigms will be best suited for specific kinds of learning; it is, it seems to me, no shame for a curricular model to be strong on one front and weak on another. What would be a shame is the blind use of a model in a setting for which it is unsatisfactory.

It is the hope of the Commission that the heritage teacher who has been prejudiced against a "systems" approach or the Dartmouth-type teacher who feels that a lecture format spells doom will be able to use the occasion as an opportunity to create movement in teaching by opening up to the well-articulated views of others. Thus, I am arguing for a true and strict eclecticism: selection from what appears to be the *best* in various doctrines, methods, or styles. A teacher needs to discover, without reinventing the wheel, that there are strategies and schools of thought designed to get the job done. This volume is designed to give maximum support in developing the teacher's eclecticism. It attempts to provide models of curricular behavior that the reader may examine, endorse, share with colleagues, reject, borrow from, or use as stimulation for thought.

VII. The Organization of the Collection

Each of the five parts of the collection opens with an essay that discusses the general problems and challenges of schooling at one educational level. The opening statement thus creates a general context or field for the three paradigm essays that follow. The paradigm essays—each based on a competency, process, or heritage approach—focus on a particular "content" in the school system.

There are four ways to read this book. The first and most ambitious is from cover to cover. The second way, especially useful for classroom teachers, is to read the section that pertains to the school level at which one works. The third way of reading the book would be to trace a paradigm up through the years of schooling. I imagine that this last approach would be especially valuable for curriculum designers, supervisors, and administrative personnel. For this beleaguered group, whose influence is so directly felt by the teachers whom they supervise, the book would raise and hopefully answer such questions as: Does *competencies* mean the same thing in high school and junior college? Can junior college students be trained in the reading of literature in a heritage approach that will prepare them for an upper-class English major at the state university without violating the mandated procedures of the two-year college? Does *process* mean the same thing in third grade that it does in tenth? Or in college?

There is, finally, a fourth way to read this book. Too often a teacher at one level, committed to a particular curricular approach which seems appropriate at that level, is unaware of the implications of sending students on to the next level of instruction where an entirely different approach is used. Very often, for instance, the new sixth grader is traumatized by the frequent tests of competencies in the middle school, tests that may have been unheard of in the process-oriented elementary school. For this kind of reader, moving backwards and forwards in the book may be appropriate in order to examine a paradigm as it appears at both lower and higher levels of education.

Readers will read however they read. But I do want to stress that this is the sort of publication that welcomes and encourages educated dabbling on the one hand and more intensive focusing on the other.

Acknowledgments

This book is the product of many hands. The authors, acknowledged leaders in language-arts teaching, cooperated in all ways to bring this book to successful publication. I wish to thank all members of the Commission on the English Curriculum (1978 and 1979) for their full support in refereeing chapters and advising the editor: Marlene Caroselli (associate director of the Commission), Jane Christensen, Ouida Clapp, Jayne DeLawter, Allan Dittmer, Ruth Gallant, Barbara Lieb-Brilhart, Elisabeth McPherson, Jasper Neel, William D. Page, William J. Strong, Dorothy J. Watson, and Lois Williams. Thanks also to the original planning committee consisting of Robert Hogan, Charles Suhor, Arthur Applebee, Alan Purves, and Marlene Caroselli.

There has been an enormous amount of correspondence and typing in the preparation of this material. For their good work and

relentless cheerfulness, I would like to thank Gloria Cohn and
Katherine Schroeder, secretaries in the Douglass College English
Department, Rutgers University, and Jo Ann Zsilavetz, secretary
in the Douglass/Cook Writing Center. Finally, I would like to pay
special tribute to Carol Smith, friend and colleague, who shared
the path with me.

I Pre-Kindergarten through Grade Five

2 American Schooling: Pre-Kindergarten through Grade Five

Walter T. Petty
State University of New York at Buffalo

The American elementary school is neither a mirror of society nor an institution isolated from it. The school responds slowly to the changes taking place around it, but decisions concerning what the school should be like, what it should attempt to do, and how it should go about doing that are essentially society's. Thus, the problems, needs, desires, and expectations of society are the major forces influencing schooling.

This has been true throughout the history of American schools. In Colonial times the strong religious beliefs and narrow vocational concerns of society limited both the curriculum and the purposes of schools. The impact of formal education had a lesser impact than it does today because not all children attended school and family structure was such that many educational tasks now ascribed or relegated to the school were performed by the family, the church, or even the community itself. But new needs inevitably arose, and just as inevitably, they exerted a profound influence on the role of the school. With the emergence of the new nation, many citizens felt the need to develop a program of schooling that would encourage a sense of national unity among the diverse groups making up the population. And as the nation grew and expanded, not only geographically, politically, and economically, but also intellectually, there arose a desire to transmit to new generations knowledge of this culture, as well as that of other nations and peoples. In addition, the growth of industry and technology produced many new vocational opportunities, which in turn brought greater emphasis on the basic skills taught in the school, an emphasis that included broadening the definitions of both *basic* and *skills* as well as raising the level of performance expected from teachers. Along with these social changes that impinged on the school came dramatic changes in the school itself: education was no longer the prerogative of males only or of the upper class, and the length of required schooling of both sexes was increased.

These changes, of course, did not occur rapidly or all at once, but by about 1870 the American school system resembled its present form in organization, financial support, and curriculum. The system of grade levels had appeared; expansion of the basic skills had led to the institution of subjects as we now know them, accompanied by series of graded textbooks; and the prevailing instructional approach was that of "re-citing" what had been read in the text or prescribed by the teacher. Today, as a hundred years ago, elementary schools remain almost exclusively organized so that children of a particular age group are in a specific grade-level classroom. Unfortunately, the children's school day remains, more often than not, a routine of time slots that focus on isolated bits of subject matter. Too often the instructional mode still consists of having children regurgitate information that has been fed to them. Both reflecting this instructional mode and guiding it, textbooks still dominate the curriculum, supplemented by products of twentieth-century technology and nineteenth-century thinking, such as a highly developed program of commercial tests and dittoed sheets for writing in blanks or checking among choices. Thus, the notion that children of a particular age are a homogeneous body of individuals continues to prevail in the school, with textbooks, testing programs, teacher action, parental expectations, and the children themselves reinforcing that notion.

The Characteristics of the Modern School

The strength of tradition should not blind us to the changes that have taken place over the past hundred years. Classrooms and buildings are obviously more attractive today, chairs and desks are no longer fastened to the floor, and the atmosphere in classrooms is generally open, bright, and cheery. The content of textbooks has changed from that of earlier days; and changes periodically occur to reflect current emphases, although there is still much in textbooks unrelated to children's present or future needs. Teaching materials are not limited to printed matter, however; there are many opportunities for children to learn through films, slides, tapes, displays, and trips away from the classroom. Schools now have libraries and resource centers, facilities and equipment devoted to art, music, physical development and health, as well as special programs for children whose educational needs cannot be met in conventional classrooms.

Advances in teacher education have also brought about many changes, even though teaching procedures generally have changed surprisingly little. Many classrooms are no longer modeled after the quiet ones of some years ago. Such classrooms reflect two understandings that are basic to effective teaching: (1) the importance of talking and exchanging ideas in children's development, and (2) the need for investigation and discovery, as opposed to memorization, and the activity such learning requires.

Other changes in the classroom have resulted from universal attendance at school. The diversity in abilities, backgrounds, and developmental levels of children in schools today has forced changes in curriculum and instruction. Furthermore, extension of the years of schooling, particularly the development of preschool programs that now accept children of age four or under, has obviously affected school programs, above all, those at the primary level of the elementary school.

While developments such as preschools appear to cause schools to change, the real force behind them is society itself. This century has seen many societal changes—changes in family structure, work and play habits, ethical behavior and beliefs, economic concerns, even life expectancy—which have brought about new expectations regarding the role of the school. For example, many teachers—perhaps especially those in the early grades—would argue that changes in attitudes and styles of living have resulted in the school's being expected to take over the responsibilities of the home, workplace, and community, as well as to equalize students' intellectual skills and compensate for society's economic and social problems. Whether this is true or not, there is no question that societal expectations vis-à-vis the school have undergone some changes.

Expectations regarding the schools' role in instilling a sense of nationhood now focus on transmitting the heritage of an established nation, which includes instilling the prevailing ethic of personal behavior. One aspect of the current ethic is the task of preparing future adults to recognize the rights of racial and ethnic minorities, women, and the handicapped; appreciate and conserve the environment; and adopt better health practices.

Schools, of course, are still expected to teach the basic subjects and related skills, a task that has become increasingly complex and difficult with the growth in knowledge and the number of skills considered to be basic. Related to this task is the sorting out of students' future socioeconomic roles, a task largely assigned to secondary schools, but increasingly expected by some parents and others to be dealt with in the elementary school—even below grade five. Schools today must also foster children's creativity and develop their self-reliance, both of which reflect changes in societal expectations from those of an earlier day when self-reliance was a task of the home and creativity was not thought of as a matter of schooling.

Each of these changes has had both positive and negative effects. Although the overall result surely is more education of higher quality for more children, many problems have been created for those who plan and administer school programs, and many pressures have been brought to bear upon teachers and children. For example, few would deny that the high pressure for achievement—a pressure too often fed by the media—has been strongly felt by teachers as well as children, with the feelings often running to anxiety and insecurity. Schools have reacted by competing for higher test scores, formalizing various schemes for children to "pass" from one level of achievement to another, adding to or further dividing up the curriculum, and frequently assigning specialists to teach various parts of it.

Certainly the achievement of universal schooling is laudable, yet this too has caused problems in the classroom. Teachers must deal with wide variations in ability, personality, and background among the children in their classrooms; this sometimes leads to fragmentation of their effort, lapses in the attention of some children, or overemphasis on competition. In addition, the mobility of families adds to children's difficulty in gaining security in a classroom. No longer does a child attend school with the same classmates for the greater part of each's school career. The nation's population has become a mobile one, and some children may attend four or five different schools, sometimes even several in one year, during the vital early years of their schooling. This mobility can bring about teaching and learning problems when coupled with such factors as changes in teaching methods and textbooks, dialect differences, and the potential emotional difficulties of adjusting to a new environment. Moreover, instability in a school's population can be a problem for learning and security—if the two can be separated—because of various integration endeavors, declining enrollments that bring on redistricting, and organizational changes resulting from declining fiscal support of schools.

Finally, the broadening of the curriculum has had some negative effects on teachers and their students. Teachers sometimes experience frustration at the number of things they are expected to crowd into the school day, even in the earliest grades, and wonder whether they have the time or the knowledge to accomplish their teaching with even a modicum of success. Thus, although today's children do have the opportunity to gain knowledge and skills in areas that children formerly did not, there is the danger of fragmentation and lack of depth that surely does not work to the children's advantage.

Strengths of the Modern School

While we must heed the warnings of the negative, the positive aspects of the modern school are many. One such aspect of the elementary school is the teachers. These teachers are likely to be the most dedicated of all those that children will encounter in their schooling. They are interested in "their" children, they are friendly and understanding, and they are optimistic about how successful they are as teachers. They have many advantages over their predecessors of earlier generations; and though more is expected of them, they are better educated. They know at least something about children's growth, development, and the way they learn. The large majority of elementary school teachers work hard at their teaching, even if they do not always use the best teaching practices or are handicapped by ill-advised organizational schemes, improper or inadequate materials, and school leadership lacking in knowledge of children and the curriculum. They are often closer to parents and, hence, to the expectations of society than are teachers of older children and those in control of school systems.

The most positive aspect of all, the one that must be foremost in our minds in our thinking and planning, is the children themselves. Children of today, like those of earlier days, have a great deal of resiliency; it takes much to get them down and even more to keep them there. They endure the too frequent "slicing up" of learning situations, experiences with poor teaching, and irrational things they may be asked to do. For some, schooling does become distasteful or worse. Too, there are children who come to school with emotional or learning problems; worse yet, there are some whose problems become more serious or even begin because of the pressures of schooling. Most children, however, come to school expecting and wanting to learn. We must build upon their expectations, for these children are, after all, the next generation that will shape the schools of the future.

3 Competency-Based Approach to Language Arts: Pre-Kindergarten through Grade Five

Betty O. Mason
North Texas State University

Sara W. Lundsteen
North Texas State University

Paula S. Martinez
Wheaton College

Ideally, the competency-based approach enables the teacher to do three things effectively: diagnose, prescribe appropriate learning experiences, and evaluate. This recurring feedback loop enables the teacher to direct the child's language arts behavior in small, successful increments toward a desired objective, in this case, a language arts skill. This skill is connected to other skills in a carefully ordered program.

A look into the future suggests that the competency-based approach will stay with us. Pressures to demonstrate measurable minimal competencies will persist. These pressures will continue to encourage a method that makes short-term successes highly visible to parents, legislators, and other "significant individuals." But we also suggest that the American educational pendulum has swung in this direction as far as it will go.

A return to a balanced, more eclectic position can profit, nonetheless, from attention to some of the aspects of the competency approach. Benefits of the approach include the following. First, thinking through the measurable objectives eliminates much fuzzy planning. Second, at the beginning of their professional careers, some inexperienced teachers and paraprofessionals gain security from the approach because through it, they can teach children something visible that adds up to a set of skills. Third, some children gain needed security, a specific, short-term sense of direction, and rewarded success for their responses. Ideally, mastery strategies allow about three-fourths of children to attain the same performance standards as the top fourth of children in a class (Block, 1971). The slow students get the time and assistance that they need to achieve mastery; hence, they are failure free. Furthermore, competitive goals are replaced by individual ones, and objectives are carefully specified as to conditions and measurement criteria (e.g., 90 percent correctly punctuated sentences).

This chapter will guide the reader toward implementing a competency-based approach. It begins with the role of the teacher; moves to examples of teacher strategies; includes general and specific examples of planning for children's skills in the language arts, criteria for selecting competency-based programs and materials (along with examples), advice on how to get started, what resources are available if the educator needs help or wants to learn more; and ends with a few words of caution.

Teacher Competencies

In order to direct a competency-based language arts program, the teacher must be competent in the following areas.

Diagnosis. To ascertain pupil's problems and level in all language arts areas, the teacher may use standardized tests and informal inventories, listen to the child read and speak in formal and informal situations, analyze the child's written material, observe the child when he or she is listening in various situations, and keep records of strengths and weaknesses. Checklists are valuable.

Prescription. The teacher will design an individual program in each language arts area for each child. Children may be on different levels in each area. The teacher will take differences into account, prescribing work on the child's level in each area and keeping detailed records of progress. A skill checklist will be valuable. The teacher must carefully observe the child's pace and assign only what he or she can manage—not too much, not too little.

Identification of obstructive behavior. The teacher must observe the child in a learning situation, such as doing a written assignment in punctuating sentences, to discover what behavior is preventing the child from performing to his or her potential. For example, a student is continually getting up and standing by the window. This behavior keeps the student from attending to the task of punctuating sentences correctly.

Analysis of child's wants. If a child is behaving in a specific manner, there is a reason for the behavior. The teacher must determine the child's reason in the particular situation. For example, the student in the example above seems to be looking out of the window most of the time. Examining the situation, the teacher discovers that rather than looking out of the window, the student, a music lover, is actually listening to music in the nearby music room.

Positive reinforcement. When a teacher knows what a child wants, the teacher can strike a bargain with the child. Both the teacher, who wants a task completed, and the child can be satisfied through their agreement. For example, the child who loves music is allowed to listen to music with a tape recorder and earphones for ten minutes after successfully completing a twenty-minute assignment on punctuating sentences in the allotted time. The student will then stop going to the window and begin performing.

Individual treatment. No two children have the same wants. Each child must be observed to determine what satisfies each. The child in the previous example may become saturated with music. When that occurs, the teacher must have another reward ready. Another child may get little satisfaction from listening to music. Art may be a favorite activity, so art should be this child's reward. A third student enjoys writing poetry, but does not need a reward for this activity since in this case, the product is its own reward.

Maintaining a conducive work environment. The teacher must attempt to be aware of everything that is going on in the classroom, whether it is physical or behavioral. If the children are sluggish and do not seem to be working, the teacher will realize, for instance, that the room is too hot.

Reinforcement of correct responses. Because immediately getting to every child in the classroom is a difficult task, materials should be provided that give immediate, reinforcing feedback. Computer-assisted instruction is ideal for immediate reinforcement because each child learns at once if the answers are right or wrong in an assignment. The child is often given a second chance and then is rewarded with praise or a star.

The teacher may use tokens, which can be exchanged for prizes, when a child gives a correct response. The children will keep trying in order to get the tokens. If the teacher works with small groups, the children are more easily rewarded immediately.

Shaping proper behavior. Sometimes a child needs reinforcement in stages while working on a particular skill. In such instances the teacher may give reinforcement for partially correct responses. In a handwriting lesson, for example, praise should be given after each stroke to assure the child of movement in the right direction. A teacher must work with one child at a time to provide adequate attention. Parent volunteers or aids can be helpful.

Diminishing reinforcement. When beginning a task, a child should be reinforced after each response. Later, when the child begins to give consistently correct responses, the reinforcement may be given at varying intervals so that the child does not know when the reinforcement is coming. For example, a child who is working on spelling is given a token when spelling a word correctly. Later, a token is placed on the desk at various intervals. Finally the child receives no reward and begins to find satisfaction simply from correct spelling.

Requiring mastery (90–100 percent). When skills are developmental, it is important that each skill be mastered before the next one is presented. For example, in manuscript writing it is important that a child can make circles and straight lines before moving to letters that require both.

Allowing various responses. Language arts includes listening, speaking, reading, and writing. The teacher should provide activities that develop skills in all these areas. For example, a Language Master may be used so that children can listen to instructions, respond, and then hear their remarks. If necessary, children can change their answers until they are satisfied that their responses are correct.

Keeping records. Since a systems approach breaks language arts into small teaching units, record keeping can be time-consuming and expensive. To keep track of the skills mastered by students, a teacher must utilize a rather sophisticated record-keeping system. Some ideas for record keeping follow.

1. Profile cards and skewer. Each student has a profile card that identifies skills, determined by a pretest, to be learned. Beside each listed skill is a small hole. As the skill is mastered, the hole is extended to the edge of the card. Thus, to identify the skills needing mastery, a skewer is slipped through the hole beside a specific skill. Students whose cards remain on the skewer need instruction on that skill, and students whose cards fall from the skewer have mastered the skill. The student whose sample profile card is shown in Figure 1 has mastered skills 1 and 2, but needs instruction on skills 3, 4, 5, 6, and 7, if 90 percent is the required level of mastery.

2. Checklist. The teacher itemizes the skills to be learned. As the skill is mastered by the student, the teacher places a check beside each skill.

3. Folders. The teacher itemizes the skills to be learned. As the skill is mastered by the student, the teacher places a check by each skill.

4. Computer. Pretest and post-test data can be stored in a computer. However, programming is time-consuming and expensive.

5. Self-carboned progress forms. Skills are itemized by objectives with a place for pretest and post-test results. One copy goes in the student file, one copy goes to the parent after the pretest, and one copy goes to the parent upon mastery of a skill.

Providing opportunities for success. Competency-based education implies that children work each on their own level and can therefore successfully perform the given task. The teacher and the pupil must constantly review the student's work to insure the child's success.

Since no two teachers will agree on all the language arts skills a child needs, no attempt is made in this chapter to list specific competencies. Examples of how various programs handle writing

		Skills	Pre	Post
		Child's name		
Extended Holes		1. Rhyming words	90	
		2. Shapes	95	
	0	3. Letters	70	
Holes	0	4. Numbers	85	
	0	5. Colors	95	
	0	6. Left-right sequences	65	
	0	7. Initial consonants	55	

Fig. 1. A sample profile card for use with a skewer file.

objectives are presented later in the chapter and will be helpful in formulating a program. But the children also must have a part in identifying skills in which they are weak and in charting their progress in mastering the skills. If children are not committed to their tasks, they will not be successful in a competency-based language arts program. Time spent planning and conferring with pupils is time well-spent.

Selecting a Competency-Based Language Arts Program

If teachers choose to teach language arts by the competency-based method, they have several options. First, they can sit down alone or with a team and formulate objectives, but this process is very laborious. Second, the teachers may search for programs already developed and follow the best program for their purposes. However, a third procedure probably is best, one in which the teachers study other programs and then formulate objectives specifically tailored for their own program.

Successful competency-based programs will have objectives with evaluation procedures built in. Appropriate objectives meet these criteria: (1) they describe the terminal behavior of the student, (2) they indicate the conditions under which the behavior is exhibited, and (3) they indicate the quality of performance that is to be expected. A clear objective should be stated like this: "When presented with a list of sentences, the student can classify each with 90 percent accuracy as interrogative, exclamatory, imperative, or declarative."

For a competency-based program to be effective, the program should include objectives for several grade levels so that the child's level can be adequately met. An effective program will include diagnostic and evaluative procedures. The objectives should be listed in a developmental order if possible, with each skill leading logically to the next. A comprehensive program will include high-level thinking skills such as application, analysis, synthesis, and evaluation (Smith and Adams, 1972). Often time will be needed between introduction and mastery of a skill. An effective competency-based program will provide repetition throughout the program for continued reinforcement of a skill.

Competency-Based Programs

As stated above, the best procedure in developing a competency-based program is first to study existing programs. These programs can then serve as resources from which teachers can develop appropriate objectives for their particular situations. The programs listed below are a few of the available competency-based programs in language arts; more can be found by searching the library. The programs listed below have some or all of the characteristics of an acceptable program. Any of them can be adapted for a teacher's special needs.

Language Arts Instruction K-12. (Oregon State Department of Education.) Skills are broken down into the following areas in this goal-based language arts curriculum: Listening; Speaking; Reading, Decoding, and Comprehension; Writing; Study and Critical Thinking. Each skill category is further broken down into subskills. Listening, for example, comprises listening to acquire information, listening to follow directions, listening and asking questions.

Verbal Communications Competencies, K-6. (Pittsfield, Mass., Public Schools.) Language arts competencies for kindergarten through sixth grade are listed, indicating the grade levels at which skills are introduced, developed, and mastered. There are tests to measure students' progress in listening comprehension, composition, grammar, writing mechanics, and usage.

111 Writing Activities: A Thinking Teacher's Guide to Writing Activities. (Roy R. Grindstaff and T. R. Shepherd.) Specific activities are presented to help elementary students develop creative writing skills. Suggestions are given for ways to begin and to develop each activity and for follow-up. A performance checklist is included.

Language Arts Curriculum Guide, Performance Expectations, K-12. (Northern Valley Regional High School District, Closter, N.J.) Language arts objectives are identified in terms of the "average" student, and the grade level at which each concept or skill should be introduced, then reinforced, and finally mastered.

Language Arts. (Selby County Board of Education, Memphis, Tennessee.) Composition skills, language skills, and literature skills are listed for each grade level. Specific ideas and activities are given in a "Continuum of Skills." Approximate time that should be spent on each skill area is suggested. This program includes traditional, structural, and transformational grammar.

Behavioral Objectives—Composition, Grades K-12. (L. C. Leach and the Arkansas State Department of Education.) Behavioral objectives are listed for written language skills. Activities listed for oral and nonverbal communication are used to develop concepts.

Wisconsin Design for Reading Skill Development, K-6. This self-directed, interpretive, and creative reading program is divided into seven levels and provides an objective-based management system from kindergarten to sixth grade. Pupil profile cards, a planning guide, a teacher resource file, and a wall chart are required for implementing the program.

NDN (National Diffusion Network) Exemplary Programs. The NDN disseminates many types of programs, some of which use a competency-based approach to the teaching of language arts (U.S. Department of Health, Education, and Welfare, 1977). An example of one of these programs is "Individualized Language Arts: Diagnosis, Prescription, and Evaluation." A description of the program follows.

> At least three times a year, the teacher evaluates writing samples composed on self-selected topics by each student. Utilizing criteria common to nearly all language arts programs, he/she then is able to assign priorities to the needs of the class as a whole, of groups of students, and of individual youngsters. For each objective stemming from this diagnosis, a teacher's resource manual prescribing a variety of prescriptive writing or rewriting is strengthened by a "communication spiral" that links composition to the other language arts and to real-life experience. A record-keeping system permits the student, as well as teachers, administrators, and parents, to observe growth in writing proficiency from month to month and grade to grade. The program can be combined readily with pre-existing language arts curricula and objectives.

Another program that uses a systems approach to teach the language arts is the "Dale Avenue Early Childhood Education Project." A description of this program follows.

> The Dale Avenue Project provides an ongoing needs assessment and skeletal curriculum for children in pre-kindergarten through third grade in the ten areas of: Listening, Naming, Observing, Speaking, Writing and Motor Skills, Perceptual Motor Skills, Encoding/Decoding, Math, Classification, and Seriation.
> Constructed from a base of a sequential, developmental, skill-oriented array of Performance Objectives, this program provides (1) a pre- and post-test mechanism; (2) a minimal curriculum; (3) a device for grouping, individualizing, record keeping, parent reporting, and summarizing the year's skill mastery.

Exemplary Center for Reading Instruction (ECRI). ECRI is a reading-language arts in-service program that identifies teacher behaviors that are critical in preventing reading failure. Teacher behaviors identified in this program include eliciting correct responses from students, establishing mastery levels with performance and rate used as criteria, correlating language arts activities to increase responses and save time, utilizing effective management and monitoring systems, and diagnosing and prescribing instantly. These techniques are incorporated into reading, oral language, spelling, dictation, creative writing, and penmanship instruction. Advancement of students depends on rate of mastery, which is set at 95–100 percent.

Selecting Materials for a Competency-Based Language Arts Program

Teachers can prepare their own materials for a competency-based program; however, doing so is time-consuming and often expensive. Since many commercial materials are available, most teachers will use a combination of their own and commercially prepared materials. Also, many textbooks can be adapted for use in competency-based programs. This adaptation will require formulating adequate objectives based on the text material.

Prepared materials that can be used in a competency-based program can be found in these areas: creative writing, English, general communication, library skills, listening, phonics, reading, speech, spelling, and writing. Some of the most effective programs are listed under special education, since these programs usually are broken down into specific skills.

Teachers can find commercial materials in stores carrying school materials, in special centers provided for teachers by the school district or state, from representatives of educational companies, or at convention display rooms. A commercially prepared package should include a list of specific objectives and methods for pre- and post-testing. The instructional materials need to stimulate the pupils; they can include tapes, slides, filmstrips, pictures, records, as well as worksheets and hands-on materials. Laminated, reusable worksheets should be self-correcting when possible. Manuals and profile sheets should be provided for the teachers.

Teachers will not be able to find or afford all of the materials that they would like to have. Although making materials will take time, a teacher can begin a collection by making materials a few at a time. These should be laminated so that they will last. Teachers may look at commercially made materials and books to get ideas.

One simple way of preparing individual skill lesson materials is by using file folders onto which the skill lesson is laminated. The child can write directly onto the folder with a felt pen and then erase the answers. Answer sheets can be placed in a box nearby so that the child can correct his or her own work. The skill title is written at the top of the folder, and the folder is filed in a box. After the children have had their needs diagnosed and a program prescribed, they can look through the file and select the proper assignments.

How to Adapt-Adopt a Competency-Based Approach

An individual school desiring to systemize its language arts program must consider planning, cost, funding, and training of school personnel. Steps in planning should include the following:

1. Assessment of needs to determine priorities and to provide direction for planning
2. Establishment of a schoolwide philosophy so that all personnel are aware of the direction of the program
3. Establishment of goals: what needs to be taught to whom
4. Visits to schools with exemplary language-arts programs to gain further insights for planning
5. Plans for implementing the new program

The U.S. Office of Education (USOE) provides assistance to schools adopting or adapting exemplary programs. The USOE publishes an annual catalog of these programs, entitled *Educational Programs That Work*, which describes programs that have been successfully developed and implemented by local school districts. The USOE offers further assistance through the Division of Educational Replication by supporting the National Diffusion Network (NDN). The NDN is a nationwide system established to help schools obtain the materials or assistance they need to adopt or adapt any of the programs that are listed in the USOE catalog. For further information, contact the state facilitator in your state department of education or the USOE.

Conclusion

We cannot leave this topic without a few words of caution. Typically the competency-based approach tends to exclude the subjective judgment of teachers and children. Subjective judgment, however, should be a central and essential part of evaluation when the judgment is cautious, deliberate, reasoned, and accurate.

The worth of a language-arts curriculum is seldom indicated by the objectively measurable achievement of the children. The worth of the curriculum depends instead on its relevance to other curricula, its effect on teacher and child morale and on long-range attitudes, and on its relevance to the goals of the community it serves. Practitioners using competency approaches that ignore these dimensions of worth to concentrate on objective measures of achievement are potentially irresponsible.

Specifically, we object to programs that limit divergent thinking and open-ended activities; limit inspired teaching, enthusiasm, and the inductive discovery of exciting new information; make language something to master rather than something to use and enjoy; fragment language learning and prevent integration; and isolate children from each other and from their teacher, i.e., deny a social, interactive context that is intrinsically motivating. Our advice is to keep these cautions firmly in mind when involved in competency-based approaches and in formulation of guidelines for such a curriculum.

References

Block, James H., ed. *Mastery Learning: Theory and Practice.* New York: Holt, Rinehart and Winston, 1971.

Exemplary Center for Reading Instruction. *ECRI.* Salt Lake City, Utah.

Grindstaff, Roy R., and Shepherd, T. R. *111 Writing Activities: A Thinking Teacher's Guide to Writing Activities.* ED 139 016. Macomb: Western Illinois University, 1976.

Leach, L. C., and State Department of Education. *Behavioral Objectives— Composition Grades, K-12.* Little Rock, Ark.: State Department of Education, 1976.

Northern Valley Regional High School District. *Language Arts Curriculum Guide, Performance Expectations, K-12.* ED 140 329. Closter, N.J.: Regional High School District, 1976.

Oregon State Department of Education. *Language Arts Instruction, K-12.* ED 144 064. Salem: State Department of Education, 1977.

Pittsfield Public Schools. *Verbal Communications Competencies, K-6.* ED 134 997. Pittsfield, Mass.: School Department, 1976.

Selby County Board of Education. *Language Arts.* Memphis: Selby County Board of Education.

Smith, Fred M., and Adams, Sam. *Educational Measurement for the Classroom Teacher.* New York: Harper and Row, 1972.

U.S. Department of Health, Education, and Welfare, Office of Education. *Educational Programs That Work.* Vol. 4. Washington, D.C.: DHEW, 1977.

Wisconsin Research and Development Center. *Wisconsin Design for Reading Skill Development, K-6.* Madison: Wisconsin Research and Development Center, 1975.

4 A New Heritage Approach for Teaching the Language Arts

Eldonna L. Evertts
University of Illinois

A heritage approach to teaching English has produced a less than satisfactory literature or language-arts curriculum during the past quarter of a century. Because listening, speaking, reading, and writing are skills and, as such, have no content, curriculum designers have relied upon literature to produce the content. Rather than being of interest to and appropriate for children or adolescents, the study of literature in the schools has dealt with established cultural values and interpretations of life, which were treated as firmly fixed. The view of life presented in the works deemed worthy of study did not allow for the life experiences of children; it ignored their backgrounds and personal responses to the real world. The preselection of works for study froze the curriculum and disregarded new publications. Because this model was text centered, it largely confined itself to the written language and the development of mechanical skills. It ignored the value of oral interaction, and it failed to explore how language develops and how it helps children gain control over their experiences or give order to their universe. The printed page, not the child, was the center of the educational experience. Convergent thinking was urged; children were not encouraged to explore or discover on their own.

Yet, rather than dismiss the heritage approach because of the weaknesses just described, curriculum developers should give attention to a *new* heritage approach that places the student in the center of the educational setting and coordinates oral communication, language development, exploration through literature, and personal growth and experience.

This chapter will describe a heritage paradigm for the elementary school that blends the development of communication skills (listening, speaking, reading, and writing) with a body of content (literature and language), while at the same time addressing itself

35

to the communicative, personal, social, intellectual, and creative experiences of the pupil.

Although the term *language arts* implies specific language skills, this approach provides for growth in areas other than the oral and written. Provision is made for achievement of competence in the basic skills, logical and creative thinking, and modification of life and literary experiences. This new paradigm provides to the fullest extent for individual needs. The gifted child, the recently mainstreamed child, the average child, the non-English-speaking child— all must be served if the curriculum is to be worthy of implementation. Thus, no predesigned book list will suffice. Old favorites, new titles, and special books to meet individual needs and interests will appear in the curriculum, and the books used will vary from class to class each year.

Acquiring Communication Skills

The new heritage approach must provide ways to develop competence in communication skills. These skills, the acquisition of which comprises between 40–60 percent of the primary or intermediate school day, include reading and language study and involve handwriting, spelling, composition (prose and poetry), listening, usage, and perhaps grammar, vocabulary development, improvisation, talking, creative drama, choral reading, storytelling, dictionary study, and the history of English. These components of language arts are not treated as separate disciplines; they are to be used as ways to explore the nature of language and its use.

In the elementary grades, it has been a common practice to use the term *language arts* rather than *literature.* Therefore, a heritage approach at the primary or intermediate level must include activities related to the entire spectrum of the language arts. Instruction in the various components of the language arts, including literature, may take many forms, some of which possess limited value although they are commonly used. The teacher may follow a language arts textbook or use it for reference. Contrived pencil-paper activities should be avoided and the focus placed on talking—questioning, seeking, hypothesizing, evaluating—because children use talk to clarify ideas and to understand their experiences. A discussion of literary works can be a neutral ground for testing one's own beliefs, insights, or feelings. The new heritage approach, with its broad base of literary experiences, provides a common class experience for total group discussions, for small group projects, and for individual pursuits and inquiry.

A New Heritage Model

Literature is the central focus, but it is not the boundary of the many and varied class and individual projects flowing from its study. Through the teacher's oral reading of stories and the children's individual reading, the way is opened to discover and discuss what it means to be human and have feelings and desires, to seek fanciful and scientific explanations of phenomena, and to assume responsibility for one's own learning. Literature provides the setting for oral communication, for language growth and development, and for improvement of reading and writing skills. Unique to the new heritage model is the emphasis upon the development of the whole child (mental, social, moral), including an ultimate growth in appreciation, discrimination, self-awareness, and critical thinking.

The model fosters an attitude of questioning, seeking, and evaluation rather than one of mere absorption of truths or insights achieved by others, blind acceptance of values, or passive acquisition of skills. Such an approach requires much planning by the teacher for involvement of children in a variety of activities.

This model includes the following elements, the order of which may vary. It assumes each activity will involve student-teacher exploring, planning, action, and evaluation, which move toward objectives established in previous discussions. A further assumption is that small learning centers, student committees, and independent individual activities will accompany large group activities.

Planning by the Teacher

The teacher begins with a number of suitable themes or topics for a specific class. First-grade themes, for example, could be animals or nature. In the sixth grade, the teacher could consider the Middle Ages, Egyptian art, volcanoes, or conflict. Other topics might be inventions, sports, geographical places, or aspects of the human experience, such as loneliness, fear, death, humor.

Together the teacher and students investigate available resources. A visit to a museum, a class visitor, a television program, or a special display could initiate the project. The teacher needs to take into account the resources close at hand, the interest of the students, the availability of books, the academic skills to be encouraged, and the types of literary experiences that would be valuable. The teacher might begin with a literary concept and then find as many ways as possible to explore this concept. A helpful reference is *Topics in English* by Summerfield (1965), which illustrates the wide range of assignments, particularly in composition, that can flow from literature.

Selection of Theme, Topic, or Unit

For a unit and its principal work of literature to be meaningful to children, it must be cooperatively selected on the basis of mutual interest by both class members and teachers. After the students have completed several units, they will be able to enter more actively into the planning of a new unit or project. The time will come when students will discover another topic to explore as they are working through the current one. An intense interest on the part of one student can lead to valuable, independent study.

Expanding the Topic through Discussion

All topics or units can be expanded to accommodate special interests of the students and to extend their knowledge and understanding. A unit on China, for instance, could include the history of China, the nature of the Chinese theatre, biographies of its leaders and cultural figures, the characteristics of Oriental art and design, the changes of dress design over the centuries, the family structure, and the recent opening of China to Western visitors. Discussion at this time allows students to synthesize what they already know and to become aware of areas for further study and reading. Students can be on the alert to discover additional resources in the immediate environment. These may be library books, objects from home, or neighbors who have had a firsthand experience related to the topic. Discussions could continue for several days. Not only do they move the unit forward, but they provide practice in oral communication; organization, location of reference materials by using the card catalog, the index, or table of contents; classification and comparison of information; and observation and thinking.

Experiencing Literature

This is the heart of the heritage approach—the planned literature program. The teacher reads many selections from the body of children's literature. If the topic were snow, the teacher could read poetry or haiku on this subject, books on the Ice Age, novels describing survival during snow storms, myths and legends explaining the origin of snow, biographies of arctic explorers, or passages from other works. Since these books will be read by the teacher, they may be on a higher reading level than those the children read independently. Oral reading of literature by the teacher should continue daily throughout the unit. Needless to say, the teacher should make a great effort to read well, with appropriate inflection.

Individual Exploration of Literature

A wealth of children's books representing a variety of types and reading levels should be available for student reading in the classroom. Trips to the library can be planned so students can make their personal selections. These books may be shared with the class through creation of dioramas, adaptation of the story or folk tale for readers theatre, or presentation of a drama based upon an old legend—group activities that stimulate creative and critical thought. The successful completion of these projects attests to the students' command of basic academic skills. Should lack of skills become apparent during the progress of the project, the teacher should take time to teach the needed skill.

Discussion

At times there will be large group discussions, especially after the reading of a selection to the class. At other times the teacher may read orally to only a small group. After the reading, the teacher should let students comment on the story and what it meant to them. The teacher can learn much about the needs and growth of individual children from listening to their responses to literature. Only after the students have ceased to volunteer ideas should the teacher enter with questions, which should encourage divergent responses.

Understanding Different Points of View

Because there are many cultural and social groups in society, the wide range of personal differences and outlooks on life produces varying points of view. The study of literature often brings these patterns, conflicts, or values into focus, where they can be discussed and evaluated. Books presenting differing positions might be explored.

Interpreting Conventions of Writing in Print

The writing system employs only a few conventions to interpret the features of oral language, so these must be carefully noted to assure comprehension. Italics, boldface type, underlining, capitalization, punctuation, and spacing are some of the conventions that assist the reader. The teacher should help pupils become aware of these aids to meaning and oral interpretation. At times sentences from a library book may be written on the chalkboard for study and analysis. At other times a language arts textbook or reference work may be consulted to clarify points under study. In these ways students can gain a practical understanding of how the English language functions and is recorded in print, and how the structure and form can affect meaning.

Competence in Composition

Students can use the literary selections discussed in class as models for their own writing. An understanding of the basic plot elements gives a framework for constructing original stories. Although such writing may be derivative, it helps students to understand literary structure. Most teachers are alert to other opportunities for writing or sharing—friendly letters, thank you notes, letters of inquiry, notices, or invitations. Children learn to write by writing, and the heritage model provides many opportunities to write. Sharing a completed composition with peers is important. These compositions also indicate to the teacher where further instruction is necessary.

Learning Centers

The centers can make a valuable contribution to skill building and assist other learning tasks. A particular learning center may exist for a long or short period of time. A center for creative writing with paper, pencils, pictures, dictionaries, student folders, and a display area may be more or less permanent, while a center for a specific skill, such as capitalization, may exist for a short time but be fequently repeated with activities varying according to individual needs. Other centers can be devoted to word games, crossword puzzles, bookmaking, reading books, creation of illustrative materials to accompany a library book, spelling, or punctuation.

Use of Creative and Expressive Arts

Literature stimulates the imagination. This mental activity can find creative expression through the arts. Students who are unable to move forward in composition may need to develop in another creative area before they can move forward in writing. Therefore, the wise teacher does not regard improvisation, creative drama, poetry, choral reading, or puppet shows as idle activities but as means to experience life.

Utilization of Media

The use of media can help to expand a topic. Pictures, slides, or films transcend time and space to broaden concepts. Students can preview and select materials for class viewing. They can also create materials for use on the overhead projector to illustrate their own projects.

Student Preparation of Learning Modules

Small groups can engage in peer teaching by making a cassette tape giving data about objects on display and a short comprehension test. Younger children may need closer teacher supervision and support, but older children can function independently with the teacher checking only the final information for accuracy. Individual learning modules created by students are a valuable experience for both the creators and the users.

Storytelling

Many stories we enjoy today evolved as part of the oral tradition. The Brothers Grimm recorded the folk tales of Germany, and now tales from all corners of the world can be found in books. The time has come for these stories to be told orally again. Teachers may invite librarians or other adults who engage in storytelling to visit their classrooms and share this literary experience.

Culminating Activity

Each unit needs to be terminated so that a new unit can be undertaken. The culminating activity is frequently an informal sharing (perhaps called a program) for parents or another class. The students explain their activities and share the products—a poem, puppet show, scrapbook, play, dance, or illustration.

Contributions of Literature

Even though young children may not be consciously aware of it, literature can make a valuable contribution to their lives. It can help them gain insights into their personal experiences and problems, understand how others approach and meet life's vicissitudes,

"try on" roles not possible in reality and enter the world of fantasy.
A book such as *Why Mosquitoes Buzz in People's Ears* by Aardema
can help children understand the consequences of lying better
than direct instruction or preaching. Similarly, a realistic book like
Time of Wonder by McCloskey can help the younger child grasp
the concept of time or changing seasons and weather. Other stories
can stimulate the imagination and enable children to consider life
patterns that may be quite different from their own. For example,
Madeline (and succeeding titles in the series) by Bemelmans describes the experiences of a little girl living in a boarding school in
France. Preschool children enjoy *Where the Wild Things Are* by
Sendak and delight in the humor of *Harry the Dirty Dog* by Zion
while most seven and eight year olds are receptive to the impossible
predicament described in *Strega Nona: An Old Tale* by de Paola.

A Planned Literature Program

The body of children's literature is too vast to allow random book
selection. Of course, free choice has a rightful place. The individual
needs to read for enjoyment, but the goal of a literature program
is to provide opportunities to understand feelings and to encourage
and nurture personal growth and development. To achieve this goal,
a planned literature curriculum is essential. To leave selection to
chance represents lack of understanding on the part of those en-
trusted with curriculum responsibility and decision making.

A planned program does not begin in kindergarten or the first
grade but in the home and nursery or child care facility. The origin
of the literature program is in Mother Goose, finger plays, jingles,
poems, wordless books, alphabet books, concept books; indeed,
even picture books are part of this world of literature.

A planned program implies that literature will be found throughout the school curriculum. Unfortunatly this is not the case. A
review of the status of literature in schools reveals that its prominent role in the primary grades decreases during the intermediate
and high school years. There should be literature programs at all
educational levels, and they should be in harmony with each other.
Articulation is essential: the early literary experiences should become the basis for reading, study, and enjoyment in the later years.

A planned program should not become frozen. Provision must
be made in a curriculum for current, appropriate literature in the
areas of interest to students, on topics being studied in class or on
current issues in society. Teachers, students, parents, and other interested persons should review and analyze new books for their

potential contribution to the literature program. However, final responsibility for the success of the literary heritage model rests upon the classroom teacher, who must arrange for an extensive collection of books in the classroon for individual selection, plan time for reading and discussion, and plan with teachers at other levels.

A Balanced Literature Program

That a literature program is planned is not sufficient; it must also be balanced. A literature program is balanced if it meets four requirements. First, a balanced program is one in which no form or genre of literature is omitted; it would include works representative of various types—comedy, epic, lyric, myth, legend, fable.

Second, the literature curriculum cannot be limited to works associated only with the Judeo-Christian tradition but should include works from other cultures as well. A criterion for selection should be the exposure of young people to the literary contributions of all peoples. Representative literary samples from many societies should be included.

The recent focus in education on the multicultural composition of American society necessitates finding legends, myths, or folk tales illustrating the literary heritage of all segments of our society. Those planning this component of the curriculum will find *Folklore and Folktales around the World* (Carlson, 1972) useful. Another source for myths and legends is the Oxford University Press, which publishes a broad selection of tales from Yugoslavia, Japan, China, Africa, the West Indies, and other areas (see, for example, Arnott, 1978, and Downing, 1978). Teachers and administrators who are interested in international children's books should investigate the resources available through the International Board on Books for Young People. (For information write John Donovan, Secretary, International Board on Books for Young People [IBBY], in care of Children's Book Council, 67 Irving Place, New York, New York 10003.)

Third, the program should be balanced according to group and individual needs. Teachers should consider the ages of students, their life experiences, their academic growth and development, their learning styles, their personal requirements, and their social and intellectual abilities as they select the books for units and group activities. It becomes increasingly important to individualize instruction as students who were previously placed in special education classes return to the regular classroom or as students with special needs remain with their peers. Books appropriate for one class may not be of the same value for a different class. Therefore, a balanced literature program offers a reading list unique for each group of children and for individuals within that group.

Fourth, a balanced program will include works of literary quality. Without a planned curriculum, excellent books can be overlooked. The study of literature should reflect, in both form and content, the diversity of life itself. Children certainly should be free to select books for their personal reading without being subjected to criticism, but at the elementary school level, the books read aloud in class should be meritorious.

Response to Literature

Discussion provides an opportunity for students to respond to literature and evaluate the selection in terms of their own personal experience. What pupils derive from their reading is colored by their past experiences with life and literature. These experiences provide them with a base of information and feelings with which to respond to new literary selections and to form their own values and set goals. They need a quantity of literary experiences to be able to generalize and to respond in more mature ways.

Responses to literature can be either affective or cognitive. To encourage affective responses, questions should probe the student's feelings about the events or characters in the story. Questions that help the student recognize structure, irony, hyperbole, symbols, or archetypes encourage cognitive development. These literary terms need not be used, but the concepts can be isolated, identified, and then discussed (Anderson et al., 1972).

Oral Reading of Literature

Although most oral reading of children's literature will be done by the teacher in the elementary school, students can share in this activity. The use of a cassette recorder permits repeated recording of readings until students are satisfied with the results and wish to share them. It is recommended that the teacher prepare for oral interpretation of literature by silent reading and private oral practice.

Oral reading of literature has three contributions to make to literary awareness and language development. First, students become acquainted with the whole of a literary selection—its plot structure, character development, and other characteristics. Because the pupil is listening and not reading silently, the story unfolds without any clouding of meaning caused by difficult or unusual words.

Second, the students hear sentence patterns or constructions that they may never have heard or used before. Edited prose has tighter structure than free, unrehearsed conversation. Sentences are expanded; elements are embedded. If pupils are to comprehend formal prose constructions in their own silent reading, they need to hear these patterns read aloud with a thoughtful interpretation.

Finally, oral reading of literature throughout the elementary years is not a luxury but a necessity, as it provides students with both an experience with literature and with the written form of language. Therefore, oral reading is of prime importance in the new heritage approach.

The selection of works for oral reading should include myths, legends, folk tales, and "pourquoi" stories. These stories are important, not just because they are part of the literary heritage, but because they parallel the thought development of children. As children adjust to their world, they seek explanations of events and they explore solutions—often imaginary—as they give shape, form, and organization to the world. The role of traditional literature in the schools is supported by Cullinan and Carmichael (1977), Huck (1976), Bettelheim (1976), Heins (1977), and others. Folk tales and fairy tales are vital in the psychological development of the child, for handling fears and for encouraging humor and fantasy.

Storytelling has been developed by librarians in recent years. The story hour in the library needs to be repeated in the classroom, home, and in other settings. A helpful publication for those interested in storytelling is *Storytelling: Art and Technique* (Baker and Greene, 1977). While storytelling is commonly regarded as an art, it is an art that can be learned and engaged in at many levels of ability. The eye contact between storyteller and listerner—the one-to-one contact—is a rich experience satisfying to both speaker and listener.

Storytelling is a bridge between the informal, oral discourse children engage in every day and the tight, frozen style of the printed page. Most teachers and storytellers today find a recorded or printed version of the tale they wish to tell. Thus, the raw material is in a form that has been carefully edited. The retelling by the storyteller then is a type of spoken discourse that is unlike both free, oral conversation and frozen, printed prose. It becomes a bridge between these two; it relaxes the printed form, yet retains its distinguishing elements. Thus, storytelling can provide the child with an experience with language that can be obtained in no other way. It also lets the child participate in the "literary" experience as people did long before printing, reading, or writing flourished.

Oral literature, then, whether in the form of reading, storytelling, recording, or film, must be a segment of any well-planned model for the new heritage approach.

Since time does not permit reading all the children's books in print, careful selection and planning is necessary. The literature program should include the best, the enduring, and the appealing. Some works should be read in class for the literary experience of all. Other works should be selected to meet individual needs. Always, the need is to make the literary experience vital for the present—then it will continue to grow.

References

Aardema, Verna. *Why Mosquitoes Buzz in People's Ears: A West African Tale.* Illustrated by Leo and Diane Dillon. New York: Dial Press, 1975.

Anderson, William, et al. *A New Look at Children's Literature.* Belmont, Calif.: Wadsworth Publishing, 1972.

Arnott, Kathleen. *African Myths and Legends.* New York: Oxford University Press, 1978.

Baker, Augusta, and Greene, Ellin. *Storytelling: Art and Technique.* New York: R. R. Bowker, 1977.

Bemelmans, Ludwig. *Madeline.* New York: Viking Press, 1939.

Bettelheim, Bruno. *The Uses of Enchantment: The Meaning and Importance of Fairy Tales.* New York: Alfred A. Knopf, 1976.

Carlson, Ruth Kearney. *Folklore and Folktales around the World.* Perspectives in Reading Series, no. 15. Newark, Del.: International Reading Association, 1972.

Cullinan, Bernice E., and Carmichael, Carolyn W., eds. *Literature and Young Children.* Urbana, Ill.: National Council of Teachers of English, 1977.

de Paola, Tomie. *Strega Nona: An Old Tale.* New York: Prentice-Hall, 1975.

Downing, Charles. *Russian Tales and Legends.* New York: Oxford University Press, 1978.

Heins, Paul, ed. *Crosscurrents of Criticism: Horn Book Essays, 1968–1977.* Boston: Horn Book, 1977.

Huck, Charlotte S. *Children's Literature in the Elementary School.* 3rd ed. New York: Holt, Rinehart and Winston, 1976.

McCloskey, Robert. *Time of Wonder.* New York: Viking Press, 1957.

Potter, Beatrix. *The Tale of Peter Rabbit.* London: Warne, 1902.

Sendak, Maurice. *Where the Wild Things Are.* New York: Harper and Row, 1963.

Summerfield, Geoffrey. *Topics in English.* London: B. T. Batsford Ltd., 1965.

Zion, Gene. *Harry the Dirty Dog.* Illustrated by Margaret Bloy Graham. New York: Harper and Row, 1956.

5 Process-Oriented Instructional Activities: Pre-Kindergarten through Grade Five

Russel G. Stauffer
University of Delaware

From the time that very young children use both imitative and spontaneous speech, the functional use of language is based on personal speech activities in a speaker-listener context. Personal and social actions advance the process of learning about language. In a school setting, it is important that these "activities" be practical, functional, and, above all, energized by the learner's grasp of why and how the activities function. Piaget's work is useful in this regard, particularly the clarity he gives to the role of action and interaction in his descriptions of children's development. Children learn to know about persons, places, things, and events through their interactions with them. This is particularly so for language learning. It is the "perceptual-cognitive underpinnings, the ability to grasp meaning, that seem to account to a good degree for the nature and degree of language development" (Bloom, 1975, p. 290).

Because conventional instructional activities are all too often referred to as "skills" and are assembled in "skillbooks," they deserve a critical look. What we find is this: skillbook activities are brief; they do not stem from an immediate learner need and are seldom process oriented; they do not provide for transfer of learning to other types of situations; and usually they are administered in a setting devoid of communication context. As Glucksberg and his associates (1975) have written, "It is our view that so long as meaning, communication, and intentions to communicate are excluded from consideration as central to the interactive acquisition process, efforts to deal with acquisition of syntax *per se* or lexicons *per se* are doomed to failure. . . . In learning and using language, one's real concern is to learn how most effectively to engage in communication with those with whom one comes into contact. The name of the game is messages, not words, sentences, or paragraphs." (p. 339) The message idea is attractive because it emphasizes communication, which in turn accents purpose, function, and immediacy, and because it involves the functional use of language.

It is also attractive to consider an instructional approach in which messages are for the most part produced through the initiative of the learner. Learner-generated activities amplify the purpose to be accomplished; the motive that prompts the message; the means, or the nature of the message; and the effect, or the envisioned outcome. Because purpose, motive, means, and effect so compactly weave the drama of communication, they are almost totally process oriented. Thus, this chapter on process activities will emphasize functional communication in which messages generated by the learner predominate. The activities presented are merely illustrative, and their sole purpose is to help children learn how to use their language to communicate effectively.

Oral Communication

At all levels of instruction, but particularly kindergarten through second grade, it is wise to capitalize on the immediate. The following transcript of a child's description is an example.

The Phanatic

We seen the Phillies and we saw the Phanatic. He is funny. His tongue is big and yellow. This is a Phanatic pennant.

Through the use of a prop, the child's teacher had stimulated a child's personal experience that promoted talking and then attended to it. Such occasions are always enriched when supported by a prop—in this instance, the Phillies Phanatic banner. The members of the class were not only attentive—listening, seeing, reflecting and imagining—but also saw the banner, felt it, waved it, paraded with it, asked about it, and responded to the child's spontaneous oral accounting with further sharing of ideas through language. The teacher spontaneously structured the activity by capitalizing on the immediate, in this case the vividness of the event to the children and the presence of the concrete object, the banner. The teacher used an action-oriented experience to help the children link oral language to what they did perceptually and cognitively.

Oral language activities may be more formally structured. For instance, the teacher may have the children participate in a pre-planned activity such as making applesauce, planting seeds, or playing with a new class pet. In such activities the teacher is alert to the possibilities for encouraging language among the children which is related to the activity in progress. These action-oriented activities also provide opportunities for further, more formal discussion. Group discussions may also be arranged for a specific topic, such as "My Favorite Toy," "My Home," "My Costume," and so on. The stimulus should be general in nature and open-ended in order to draw upon a child's own circumstances and recall.

From Oral Language to Printed Language

The Bullock report (1975) concluded its review of publisher programs by stating, "We believe that an improvement in the teaching of reading will not come from the acceptance of simplistic statements about phonics or any other single aspect of reading, but from a comprehensive study of all the factors at work and the influence that can be exerted upon them (p. 78)." It is in this respect that the Language Experience Approach reflects a comprehensive global approach. The Language portion encompasses the four facets of communication and is founded on the purposeful social-personal use of language. Experience encompasses an individual's perceptual and conceptual world, interest and curiosities, creativity, culture, capacity to learn and to use, and, above all, a person's extraordinary flexibility.

Since at ages five and six, children are eager to learn to read, an immediate reading start is paramount. This can be accomplished by means of student-dictated accounts of a structured firsthand experience. The teacher makes available a prop that will capture and hold pupil interest, something they can act upon and interact about. For instance, one teacher on the second day of school brought a box turtle into her room. The children gathered around and watched it crawl, withdraw its feet and head, then felt its shell, described its colors, size, and movements, noted its reaction to being lifted, and so on. The teacher asked open-ended and attention-focusing questions such as, "How does it walk?" "How is the way it walks different from the way you crawl?" "What do its colors remind you of?" "How does its shell feel?" "Why do you think it feels that way?" The children then dictated the following account:

The Box Turtle

Reginald said, "He lives in a shell." Jeff said, "When you pick him up, his head goes into his shell." James said, "He can swim." Charisse said, "He is black and yellow." Regina said, "He has two eyes and four feet." Lisa said, "His tail is short." Tyrone said, "He crawls around in his box."

The teacher then read the recorded dictation to the class, pointing to each word as she pronounced it. Then she paced the children through an oral reading and finally had each of the eight children who had contributed read the account with her. Each child was then asked to draw a picture of the box turtle, and the teacher wrote the title "Box Turtle" on each drawing, thus facilitating the recognition and recall of the two words. Picture clues and language clues provide logical, meaningful aids to recall and are more effective than rote memorization or skillbook activities. Both forms of clues have a tremendous potency because they are produced by the original language creator and artist.

Word Recognition

The next two days the class read and reread the dictation and examined each other's drawings. In addition, some words were identified in isolation: *Box, Turtle, shell, eyes, feet, tail, Tyrone.* These words were chosen because of their significance to the children, which made the words more likely to be recalled.

These words were also located by the children in books, newspapers, and magazines that had been placed on the classroom library table. These different contexts provided superb word recognition training through use of a basic law of learning—transfer of knowledge to a new situation. Locating the words was also a marvelous use of configuration or visual discrimination clues coupled with meaning or semantic clues. At the same time, the use of the classroom library for the activity built up receptivity to a wide variety of reading materials.

On the third day, each student received a copy of the dictation, which was dated and placed in the student's own notebook. (The notebook provides a chronological organization of dictations, illustrations, and known words.) On the copies the teacher showed the children how to underline any word they could name. The words underlined were then read to the teacher on an individual-by-individual basis. To be sure that the child could identify the word in isolation, the teacher used a $3''$ x $5''$ card in which a word-window had been cut, thus isolating the word from its context.

Word Banks

Each word recognized through the window was placed on a card stored in a small sturdy box known as a "Word Bank." Thus, each student had a sight vocabulary file that varied directly with his or her ability to recognize, retain, and recall. Bright children progress rapidly and soon underline all the words in an account. The less apt underline fewer and sometimes fail to recognize these twenty-four hours later. It is wise to have these children underline "known" words a second time to determine if they are well enough established to place in a word bank. This kind of pacing geared to the individual helps provide success for each child and minimizes demands and restrictions.

The use of windows and of word banks provides a good opportunity for learning word-attack skills. The children are plied with their own window-cards to test themselves and others; this allows children to pair up and play window-card games. Similarly, words can be lifted from a word bank and used for a variety of purposes.

Alphabetizing

Once the number of words in a word bank exceeds thirty or more, alphabetizing can be helpful. A good plan is to provide a small envelope for each letter in the alphabet. In a short time, alphabetical order is appreciated because the letters serve a function. Children note letter order relationships: *B* is up front, *S* near the end, *L* in the middle, and so on. At this point an abridged elementary dictionary may be used to compare letter order, word location, page organization, and the like.

Developing Word Recognition Power

Context or meaning clues are based on the psychological principles of closure and projection. Both refer to closing a gap through a relentless search for meaning. At the earliest stages of learning to read, children should receive systematic instruction in the use of meaning clues, with the teacher constantly and deliberately promoting the training by rereadings, use of window cards, locating words elsewhere, and so on.

The way to start making children articulate the phonological wealth represented by their speaking vocabularies is through rhyming and alliteration. Training in rhyming is easily initiated by using a student's name, one with a readily distinguishable ending sound such as *Bill, Jane,* or *Tom.* Ask Bill to stand up and then say, "I am going to say a word, you tell me if it sounds like Bill." The teacher says, "Hill, will, still, Jill, stop." This provides training in likeness and difference, with emphasis on likeness or rhyme. Alliteration is not as readily grasped by some children, but when three words are grouped in a semi-sing-song fashion, the beat and rhythm can be helpful. Three words like *"Big boy Bill,"* *"Down the deep ditch,"* or *"Lisa likes lemons"* can be spoken by the teacher with stress on the beginning sounds. The words are repeated by the children so that they can hear the alliteration. This training in auditory skills precedes and then parallels auditory-visual discrimination.

Auditory-Visual Training

As soon as one word is recognized, auditory-visual training can be initiated. For example, by the end of the second day, all the children in the class that observed the box turtle could recognize *box* and *turtle.* Instruction might proceed as follows. The teacher prints the word *box* on the chalkboard. When all eyes are focused on the printed word *box* (with the letter *b* underlined), the teacher says a word like *big,* and the children are asked to determine if the spoken word begins with the same sound as the printed word. Next, the teacher says such words as *book, bank, barn, tree* and like decisions are made. Such auditory and auditory-visual training must be done every day. The more proficient the children become, the more apt they will be to utilize the skill to unlock words in their own dictated accounts and in those of their classmates; and they in turn become increasingly more skilled at transferring the decoding skill to books.

Moving from this skill to letter substitution is readily accomplished. The procedure is simple. Words are placed in columns to facilitate comparisons.

Bill	boy	make	sun
hill	toy	take	run
fill	joy	lake	fun
pill	Roy	rake	bun

Once children grasp the idea, they can use their word bank for substitution work.

Conceptual Classification and Word Usage

Words can be assembled into classes or categories, e.g., names of things and names of friends. Words in the word bank may be used initially and then augmented by words from books and other sources.

Words in a word bank can also be arranged and rearranged to create sentences. This kind of idea structuring not only develops word recognition and concept power, but also sets the stage for creative writing.

Creative Writing

By the time children are of school age, they have had much experience in using language creatively (Bloom, 1975). Creative use of written language may be defined as writing that reflects a child's own choice of ideas, words, grammar, and punctuation. The content may be nonfiction or fiction, documentary or imaginative, expository or narrative. The subject of the writing may be selected by the student, the class, or the teacher.

When children reach the stage where they try their hand at creative writing, they have already acquired a sensitivity to letter order within words and to phoneme-grapheme relationships. It is of utmost importance, however, for children to realize that in creative writing their ideas, vocabulary usage, and language structure are more important than spelling. While the ability to encode by producing standard English spelling is a long-range goal, phonological encoding is acceptable at this stage. The important thing is the communication of ideas.

The story below was a first attempt at creative writing by Denise, a first-grade girl.

Wndr Wmn

I wsh I wz Wndr Wmn. I will bet up the Nzzis. I will jump of the mpir Stat billding.

Note the strengths displayed by Denise: (1) she has a title that is placed appropriately; (2) she uses capital letters when appropriate; (3) the words *I, will, up, the, jump* are spelled "correctly"; (4) other words show astonishing alertness to letter-sound relationships; and (5) she expresses her ideas in logical order.

By the third grade, productions become lengthier, more involved, and more "creative." Writings reflect increased maturity, language-usage power, and continued instruction. The following is an example.

Sunny the Funny Bunny

Once there was a funny bunny. He always told jokes. The animals got tired of his jokes. He had a problem on his hands. He had to find someone who liked him. That would be hard because he told jokes to everyone in the forest. He would have to go somewhere else. He asked the owl where to go. The owl said he should stay where he is but not tell jokes. So he did and he never told jokes again.

Even though children find objects, events, and people interesting to write about, the teacher should be prepared to supply subjects for creative writing. The curriculum itself is a good source: science activities (classifying leaves), health (jogging), social studies (Norwegian houses), arts (sketching, carving), music (folk songs), and so on. Current events such as storms, contests, elections, Halloween parades, and the first snowfall are also excellent subjects.

Editorial effort enters into the writing almost from the very beginning, but usually in an informal manner. Students reread what they have written and often want to make changes, additions, or corrections. This editorial effort is to be encouraged on a "discovery-learning" basis, but it must not become a preoccupation and thereby shut off interest and performance. When the writing habit has been established, usually by fourth grade, structured editorial work can begin; it should, however, proceed at a modest rate and be conveyed through approval. After successes are stressed, one or two items can be selected for improvement. Eventually this leads to drafting, editing, and rewriting.

When editing is structured, instruction should introduce only one type of editing activity at a time. It is often helpful to remember that editing is also a process. Before focusing on capitalization, punctuation, or vocabulary usage, it is beneficial to read and discuss certain passages from books, stories, and the like for vocabulary, phrasing, mood, and sequence of ideas. Student responses to the material should have a prominent place in the instruction.

Reading Strategies

The strategy of Directed Reading-Thinking Activities (DRTA) is based on student inquiry and reflective thought. The DRTA approach is designed to use as fully as possible certain assumptions about human capacities: that humans are thinking beings oriented toward the future and constantly making educated guesses or predictions; that humans by nature categorize knowledge, and that they by nature are decision makers. It behooves us then to direct reading instruction in such a way that these innate capacites of students to predict, to categorize, and to exercise free will are utilized as fully as possible.

Reading is conceived of as a process of continuous growth of the mind through increasingly refined powers of inquiry, categorization, and decision making. By declaring purposes for reading, readers engage their curiosity, their experience and knowledge, and their decision-making processes. Comprehension is thus determined by purposes of the mind because they play a regulatory role. Critical reading, or reading as reasoning, provides the instructional foundation from the moment DRTA instruction is introduced in first grade. Because making judgments is an evaluative process, the reader is required to determine not only the facts, but also the value of the facts and their consequences in light of the reader's purposes.

Divergent Thinking

The divergent thinker is the creative thinker. One good way to begin divergent thinking instruction is through use of a title. For instance, a group of six year olds was asked to predict what the story "A Newspaper Helps" might be about. A range of responses reflecting pupil experiences and maturity resulted: (1) a rainy day story, (2) a lost pet story, (3) training a pet story, (4) a painting class story, (5) a garbage story, (6) a moving day story. In another setting, nine year olds using a selection titled "The Railroad Cat" predicted as follows: (1) a pet cat story, (2) a troublesome cat story, (3) how a cat saves a train, (4) a cat and her litter, (5) a cat in a caboose. Eleven year olds responded to a nonfiction selection title "Our Fourth Coast" with varied expectations: (1) the selection would deal with Alaska, (2) it would be about Hawaii, (3) it might be about our space program, (4) it might be about the Panama Canal. In each of those instances, the predictions were supported with explanations that reflected a student's knowledge and provided stimulating ideas for others in the group.

The use of a newspaper headline or the equivalent is an excellent aid for training in divergent thinking, speculating, and purpose setting. This type of training and the resulting reading to confirm or correct can be done almost from the beginning of reading instruction.

Convergent Thinking

Instruction is also needed in convergent thinking. In this type of instruction, the reader is exposed to most of the information given in a selection and is then required to evaluate and make judgments about the one or two most likely outcomes. A good instructional procedure promoting convergent thinking is to ask a student to read all of a selection except the last page. The reader may have to cope with many facts and ideas and not only determine their relevancy, but also decide which ones point to the most likely conclusion. Since convergent thinking can prove taxing, it requires instructional opportunities at all levels.

If, for example, the children had read all of "The Railroad Cat" except the last two pages, they would be familiar with the story up to the point where the cat is riding on the train with the engineer and begins to howl fiercely. Convergent predictions are usually two-fold: (1) the cat senses danger ahead and saves the train; (2) the cat saves the train and returns to its home. Each prediction must be backed up with reasons obtained from the selection, so the reader must weigh many facts, make and defend decisions, and uncover proof.

Some DRTA's should be planned that require students to weigh evidence at different points and make educated guesses. For instance, students may be asked to read one-third of a selection and then speculate about the rest, or read one-half of a selection or two-thirds and so on.

In this type of instruction, the reader must learn how to hold ideas long enough to compare and evaluate them, to make choices among them, and to act upon the choices. This activity is what is so loosely called "reading." It reflects the ability of the human mind to anticipate, to look ahead, to project; to abstract and take out of the content those ideas that are relevant and essential; to test or use or act upon what has been abstracted. The functional kinds of critical reading instruction described here must be accomplished from first grade on up in terms of age-related growing experiences, interests, maturity, the expanding curriculum, and students' varying abilities.

Inquiry Reading

The Directed Reading-Thinking Activities described earlier involve group reading in which each member of the group reacts to the same material at the same time and under the constant, immediate direction of the teacher. Inquiry Reading procedures utilize skills acquired in group instruction, but do so quite differently. Distinguishing features of Inquiry Reading are (1) interest areas and the nature of the inquiries to be made are declared by the children, who are grouped according to interest areas; (2) students select and use materials from a range of media possibilities; (3) obtaining answers to their questions and internalizing information gained are the key factors in regulating learner growth; (4) information is shared through careful preparation and presentation; and (5) audience interaction and evaluation are obtained.

At the beginning of the three- to six-week Inquiry Reading period, inquiry interests are declared by the students. Topics such as space, oil, weather, black holes, horses, oceans, and planets are listed as they are raised and are enlarged on briefly by each proposer. On another day the class reduces the number of topics to four or five, and each student decides which topic would be most interesting to pursue.

To make the topics more definitive, ideas related to each topic are declared. For example:

Oceans

fish	oil slicks
currents	exploration
pollution	hurricanes
sharks	sailing
swimming	whales
fishing	seaweed

Again, the ideas are elaborated on briefly, and then the children decide how best they can be categorized.

Sea Life	Ocean Conditions	Things to Do
fish	currents	fishing
sharks	pollution	swimming
seaweed	hurricanes	sailing
whales	oil slicks	exploration

Categorizing ideas can prove both challenging and provocative. It requires close examination of ideas or concepts to note how they are related and how they differ. Such categorizing is marvelous training in objectifying experiences that may have existed largely as abstractions and is a fundamental step in extending and refining concepts. Categorizing as a preliminary to study also stimulates curiosity and leads to better insights into what is known and what is not known.

The activities described so far lead naturally to the raising of questions by the students. Obviously the nature and quality of the questions will reflect not only the students' maturity and experience, but also the nature of their instruction. Repeated opportunities and instruction lead children's inquiries from the what, when, where, who factual stage to the why and how conceptual stage and, for example, to such questions as, How are ocean currents formed?

or How do ocean currents affect the world? To obtain even greater commitment to the inquiry process, students are asked to speculate about likely answers to their questions. The above questions may produce such speculations as the following: I think ocean currents are formed by the moon, or Ocean currents result from hurricanes and high winds.

Now several days are devoted to locating and selecting materials. Books, periodicals, films, speakers, encyclopedias, newspapers, government pamphlets, and the like may prove helpful in finding answers. Obtaining answers to questions is done not only by reading, but also by listening, seeking, talking, experimenting, and organizing. The teacher's role at this stage is vital—locating materials, keeping students on course, assisting with concepts and vocabulary, and suggesting ways of organizing information.

The final activity, sharing information, focuses on the audience and audience-related demands: knowledge of the subject and presentation of it with clarity and style. Sharing can be accomplished by a mural, a simulated television interview, a diorama, a series of posters, demonstrations, and so on. Preparations for sharing—rehearsals, polishing lines, making props, timing presentations, working together—are as instructive for students as audience response, which promotes appreciation, social sensitivity, cooperative interactions, listening, and critical evaluation. However, teacher direction is essential to promote thoughtful, discrete, and tempered audience responses.

There are instructional advantages in scheduling teaching-learning opportunities for both Directed Reading-Thinking Activities and Inquiry Reading. Each alternate instructional period should help develop higher levels of communication, sound attitudes, and refined skills as reading becomes a means of self-realization, self-regulation, and self-relaxation. Above all, children learn to examine their interests and tastes and gain increasing appreciation for the depth and breadth of their curiosities, the nature and scope of knowledge, and different means of communication. For students the key to all these advances is quite simple: the asking of questions, an art that has been undervalued and stunted by misleading teachers' guides.

Concept Development

If comprehension is thought of as the functional constant of reading instruction, then the acquisition of concepts is of first-order importance. Children bring with them to school innumerable ideas or concepts, some of which are quite sound and functional, while others are vague and unclear. Experimenting with ideas provides a firm foundation for further cognitive development.

Basically, concept formation consists of the perception of relationships among stimuli (Vygotsky, 1962) or between constituent-part processes (Bruner, 1956). Instructional guidelines for aiding concept development as defined by Klausmeier (1968) are as follows:

1. Use the correct label or language for a concept.
2. Emphasize the attributes of a concept to be learned. Note attributes, but also compare them.
3. Provide for proper sequencing of instances or examples through objects, models, illustrations, etc.
4. Encourage and support students by fostering a questioning attitude.
5. Provide for application of the concept, especially in a new situation.

Concepts can also be taught by proceeding from attributes to functions to category. For instance, the concept of an egg-timer can be taught by first having the children define its attributes by feeling it, by watching the sand drain from top to bottom, and so on. The function of a timer can be demonstrated by timing eggs for soft boiling and for hard boiling. The category of timer can be established by comparing it to a stopwatch, an alarm clock, a stove timer, and a wristwatch.

Conclusion

The purpose of this chapter has been to show that language-learning activity should be learner-generated, process-oriented communication activity. While specific ideas for such activity have been described here, they are simply illustrative of an endless number of similar activities that teachers can use. And the best source for these activities is teacher inventiveness and judgment. Teachers no longer need be stifled by manuals, subjectively structured skillbook activities, and instruction that withers the mind. We live in an intellectually exciting world, and the instructional activities we employ should reflect and reinforce that excitement.

References

Bloom, Lois. "Language Development Review." In *Review of Child Develop-ment Research*, vol. 4, edited by Frances D. Horowitz, pp. 245-303. Chicago: University of Chicago Press, 1975.

Bruner, Jerome, Goodnow, Jacquelline J., and Austin, George A. *A Study of Thinking*. New York: John Wiley, 1956.

Bullock, Sir Alan. *A Language for Life: Report of the Committee of Inquiry Appointed by the Secretary of State for Education and Science* (England). London: Her Majesty's Stationery Office, 1975.

Glucksberg, Sam, Krauss, Robert, and Higgins, E. Tory. "The Development of Referential Communication Skills." In *Review of Child Development Re-search*, vol. 4, edited by Frances D. Horowitz, pp. 305-345. Chicago: University of Chicago Press, 1975.

Klausmeier, Herbert J., and Harris, Chester W. *Strategies and Cognitive Processes in Concept Learning*, Final Report, Project No. 2850. Washington, D.C.: U.S. Department of Health, Education, and Welfare, Office of Education, Bureau of Research, 1968.

Vygotsky, L. S. *Thought and Language*. Translated by E. Haufmann and G. Vakar. Cambridge, Mass.: M.I.T. Press, 1962.

II The School in the Middle

6 Schooling for Young Adolescents

Theodore Manolakes
University of Illinois

Whether it is called a junior high school, middle school, or an upper elementary school, the educational institution that serves young adolescents is often viewed with concern by the public. Its public image is that of a school that deals ineffectively with a very difficult age group. Whether the general impression of these schools is fair is less important than the fact that the school at this level does face some persistent problems because of its position as the school in the middle. This chapter is an attempt to define those problems and suggest some solutions.

The school in the middle exists between two long-established institutions that have goals and structures significantly different from each other. The school in the middle, then, has a very difficult and complex function. It must provide transitions in academic programs and organizational structure for its students. That it does not always do so should surprise no one.

Elementary and Senior High Schools

The elementary schools of this country have long had a publicly accepted foundational function. There is a clear expectation that they will train children in fundamental skills in reading, writing, and mathematics. Although elementary schools do other things for children, the effectiveness of their programs is judged almost entirely on the basis of children's performance in the skill areas. Elementary schools are thus organized to pursue the aim of skill development. Generalist teachers usually work with a single group of children for an entire year, taking responsibility for the major part of their educational experiences during that time. Through continuous contact, these teachers are able to monitor and reinforce the development of skills. The close contact allows teachers to know children well and to make better prescriptions for meeting their individual needs.

Though not as simple an organization, the senior high school also has a clear aim. It is expected to prepare students for higher education or for a vocation. It uses a subject matter curriculum to give learners important content in the disciplines or vocational fields. This preparation is assumed to serve students well in their future pursuits and is generally accepted by the public. The senior high school is organized to bring students in contact with teachers who have expertise in specific fields. The aim of the organization is knowledge, not skills. There is less need for continuous contact with a single teacher. In fact, contact with several teachers is considered to have the virtue of fostering independence.

The School in the Middle

Between these two very different institutions is the school in the middle. It has neither the primary skill responsibilities of the elementary school nor the special preparational responsibilities of the senior high school. In fact the institution that serves young adolescents has no publicly accepted role except that of a transition between the elementary school and the senior high school. Ideally it provides a program that prepares children for the organization and educational activities of the high school. Unfortunately, the bridging function does not make clear what the program emphasis should be. Is its purpose to continue with the basic elements offered by the elementary school? To prepare students for the high school by creating the conditions of the high school? Or is it something quite different?

Differing Roles of the School in the Middle

Because the school in the middle has no clearly defined role other than that of a transitional institution, these schools frequently assume one of several different roles, often as a consequence of local expectations. Although few schools take any of these roles to its extreme, the general emphasis is obvious in the school programs.

One role sometimes emphasized is the school as a center for review and remediation of skills. It should not be surprising that some middle schools place great emphasis on the same skill development that the elementary schools stress. The school in the middle receives children with a wide range of achievement in the skill areas. Many of these students have not mastered the skills that will be necessary for survival at the senior high school level.

As an academic mission for the school in the middle, emphasis on the skills appears to make some sense. This school should send to the senior high school students who are well grounded in fundamentals and who are ready for more advanced work in content areas. Unfortunately repetition of work does not challenge those who are ready to move on, and a strict emphasis on skills may not work for remedial students either. An approach that focuses on weaknesses and continuous exposure to what has already been found frustrating does not create enthusiasm for learning. Something more is necessary.

A second role often given the school in the middle is that of "junior" high school. The most common role for the school in the middle is based on the assumption that the best preparation for senior high school is to create a similar school for younger learners. This emphasis assumes that the students entering the school in the middle already have necessary skills to proceed in a more independent fashion by taking courses taught by specialized teachers. This approach has some benefits for the students who come to the school with better-than-average achievement and who are college bound. It does serve as preparation for the high school program. It also allows the independent student the opportunity to take advantage of the specialized resources of the school.

The "junior" high school orientation appears to serve some students well with its high-school-type program and extracurricular activities, but a large number of students may pay a price in meeting the expectations of this focus. The less mature learners are forced to make a severe adjustment from the more intimate and controlled environment of the elementary school to the large, impersonal, and independently oriented "junior" high school. Students without the skill background to handle the demands of high-school-oriented work often fail or become turned off by school. In reality the "junior" high school role eliminates the transitional function by creating a six- or seven-year senior high school.

A third role occasionally given this school is that of a therapy center. Much of the literature concerning schooling for young adolescents rejects both the notion of a skills-oriented institution and a school modeled on the senior high school. An alternative to these two roles uses the age group itself as a basis for program direction.

Students at this age are going through a difficult time. They are often described as a dismal lot, undergoing dramatic physical and social changes. They are viewed as distracted from school work because of all the stress they face and as being more interested in the opinions and judgments of peers than adult authority. In general they are assumed to be going through a very difficult time of life. More extreme descriptions lead one to conclude that these youngsters are suffering from a form of temporary insanity.

The school as a therapy center obviously gives less attention to substantive academic activities. Students are helped to develop self-understanding. The aim is to assist them in coping with growing up. Such a school attempts to create a positive and accepting atmosphere, stressing the social dimensions of school over the academic aspects. Its emphasis is humane and developmental.

While the idea of creating a humane "holding tank" for this group has some appeal, it suffers from two basic problems. First, it disregards the nature of the school, which is an academic institution. The major organizer for a school should be its academic program. The second problem is that it is based on a negative concept of this age group. It is also possible to view the young adolescent positively as having a strong language base, a great ability to think abstractly, a very strong concern for social problems, and a very high degree of physical energy. It can be argued that playing only to the social and emotional dimensions of the school program is doing learners harm.

None of the roles discussed above in fact offers a clear direction for the school in the middle. The roles are based on a narrow and often inappropriate approach to the education of young adolescents. Clearly a better conception, which more adequately focuses the transitional activities of the school, is necessary.

Goals for the Transitional School

If the school in the middle is to carry out its complex transitional function, it needs a clear focus to evolve effective educational programs. The following goals keep the transitional function in focus while providing substance and direction to programs.

1. Intellectual development should be the primary concern of the school. There should be no question as to the intention of these schools. They do not exist to provide therapy or socialization or to act as holding tanks. They exist to develop

individuals through academic activities. Other goals may be worthy and receive attention in the schools, but they are not and should not be a primary focus.

2. Extension and enhancement of skills should be a primary organizer for the curriculum. This school cannot ignore its basic responsibility to continue the skill development of learners. Stress on application and on higher-level skills should be a major concern. This does not mean a return to the elementary school curriculum but a natural continuation of its function.

3. The academic disciplines should increase learner knowledge and enhance basic skills. The transitional school should give systematic attention to the content of academic subjects while having students use skills in reading and other language areas.

4. The arts should be part of the school experience. The arts and cultural activities support the primary emphasis on the academic skills. Because they enlarge the domain of expression and add new dimensions to the lives of students, they should receive more than passing attention. They should be part of the central academic program.

5. Instructional modes should suit the background and developmental level of the learners. The transitional school should organize its instruction using neither an elementary nor a senior high school model. The methods of instruction should appeal to the positive characteristics of students at this age.

6. The organization of the school should reflect its aim. Too often in the past the organizational patterns of schools in the middle have not reflected their educational intentions. It is clear that if the school is to place emphasis on skill development, its organization must make it possible for teachers to reinforce and increase skills. It is also clear that an elementary school organization with a single class teacher will not suffice. Teamed or cooperative patterns are necessary because they allow teachers to have increased contact with a limited number of students.

This list of goals provides a positive focus for an institution that has long suffered from a negative public image. It is important that serious thought be given to the programs at this very important level of schooling. In many ways the schools that educate young adolescents are an educational fork in the road. The school can either encourage youngsters to seek academic achievement through knowledge and skills, or it can discourage, frustrate, and bring about failure. For successful attainment of many of the attitudes and behaviors desired in the educational process, the elementary school may be too early and the senior high school may be too late. This makes the middle institution critical in our system of education.

7 Competency Paradigm: Grades Six through Nine

Donna Townsend
Texas Education Agency

Janus-like, the middle school looks both forward and back as it provides instruction for students in grades six through nine. It seeks to consolidate those fundamental skills, behaviors, and attitudes that students have developed in the elementary school and to extend them toward the more advanced learning of the high school. Whatever the approach to teaching and learning—a process, heritage, or competency model—this characteristic of the institution exists. Thus, the middle school is aptly named.

This section deals with the competency model for language arts instruction in the middle grades, but it does so from a nondogmatic stance that many adherents of competency-based education may find heretical. Probably none of the definitions, examples, or terminology used here will satisfy a competency purist. This writer is not concerned with the trappings of the competency movement, for instance, rigidly stated behavioral objectives (e.g., "When presented with a random list of 10 words the learner will write 3 rhyming words for each word with 100 percent accuracy" [Morreau, 1972, p. 42]). Nor is the writer concerned with the distinctions between exit objectives, enabling objectives, performance objectives, and learner outcomes. Instead, the concern is with the competency movement's general philosophical basis of defining the outcome of insturction in terms of student behavior.

The Competency Curriculum

Of the instructional approaches considered in this volume, the competency approach is the newcomer on the educational scene, but its newness is defined not so much by what content it includes in language arts as it is in how that content is formulated, that is, in terms of student behavior that gives evidence of a student's having learned whatever skill, behavior, or attitude has been the subject of instruction. Either the familiar quartet of language arts—listening, speaking, reading, and writing—or the traditional model of the language, composition, literature triad provides the major segments of content for most competency curricula in language arts programs around the country. Sometimes these models are combined at the middle school level since the arts model is usually identified with the elementary school and the triad with the high school. Frequently they are extended to include recent curricular concerns that have found their way into English language arts, such as visual literacy, career education, and survival or coping skills.

Anything of significance within the discipline of Enlgish language arts can be treated in some way in the competency approach. Clearly some skills, behaviors, or attitudes are more easily definable and more easily identifiable than others, but even higher-order thinking skills and affective skills can be dealt with adequately within this approach. In an essay appearing in a 1970 publication of the NCTE Commission on the English Curriculum, Hoetker provided an early caution on the dangers of inflexible adherence to the behavioral objectives approach to learning. That approach has since evolved into the full-blown competency movement omnipresent on today's educational scene. His caveat is therefore still timely, and so are his distinctions among kinds of observable behaviors:

> There are three sorts of behaviors that educators are concerned with. I am going to call these "can-do" behaviors, "may-do" behaviors, and "will-do" behaviors. "Can-do" behaviors are those specific things that a student can do at the end of a particular unit of his education that he could not do at the beginning of it; in terms of Bloom's *Taxonomy*, the "can-do" behaviors include knowledge, comprehension, and the application of knowledge in familiar situations. "May-do" behaviors are things a student may be able to do in a novel or unfamiliar situation because he has mastered certain "can-do" behaviors. These would include, among cognitive behaviors, the application of abstractions in novel situations, analysis, synthesis, and evaluation; plus, among affective behaviors, attending, responding, valuing, and, in some cases, organizing. "Will-do" behaviors are the choices and preferences that describe the quality of an adult's life, and which are present only fractionally during the school years. The affective *Taxonomy* refers to "will-do" behaviors as "characterization by a value or a value complex." (p. 49)

Conceptually, then, competencies need not be limited to low-level cognitive skills, or even only to cognitive skills. Both higher-order thinking skills and affective behaviors can and should be included in an enlightened view of competency-based education. That they are not—in all too many instances, at least—is a failure of the execution rather than of the design.

Activities

The choice of classroom activities available to the teacher in the competency approach is not limited by the approach itself. Anything that will contribute to the development of the desired student outcome, that is appropriate to the interest and developmental level of young adolescents, and that is educationally defensible is appropriate. Students at this age level benefit from activities that allow them to become involved both with the subject matter and with each other in varied and meaningful ways. They need frequent opportunities to practice skills, but this does not mean repetitious and boring drill. It does not mean the endless skill sheets and workbooks that are frequently but erroneously taken to be synonymous with "competency approach." Role-playing, acting out various points of view that could be developed in a composition assignment, and dramatizing stories or poems—activities that are most frequently associated with a process-centered approach—are all useful activities, not only for students to practice skills or behaviors, but also for them to demonstrate whether they have acquired those skills and behaviors.

Activities to develop composition skills may employ sentence-combining techniques, journal writing, peer evaluation of compositions, and opportunities to engage in various forms of creative, explanatory, and persuasive writing. As much as possible, writing should be done in meaningful situations or in simulations of them. The following example, an adaptation of a writing exercise used by the National Assessment of Educational Progress (1977) with thirteen year olds in 1973-74, is illustrative of this kind of writing and of the way a teacher can define the criteria for success with the task.

> Imagine that your principal asked for suggestions about how to make things better in your school. Write a letter to your principal telling him just ONE thing you think should be changed, how to bring about the change, and how the school will be improved by it. Space is provided below and on the next three pages. Sign your letter "Chris Johnson."

NAEP's evaluation of the writing resulting from this stimulus consisted of placing papers into one of four categories describing how well a writer achieved the purpose of the writing assignment. Level I papers did not identify a problem or defend a change. Level II papers identified a problem and explained either how to solve the problem or how the school would be improved if the problem were solved, but the reasoning was undeveloped. Level III papers identified a problem, successfully explained and defended a change, and told how the change would benefit the school. Level IV papers met the same requirements as Level III papers, but they also *systematically* defined and defended a change.

The criteria for success with this composition assignment were built into the assignment itself. The four scoring categories, then, describe to what degree the student has solved the writing problem posed by the situation. Teachers can readily adapt this procedure for classroom use by making explicit the competencies implicit in any composition assignment. By asking themselves a series of questions designed to illuminate what features will be present in a successful piece of writing resulting from an assignment, teachers can establish in a systematic way both the competencies students will exhibit and the criteria for evaluating the writing products of that assignment. Further, they may provide continuity among composition assignments by structuring them to focus on those designated competencies over a period of time.

Middle school teachers of language arts know that their students respond especially well to either real or fictional accounts of young people, especially those who face and overcome some difficulty. This explains the continuing popularity of such books as *Mary White, Brian's Song, Death Be Not Proud, Flowers for Algernon, The Miracle Worker*, and *The Diary of Anne Frank*. Students will respond to poems that deal with similar topics as well as those that use language vividly and originally, like John Tobias's "Reflections on a Gift of Watermelon Pickle." The adventure and repeated rhythm found in most narrative poems and the playful use of language in concrete poems and limericks are also appealing to most students at this age. These kinds of literary works should be included in abundance in any middle school language-arts curriculum. However, they need not be the only selections that provide students experience in developing literature competencies. Traditional selections such as Greek myths, Arthurian legends, Aesop's fables, *Huckleberry Finn, Treasure Island*, and the time-honored works of Wordsworth, Dickens, Tennyson, and Browning, for example, serve equally well in this regard. Indeed, in a broadly defined competency curriculum, they become essential, for they help to develop an array of competencies dealing with students' abilities to recognize and to draw upon their literary and cultural heritage.

Competency statements for responding to, interpreting, valuing, and evaluating literature help to define what has long been the most amorphous part of the English curriculum. Competencies that deal with the literary element of setting, for example, may be developed through a variety of activities that give the student an opportunity to become engaged with this concept. The following activities (based on material by the New York State Education Department) can be easily adapted to any specific literary work when the teacher is planning experiences to develop the following competency: "The student is able to identify the aspects of place, time, and the customs and practices of people in a given literary work and to describe orally or in writing how these aspects make up the setting of that literary work" (New York State Education Department, 1972).

1. Individual students or small groups list the details of a work that describe or suggest such aspects of setting as geographic background; structures; work, social, and personal habits of people; kinds of people; and occupations.

2. Findings are reported to the entire class (the display of pictures might be helpful); the class establishes which of the customs and details of time and place are the most important in terms of the complete selection.

3. Students consider questions such as:
   a. Do the characters act in ways that are peculiar to the era and environment in which they live?
   b. What effect would there be on the theme of the work if the setting were changed? If it were given little importance?
   c. What do the details of time, place, and customs suggest about the daily lives of the people in the story?

4. For selections in which the geographical setting is complex, students draw maps of the setting and compare results.

Many language-arts skills are described variously as "survival," "coping," or "life" skills and are frequently defined in terms of what students will be able to do as they leave high school and enter adult life. The implication, then, is that instruction at each educational level leading to graduation will contribute to the ultimate acquisition of the skill. This means that classroom activities in the middle school often simulate "real-life" situations or otherwise provide meaningful learning contexts for these skills. For example, the Speech Communication Association (1978) has published *Guidelines for Minimal Competencies in Speaking and Listening for High School Graduates.* Among those competencies, under the section headed "Oral Message Evaluation," is the competency "distinguish facts from opinions." Examples for application are then given in three categories corresponding to the purposes in adult life for which speaking and listening skills are used: occupation, citizenship, and maintenance. The curriculum problem arising from this competency becomes one of meaningful translation of this concept and its attendant skills into learning activities appropriate for students at a given stage in their schooling.

The following example illustrates how this might be done in a sixth- or seventh-grade language-arts classroom. The performance objective states, "The student will be able to identify an occupation of personal interest and relate how the ability to distinguish between fact and opinion would be important in that work." Activities to bring about the development of this competency might include the following (the activities are based on material in Partners in Career Education, 1977).

The student will:

1. Read the section on fact and opinion in *New Directions in English*, pp. 135–139.

2. With a partner, orally identify the sentences in the text in which opinions are expressed and those in which information is given.

3. On one card write a sentence expressing an opinion and on another write an informative sentence. After all of the cards have been placed in a container, take turns selecting cards, reading the sentences, and telling the type of sentence each is.

4. Discuss with a variety of community workers instances in which they must distinguish between fact and opinion and ways in which their work relates to factual information and opinions. (Suggested resource persons: Chamber of Commerce manager, nurse, salesperson, radio announcer, minister.)

5. Select a personally interesting occupation and relate how the ability to differentiate fact from opinion would be an asset in that occupation.

Evaluation

Pretesting and post-testing are not terms that were coined by the competency movement, but they have come to be associated with it so closely that they have for many people become the catchwords for the movement. Logically, one should determine whether instruction is necessary—the student may already possess the competency—and to what degree. Pretesting serves the dual purpose of diagnosis and placement. If, for example, a teacher wants to know if students in a middle school class can show that language is a source of pleasure, that teacher might construct a diagnostic procedure that identifies which students can perform a series of activities that define the competency: playing word games such as Scrabble or Perquackey or doing crossword puzzles; composing original sentences that express the same idea with and without using figurative language; or experimenting with new meanings and arrangements of words by constructing new and unusual metaphors or puns or by deliberately using malapropisms (Indiana Department of Public Instruction, 1978). Although "pretest" usually connotes a multiple-choice commercial test, these examples indicate that the pretest need not be so limited. It should give the student an opportunity to demonstrate, as the competency statement indicates, the knowledge and skills possessed in the area defined by the competency statement. It also need not be limited to the "can-do" level of behaviors discussed earlier. These items certainly deal with "may-do" behaviors and, at least by implication, with "will-do" behaviors.

Once a teacher has determined that a student can demonstrate nothing at all in regard to a given competency or some aspects but not others or the total set of desired behaviors, appropriate instruction can be designed for that student. The student may be grouped with others within the class who have shown a similar level of competence on the diagnostic pretest. The teacher then provides activities similar to those used in the diagnostic process, and students are given ample opportunity to develop the desired skills. At any point during the instructional period, informal observation by the teacher or the student's feeling of having gained the skill may lead to post-testing. The post-test, in the case of the example used here, may very well be the same set of procedures as the pretest. Its purpose is to verify that a student has gained the level of competence necessary to move on in the instructional sequence.

Need for Individualization

As the foregoing discussion on testing clearly indicates, students within a classroom will vary considerably in their level of competence on a given skill or across a continuum of skills. Therefore, a variety of instructional activities must be made available. Teachers will sometimes engage in direct instruction with the total class or with small groups within the class who are performing at a similar level on a specific task. Sometimes a student may work individually at an activity. In any of these instructional situations, teachers will be using a variety of instructional materials and strategies, such as textbooks, teacher-developed materials of various kinds, visual and auditory media, and learning centers. The classroom should become a place where there are many options for students to gain the competencies expected of them. Individualization of instruction is a necessary feature of the competency approach.

Advantages of a Competency Approach

An enlightened use of the competency approach yields several advantages for the instructional process. First, this approach states in explicit terms the object of instruction. It describes the skills, behaviors, and attitudes that students should exhibit if instruction has been successful. Students, teachers, and parents are able to understand what constitutes success or lack of it. At its best, a competency approach reduces the ambiguities that have long plagued teaching and learning. Second, it generally defines learning in smaller segments that can be more easily attended to in instructional planning. Third, this approach enables teachers to increase the efficiency of instruction by examining all classroom activities and learning materials to see if they contribute directly to students' gaining the competencies designated for a day's lesson or for a year-long course.

Application of the competency approach to the teaching of language arts has in many instances resulted in a perversion of the approach. Nothing within the competency paradigm is antithetical to the largest intellectual conception of the English language arts or to the humanistic values associated with them. The potential disadvantages of the competency approach are well known: trivializing the curriculum by focusing on relatively insignificant but easily measurable skills; requiring a great deal of time for testing to see if competencies have been mastered; causing an imbalance in the curriculum by dealing only with cognitive areas and narrowly defined life skills. The material presented in this chapter suggests, however, that, as far as the language-arts curriculum is concerned, these disadvantages need never appear. At the same time, it is true that if careful planning is not done, these negative aspects all too easily occur. The challenge for those using the competency-based approach at any level and in any area of the curriculum is to avoid the pitfalls of the approach so loudly and frequently proclaimed by its critics and to capitalize on its very real strength: definition of a clear set of teaching and learning goals.

References

Hoetker, James. "Limitations and Advantages of Behavioral Objectives in the Arts and Humanities." In *On Writing Behavioral Objectives for English*, edited by John C. Maxwell and Anthony Tovatt. Urbana, Ill.: National Council of Teachers of English, 1970.

Indiana Department of Public Instruction. *Basic Objectives in Language Arts, K-12*. Indianapolis: Department of Public Instruction, 1978.

Morreau, Lanny E. "Behavioral Objectives: Analysis and Application." In *Accountability and the Teaching of English*, edited by Henry B. Maloney. Urbana, Ill.: National Council of Teachers of English, 1972.

National Assessment of Educational Progress. *Explanatory and Persuasive Letter Writing*. Denver: National Assessment of Educational Progress, 1977.

New York State Education Department. *English Language Arts*. Albany: State Education Department, 1972.

Partners in Career Education. *Teacher-Developed Infused Curriculum Modules: Grade 6*. Arlington, Tex.: Partners in Career Education, 1977.

Speech Communication Association. *Guidelines for Minimal Competencies in Speaking and Listening for High School Graduates*. Falls Church, Va.: Speech Communication Association, 1978.

8 The English Program, Grades Six through Nine: A Heritage Model

Richard E. Hodges
University of Puget Sound

As the principal means by which the cultural heritage is preserved and transmitted, written language has historically occupied an especially important place in the American school curriculum. It is not merely for alliterative effect that the core subjects of the curriculum are termed the "3 R's"; for one's abilities to read, write, and compute are common measures of educational attainment. While curricula are planned to accomplish other important educational and social objectives, the fact remains that competence in language has traditionally been one of society's chief standards for judging the effectiveness of our nation's schools.

No other subject matter pervades the school curriculum to the extent that language does—especially written language. Not only is written language a subject of formal study when one is learning to read and write, but it is also the principal medium through which most other school subjects are presented. Schools are, in short, mainly verbal institutions, to which this volume on the English curriculum gives further testimony.

Yet while there is little question that English language study is of primary importance, both the content and the manner of instruction can be and are quite differently viewed. It is the purpose of this chapter to examine one such view of the English curriculum—the heritage model—as designed for students in the middle school/junior high school years. However, before doing so, we should first review two relevant factors: (1) the view of language study in a heritage model and (2) insights into the young adolescent's intellectual and social development.

Review of the Heritage Model

The heritage model described in the Introduction to this collection is based on the classical view that the fundamental purpose of education is to preserve and to transmit the cultural heritage. Since the bulk of this heritage is accumulated in written materials, the ability to read and write is essential. Moreover, because written language is so highly valued, its study also includes our literary heritage so that the student can experience and subsequently appreciate exemplary uses of the language. In sum, competence in using the language and appreciation of its notable uses are considered attributes of the literate person.

Thus there have emerged three aspects of English study: (1) knowledge about the language (grammar), (2) facility in using the language (composition), and (3) appreciation for the language (literature). As for instructional method, the manner of teaching has typically been expository, and learning has commonly been regarded as assimilative.

Given these traditional aims and the emphasis on teacher-directed learning, textual materials play a fundamental role in the English curriculum. In many respects, books are the core of the heritage-based curriculum. While textbooks have their limitations, those who advocate their use cite particular advantages. For one, a well-designed series of texts can provide continuity to the English curriculum throughout the grades, in keeping with Muller's (1967) observation in his report of the Dartmouth Conference, "Nothing is plainer than that the English curriculum should have some kind of continuous, cumulative development from the first grade to the end of high school, corresponding to the simple fact that children keep growing up" (p. 39). In this regard, heritage model proponents would say that a text series provides a better sequence to the English program than that which might result when teachers prepare or students select their own instructional materials.

A second advantage of textual materials concerns the scope of content that is covered in the English curriculum. Because publishers are generally conventional in the manner in which content is covered, textbooks provide a common denominator of information about the English language. While there are exceptions, of course, published materials constitute a kind of national curriculum, insuring that most students will cover somewhat the same content in grammar, composition, and literature.

A third advantage sometimes cited to support the use of textbooks reflects on the preparation of teachers of English, particularly in elementary grades. Because many teachers at these levels will not have majored in English or have had thorough training in its teaching, textual materials in large part determine what content is taught as well as the manner of instruction. Students' materials and teachers' manuals thus provide common guidelines for English instruction in the schools where they are used.

The Young Adolescent

Having noted some attributes of a heritage model, let's briefly review some attributes of twelve- to fourteen-year-old learners. The onset of puberty brings a dramatic metamorphosis of the human body and concomitant changes in the intellectual and emotional characteristics of the young person. These behavioral changes have important educational consequences.

The young person is undergoing qualitative changes in intellectual processes, no longer "thinking" as a child, but beginning to display adult-like intellectual functions (Kagan, 1971). These "formal operations" include increasing ability to analyze problems systematically and to consider alternative solutions to them. Young adolescents are increasingly able to organize their thoughts into higher-order, more complicated structures. They are, in short, becoming capable of understanding existing systems of knowledge and of organizing new knowledge systematically for themselves.

In similar fashion, social and moral behaviors follow developmental patterns. Kohlberg (1969) has defined three levels and six stages of moral growth through which the individual moves in developing a system of values, which at first resides in externally imposed cultural rules and which can ultimately result in a system of values based on universal ethical principles and respect for the dignity of others. Although these stages are not necessarily age-dependent (a person's moral growth may not reach the higher stages), with adolescence comes a growing orientation toward moral behavior that resides in "good" or "right" roles which conform to majority behavior. At the same time, young adolescents reflect upon the consistency of socially imposed rules, questioning their validity. Kagan (1971) has remarked, "The adolescent, unlike the child of eight or nine, is concerned with the hypothetical, the future, the remote, and the ideal" (p. 130). There is, in sum, as the parents and teachers of young adolescents know, a growing questioning of and independence from adult authority.

The adolescent's psychological growth thus results from an active attempt to make sense of experiences. Young persons seek to reduce uncertainty and in doing so continually test their knowledge of right and wrong. Young adolescents do not have to be prodded to solve problems if those problems are central to their own concerns. Here the heritage model as it has traditionally been implemented has its greatest limitation when students are regarded as passive participants in the educative process.

Yet while people tend to engage actively in tasks in which they have intellectual and emotional investment and in which they have had a hand in selecting, the important understandings and skills that are required for effective participation in the larger society should not be left to chance. For, as pointed out by Kagan (1971), if society did not demand that children develop specific talents,

> children would obviously be more enthusiastic each morning. They would select tasks in accordance with the values of their peer group, the immediacy of feedback, the likelihood of success, and the degree to which sensory and motor delights were a part of the learning experience. Spelling, arithmetic, history, and science would not rank high on their list of preferences. These academic skills were given priority by society, and the decision was partly rational. If we believe in this decision, we must tolerate the dissonance generated by the possibility that the child will not agree; we must become less pollyannish about academic mastery. Speaking, running, and climbing are natural activities that the child wants to perfect; reading, writing, and arithmetic are not. (p. 196)

Manolakes has observed elsewhere in this collection that the middle school/junior high school years are generally regarded as the time to prepare for the academic rigors of high school. It is the time to "get down to business," to remediate deficient skills, to engage students in academic studies akin to the high school experience. In short, it is the time "during which children grow from being 'babies' to fully conscious, 'self' conscious young adults" (p. 7, Judy, 1978). These are in truth the *middle* school years, midway between the challenges of childhood and the challenges of adulthood, and it is in this context that we now consider the English program from the vantage point of a heritage paradigm.

The English Program in the Middle School Years

Although the heritage model generally promotes the acquisition of knowledge for its own sake, English study can also have a utilitarian focus in which "the major purpose of [English] instruction is not to teach the student to spell correctly, to write a grammatically correct sentence, or to analyze a literary selection, but to teach him to think, to communicate his thoughts to others, to understand and to evaluate the communication of others" (Petty, 1977, p. 92).

Organized, logical thinking is a critically important objective of the heritage paradigm. Because language and thinking are integrally related, the formal study of language has a fundamental part in developing organized thinking. Using conventional textual materials, the English program becomes a guided exploration of language, affording students opportunities to use language to compose and to express their thoughts and to develop an understanding of and appreciation for our literary heritage. Let's briefly examine each element of the triad that comprises the English curriculum, language (grammar), composition, and literature, bearing in mind that although this triad has had widespread application in designing English programs, it by no means has universal acceptance.

Language

Three reasons have often been given to justify formal language study. First, a study of language makes students sensitive to the variety of ways in which ideas can be expressed. Second, such study provides knowledge with which to edit written prose. And third, formal language study provides knowledge of structure that explains how the language works. Let's look in particular at this third justification.

In the language component of the English program, the instructional outcome is meant to be a functional understanding of language. Textual materials that provide descriptions of grammatical structure and historical development and that examine social uses of the language are especially appropriate. The study of English grammar is in effect an examination of the rules by which we play the language game, rules that are intuitively learned in the early years of life and that govern our uses of spoken and written language. Just as knowledge about the rules of any game enables its players to play that game more nearly to its potential, knowledge about the rules of language can enhance one's linguistic potential.

Western (1978) articulated this point when he distinguished *constitutive* from *regulative* rules. Constitutive rules make new forms of behavior possible, as for example, the rules of chess and football. Such rules *constitute* the game; that is, in learning the rules, one learns the game. On the other hand, regulative rules control existing forms of behavior; they *regulate* behavior. The rules of etiquette, for example, are regulative; they prescribe behavior. Grammatical rules are constitutive, although they have commonly been taught as regulative. They are the natural, not the socially imposed rules of language. They are the rules that enable us to use language effectively, to "take advantage of the resources of English construction to say what one means and to say it in ways that have the desired effect upon the receiver" (Moffett and Wagner, 1976, p. 30).

While texts are readily available that provide a formal study of English grammar that is unrelated to practical purpose, there are other materials available in which language study is set in functional contexts. These materials are valuable resources in helping students understand their language and its heritage—structurally, historically, and functionally.

Grammatical structure can be explored to bring to conscious awareness students' understanding of what they already are capable of doing and to expose them to other grammatical devices, of which they may be unaware, that might be used effectively. Although researchers have yet to demonstrate that formal grammar study (especially traditional diagraming) has any significant effect upon general writing ability (Galvan, 1977, p. 168), the aim of such study ought to be to help students to understand the grammatical flexibility that is available to them. The historical development of the English language can also be studied during these school years to acquaint students with our linguistic heritage and to give them an understanding of how historical change and contact with other languages have had significant effects on our language, and particularly on spelling and vocabulary.

Still another important area for study is language use. Here formal study serves to inform students that, while socially approved standards of English usage exist and need to be practiced, linguistic ability involves being able to fit the spoken or written message to the social setting in which it is used and to the audience for which it is intended. At a time in the student's life when social awareness becomes increasingly apparent, an exploration of the ways in which language is used as determined by social context can be an especially profitable and interesting aspect of the student's understanding of the functions of language.

In summary, language study goes far beyond knowing how to construct sentences. It involves knowing about the language—

its structure, history, and use. It is knowledge that is fundamentally imbedded in the other parts of the English program—composition and literature.

Composition

While a study of language during these years is intended to extend the young adolescent's knowledge base, instruction in English composition has more direct applications. The intention is to foster linguistic fluency, and the instructional outcome is logical and persuasive expression of ideas in both spoken and written discourse. While textual materials can help structure the teaching of composition, they do pose limitations when they restrict students' writing experiences to situations that have little relationship to their world.

Linguistic fluency is not a competence that is attained overnight, of course. It is a consequence of a cluster of innate and social factors influencing general linguistic development, as Loban's (1976) longitudinal study has reaffirmed. Although Loban's research was focused mainly on spoken language development, writing samples were gathered from third grade on. His analysis of these students' growing language facility contains some important implications for the English program.

For one, the better (i.e., linguistically fluent) students repeatedly demonstrated control over the ideas they expressed. They had an overview of what they wanted to say and a plan for expressing their ideas in coherent and unified ways. They used a rich variety of syntactic patterns and vocabulary. They demonstrated greater flexibility in the use of language. In both spoken and written discourse, the more capable students displayed greater tentativeness— e.g., supposition, hypothesis, conjecture, use of conditional statements—and were capable of adjusting the mode of communication to their audiences and in return were attentive to others. Linguistic fluency showed up in both grammatical competence and the social uses of language. They exhibited what has been termed *communicative competence,* the ability to compose spoken and written discourse appropriate to social circumstances (Hymes, 1972), to use more fully the range of linguistic possibilities that grammar permits.

It is in the composition component of the English program that implementation of the heritage model, with its heavy reliance on textual materials, has limitations. Texts can at best provide only vicarious experiences for students, and a danger exists that these experiences will be largely unrelated to the real needs and interests of young adolescents. A 1963 analysis (Lynch and Evans) of high school composition texts, for example, led the researchers to conclude that most widely used texts had generally similar content regardless of grade level, but, more important, writing activities were usually based on contrived situations. Because communicative competence is the capability of using language functionally, its development requires experience in writing for functional purposes in meaningful situations.

Bearing in mind that the middle school years are a time when young adolescents are developing adult modes of thinking, instruction in composing spoken and written discourse plays a basic role in furthering students' capability of expressing themselves clearly and in organized fashion. Students' own experiences, thoughts, and feelings can be the raw material for the composing process. Literary examples, such as autobiography and biography, can be used to illustrate how other authors have shared their own and others' experiences.

Britton (1975) has described three stages in the composing process: conception, incubation, and production. The first stage—conception—begins with the individual's decision to write. While that decision may be forced, as is often the case in school, composing begins when the writer forms some idea of what it is that he or she is to do.

Time is necessary for planning and organization of the writer's thoughts, to, in Britton's words, "explain the matter to oneself" (p. 28). Often, however, composition instruction fosters the perception that unless writing is done at once, vital ideas and information will be lost. Ample time must be provided the young writer before the production process can begin.

Stephen Leacock, the Canadian humorist and educator, once responded to a high school student who had sought his advice about how best to embark on a writing career: "Don't try to *write*, try to *think*. Then when you really have something to say and want to say it very much, say it. That process is called *writing*." (I am grateful to a U.P.S. colleague, Stephen Kerr, for sharing this letter with me.) In a very real sense, writing lies beyond language and resides in the domain of general cognitive development. Effective writing is a display of organized thinking. While the mechanics of writing—spelling and punctuation—are necessary and warrant instruction in the English program, they belong in the final stage of

writing, revision. But revising one's writing is not just a matter of correcting and improving; it is, as Britton (1975) notes, the "final stage of the process by which a writer presents himself [to others].
. . . [It is] a declaration, a tacit agreement with the reader that the writer accepts responsibility for his own creation" (p. 47).

Just as we learn to speak by speaking, we learn to write by writing, and instruction must allow ample opportunity to do so in a range of rhetorical modes—narration, exposition, description, argumentation. While it is important that teachers create conditions for writing and provide guidance in the composing process, we should not lose sight of the fact that writers must draw upon their personal storehouses of past experiences so that, ultimately, individuality is imposed upon the writing process. In the context of the heritage model, the importance of instruction in composing has been forcefully summarized in Mellon's (1976) review of the 1974 NAEP tests:

> In pondering the value of writing, whether to the college bound or the early school leaver, regardless of fancies as to its "practical" value or the current extent of its use for hire, we should always be mindful of the truth long recognized by scholars of language and thought, that writing is the greatest tool of thinking ever invented by man; that it functions as an extension of the self allowing the writer to create a reality of thought, no less real for being thought, that is unique to verbal language and dependent for its ideational plenitude upon presentation in the written medium. To have achieved a degree of mastery over written language, to have known its production as a durable detached artifact of one's own mind, and to have felt the pleasures of crafting, focusing, and qualifying that artifact, is as valuable a learning experience as a human being can have, even if one never again puts pen to paper or earns a dime thereby. (p. 73)

Literature

The study of literature provides students with a means of experiencing language in its most eloquent forms. In a very real sense, a study of literature most clearly represents the heritage paradigm. For it is through writing that the cultural heritage is both preserved and transmitted, and it is from the study of outstanding writing that the student can come to comprehend and to appreciate the effectiveness with which language can be used.

The study of literature serves young adolescents in still another way, by providing access to the adult world into which they are emerging. Literature can enhance students' social understanding through vicarious experiences of the world in which they live. Young adolescents, who now begin to see the world in qualitatively different ways, can also begin to understand value systems other than their own, perhaps to see a world that is neither all good nor all bad, but with universal problems like those with which they are familiar (Donelson, 1977, p. 160). Literature study, in short, can help students to place their personal selves into the broader context of humanity.

In a heritage model, the study of literature has a fundamental objective of enabling the student to appreciate how language can be used to express writers' intellectual, affective, and aesthetic purposes. As with other parts of the English program, learning to appreciate notable writing is also a developmental process, as Early (1960) has described.

An appreciation of literature begins with readers' unconscious enjoyment of the material they read, knowing what they like to read but not knowing why. During this rudimentary stage in literary appreciation, teachers can make sure that students are exposed to a wide variety of literary forms and devices that is in keeping with their maturity and interests. The objective during this stage is to enable students to experience good writing without seeking their critical analysis of it.

The second developmental stage in literary appreciation Early has described is that of a self-conscious appreciation of notable writing, in which the individuals not only know what they like to read, but are willing to exert some effort to enhance their enjoyment of it. It is during this stage that under the teacher's direction, young adolescents can begin to explore why certain writing brings them pleasure, to attend to details that reveal setting, character traits, and other factors that are involved in analyzing literary work. Students can be helped to compare different treatments of similar themes and to examine relationships between the authors' purposes in writing and their choices of literary forms. The aim of this instruction is to help students to acquire their own sense of appreciation of good literature, to further their development toward the highest level of literary appreciaiton, conscious enjoyment, in which individuals enjoy literature, know why they do, and by relying on their own judgment can choose the material they read.

Early's essay reiterates the point that acquiring an appreciation of good literature is indeed a developmental process and that care must be taken not to force a formal literary analysis upon immature readers. Young adolescents should be exposed to a wide range of literary forms that capitalize on their interests, such as science fiction, adventure, and mystery stories about other young persons.

Although anthologies presume that all students share certain interests and needs in common (a presumption often belied by reality), they do provide a means for students to study the same materials and for teachers to focus more directly upon literary content and form. Clearly there is a place in the classroom for both commercially prepared literature anthologies and a wide range of teacher- and student-selected supplementary materials.

A Recapitulation

Hunt, in a notable book on human neuropsychological development (1961), referred to the "problem of the match." By this he meant that growth occurs when a task extends the individual beyond the level where he or she is presently, but is not so difficult that it cannot be accomplished. This "problem of the match" articulates the essential task and challenge of the English curriculum in the middle school years.

As we have seen, the foremost objectives of any English curriculum are to produce adults who are competent in communication and who display and appreciate the functional and aesthetic uses of language. We have also seen that young adolescents bring to the teaching-learning situation qualitatively different intellectual skills from those of younger children. Clearly the "problem of the match" between the objectives of the middle school English curriculum and the needs, interests, and capabilities of twelve to fourteen year olds is both potent and real.

The heritage model lends itself well to ameliorating the problem of the match by providing continuity and sequential development of language study through the use of textual materials. Knowledgeable teachers are essential, however, teachers who are aware that learning is a dynamic process, not a passive one. Such teachers can use their knowledge of the developmental characteristics of students and of the English language to create opportunities for students to apply knowledge gained from formal study to functional and socially meaningful situations.

Language is, after all,

> man's greatest invention, his indispensable tool, the concomitant and in large part the cause of his rise to dominance among Earth's creatures. With language, man informs, explains, moves, sometimes enthralls; he expresses his fear and his hate and his love; he finds structure in his universe; he passes from generation to generation

what he knows; with language man transmits his own history and the history of all earthly things; with language he conceives of gods and worships them. . . . (Hook and Crowell, 1970, p. 5)

To appreciate one's own linguistic potential and to exercise that potential in one's daily life is the aim of the total English program to which instruction in the middle school years can contribute.

References

Britton, James, et al. *The Development of Writing Abilities (11-18)*. London: Macmillan Education, 1975.

Donelson, Kenneth L. "General Influences on the Changing Literature Curriculum." In *The Teaching of English: The Seventy-sixth Yearbook of the National Society for the Study of Education*, edited by James R. Squire, pp. 158-167. Chicago: University of Chicago Press, 1977.

Early, Margaret J. "Stages of Growth in Literary Appreciation." *English Journal* 49 (March 1960): 161-167.

Galvan, Mary. "Changing Content in the English Curriculum: Language." In *The Teaching of English: The Seventy-sixth Yearbook of the National Society for the Study of Education*, edited by James R. Squire, pp. 168-177. Chicago: University of Chicago Press, 1977.

Hook, J.N., and Crowell, Michael G. *Modern English Grammar for English Teachers*. New York: The Ronald Press, 1970.

Hunt, J. *Intelligence and Experience*. New York: The Ronald Press, 1961.

Hymes, Dell. Introduction to *Functions of Language in the Classroom*, edited by Courtney B. Cazden, Vera P. John, and Dell Hymes, pp. ix-lvii. New York: Teachers College Press, 1972.

Judy, Stephen. "I Met Johnny and Jane." *English Journal* 67 (September 1978): 6-8.

Kagan, Jerome. *Understanding Children: Behavior, Motives, and Thought*. New York: Harcourt Brace Jovanovich, 1971.

Kohlberg, Lawrence. "Stage and Sequence: The Cognitive-Developmental Approach to Socialization." In *Handbook of Socialization Theory and Research*, edited by David A. Goslin, pp. 347-480. Chicago: Rand McNally, 1969.

Loban, Walter. *Language Development: Kindergarten through Grade 12*. Research Report No. 18. Urbana, Ill.: National Council of Teachers of English, 1976.

Lynch, James J., and Evans, Bertrand. *High School English Textbooks: A Critical Examination*. Boston: Little, Brown and Co., 1963.

Mellon, John C. "Round Two of the National Writing Assessment—Interpreting the Apparent Decline of Writing Ability: A Review." *Research in the Teaching of English* 10 (Spring 1976): 66-74.

Moffett, James, and Wagner, Betty Jane. *Student-Centered Language Arts and Reading, K-13: A Handbook for Teachers*. 2nd ed. Boston: Houghton Mifflin, 1976.

Muller, Herbert J. *The Uses of English.* New York: Holt, Rinehart and Winston. 1967.

Petty, Walter, et al. "Language Competencies Essential for Coping in Our Society." In *The Teaching of English: The Seventy-sixth Yearbook of the National Society for the Study of Education,* edited by James R. Squire, pp. 66-95. Chicago: University of Chicago Press, 1977.

Western, Richard D. "Grammar and Composition: Why People Disagree about Their Relation to Each Other." *The Elementary School Journal* 78 (March 1978): 284-289.

9 Process Paradigm: Grades Six through Nine

Dorothy J. Watson
University of Missouri at Columbia

This chapter will describe a process curriculum for junior high students. To do this it is necessary to focus on the students and on the teacher, for from them stems the curriculum. We will first look at the typical, if hypothetical, process-oriented (sometimes called naturalistic, humanistic, or creative) teacher, then at the students, and finally at some activities that might go on in their teaching-learning world.

The Teacher

At some point in their careers, potential process-oriented teachers become consumed with curiosity about why their students are succeeding, slipping away, or standing still. When our hypothetical teacher, Joe Green, was himself in junior high school, he received instruction in what was referred to as the language arts and later as English. As it turns out, the instruction he received had a great deal to do with learning to identify parts of sentences, spelling words on a graded spelling list, punctuating innumerable sentences, reading a prescribed list of books, and memorizing the same elegant poems his older brother had memorized ten years earlier. There were variations within limits, but for the most part our teacher received a ready-made curriculum, and by prevailing standards he was a successful student. In his undergraduate methods courses in college, he "gained insights" into how his own junior high teachers had helped him produce. His student-teaching was *déjà vu*—junior high revisited—and his first years of teaching were attempts to teach as he was taught and as he was taught to teach.

Reflecting on his own schooling, our hypothetical teacher vacillated from feeling slightly cheated to feeling irreparably misled:

cheated because he did not reflect with joy on his own schooling and misled because at the close of each day he sensed that his own students were in a continuous retreat from language and literature. The language arts he had hoped to bring to life in the minds and hearts of his students were languishing for want of proper staging. Then, one day, right before the concrete of the preexisting curriculum had hardened, our hypothetical teacher began to look around. That is when he stopped teaching as he had been taught and began searching for a solid foundation on which to build a lively language arts curriculum.

The process-oriented teacher has special viewpoints about language, literature, learners, and learning. When our hypothetical teacher began to look for alternatives to preformulated guides, he found it necessary to rediscover literature for children and youth, to investigate pedagogical research, and to investigate current information related to language. As his study progressed, he developed a guiding belief: language is alive and well and resides in the heads and on the tongues of students as well as in the plays, prose, and poetry written for young people. It dawned on him that by the time children enter the sixth grade, they have used their language to inform, proclaim, persuade, gossip, tattle, double talk, sweet talk, and outtalk—when they were motivated to do so. Our hypothetical teacher learned two important things: first, students use language when they need to and, second, the meaning attributed to their discourse does not reside in sounds or in print, not in glossaries or dictionaries, but rather in what they and those in their worlds say it means. A third truth followed: as surely as young adolescents and their worlds are changing, so is their language changing. From a realization of these truths came a teaching-learning fact: it is not profitable for children to deal with letters, syllables, words, or any other units of language outside whole language in its fullest context. Indeed, to understand what language symbolizes we must first be concerned with the concept, the reality, rather than with the symbol itself. If students understand what is being talked about, they can then use their language to help categorize, classify, and label. To introduce labels, rules, and nonsituational facts prior to reality is to pander in nonsense and to invite blank stares, yawns, and frustration.

Another important notion held by our teacher has to do with individuality. When students are encouraged to share their world and to tell about their lives in their own preferred language, the entire class can only become richer and wiser. In addition to adding another resource to the classroom, such contributions give the teacher creditable information about his students' motivations and needs and allow him to find out if students are communicating with one another and he with them. He knows that the greater the overlap in their worlds, the greater the chance for communication and the interchange of ideas. However, even when experiences are the same, he is aware that individuals perceive those experiences differently and describes them differently. Who is to say which perceiver is right or wrong or, indeed, if anyone is right or wrong?

But what of errors and mistakes? Perhaps when dealing with language learning we should accept Kenneth Goodman's (1972) more positive term, *miscue*, usually applied to reading. When a student reads something that deviates from what is printed, a miscue has been made, and until that miscue is investigated, it can't be labeled good or bad. Isn't it possible to talk about miscues in listening, speaking, and writing as well? A process-oriented teacher encourages students to forge ahead into situations in which they must take risks, hypothesize, and—quite likely—miscue.

At all times our hypothetical teacher attempts to find out what students are trying to do; he understands that if care and attention are given to the process (the risk-taking, the hypothesizing, the miscuing) by which learners make sense of their world, the results of such endeavors will be meaningful, important, and satisfying for both teacher and learner. Denial of a learner's tentative attempts, along with concern for achieving someone else's preconceived objectives and emphasis on production, misdirects the learner and distorts the learning process. Such attention causes students to doubt their own motivations and choices and inhibits even the most tentative exploration. This is not to say that learning stops when the product rather than the process is treasured; rather the lessons students learn are unexpected and unwholesome: (1) that they have little or no voice in their schooling, (2) that there is a prescribed body of knowledge they are expected to master, and (3) that there are certain acceptable ways of acquiring that knowledge.

Our process teacher is an incurable kid-watcher. He can't help himself; it is an addiction that not only delights and informs him, but is the bone and marrow of his curriculum planning. Yetta Goodman (1978) reminds us that the basic assumption in "kid-watching" is that development of language is a natural process and that the teacher should keep two questions in mind: (1) What evidence is there that language development is taking place? and (2) When a student produces something unexpected, what does it tell the teacher about the child's knowledge of language? Goodman also advises that good kid-watchers have up-to-date knowledge about language and that they understand the role of errors in language learning; errors are not random, and if we know enough about language and the language user, we can explain those errors.

Finally, our hypothetical teacher is instinctively a nongrader, and finds it difficult and unnatural to reduce a child's efforts to a black squiggle on a report card. Where is the motivation when we label a group of students with a C? Where is the process and growth when a student gets an A? Where is the context when we indicate that a child is a B student? On the other hand, our teacher has bulging folders of students' work, dated notes, and memories—all of which is used as data for discussions of the pupils' strengths and shortcomings.

The Student

Children between the ages of eleven and fifteen have been described in interesting, diverse, and sometimes unprintable terms. To make our task of learning about the learner easier, we will again produce a hypothetical character—this time a student who finds herself in an eighth-grade classroom with a teacher who is interested in why, how, and what she is thinking and doing. This can be unsettling for a youngster who for seven years has come to expect a cycle of test, prescription, readiness, drill, retest, and remediation.

Our hypothetical student spends the first few weeks looking for the cloud that accompanies the silver lining. She is uncomfortable working with a partner and in small groups, and when she does work alone, it isn't on the ever familiar purple worksheets or exercise books, nor is it even answering questions at the end of the chapter. Uprooting, redirecting, and beginning anew are tough, and our young student inches through her prevailing malaise by demanding the past, testing the innovator (something must shatter his calm determination), acting up, refusing, resisting, pouting, keeping a distance, eavesdropping, waiting, watching, listening, offering a comment, writing a thought, opening a book, and finally giving it a tentative try.

Our young student discovers that she has something to say and write and that she can talk and write without fear of interruption or put-down. Her ideas are valued, her suggestions are given consideration, her humor is appreciated, her doubts are explored, and, strangest of all, her mistakes are investigated—not counted. Slowly, our student becomes accustomed to having her strengths as well as weaknesses pointed out. The weaknesses—learned through the curious investigation of miscues—point the way for the next attempt. For the first time in her schooling, our young student hears that you learn not only by getting it right, but also by getting it wrong.

Another source of discomfort for our student has to do with major changes in the reward system. In the past the student relied on immediate approval or disapproval; there was no waiting to find out about correctness. She knew, too, that there was the final reckoning; stars or spaces, smiles or frowns, and letter grades awaited. One year she received poker chips for jobs well done, and these were traded in for free time, extended play, or Friday movies. Once in remedial reading class she received candy for doing workbook exercises. By contrast, in this new class she gets encouragement that is realistic. Now strange things begin to happen as she starts the processes of reading and writing. First, the student is encouraged to use her own strategies; no one gives her the word or constructs the sentence. She gives the whole thing a try without interruption for corrections or changes. She is never asked to read or write snippets of language about things she knows or cares little about, but now works with whole, meaningful discourse. After a while, our student begins to pay attention to receiving and producing something sensible. That leads to another curious thing: making sense is its own reward.

If the full potential of language is to be realized, it must be used in as many situations, private and public, as possible. The "sociability of language" calls for our hypothetical student not only to enjoy the privacy of reading and writing, but to share, communicate, and grow with others. Giving and receiving does not mean parading a polished production that can be compared with other polished productions. Sharing can take place in a natural, comfortable way when students work cooperatively, giving and receiving ideas, venturing speculations, and making discoveries as they work on mutually rewarding projects. But the notion of cooperative activity is easier said than done for our young student. She is familiar with competition in which her book reports, other writings, and scores are compared with those of her classmates. She knows how to hide disappointment; hurt feelings are nothing new. Now she is asked to abandon the familiar for the untried—leave competition on the playing field and accept cooperation as a way of academic life. Fortunately, the cooperative spirit takes hold quickly when students find joy in some creative venture such as dramatic improvisation, sharing readings and writings with other readers and writers, or participating in a research project with others who are participating just as fully.

In summary, a process-oriented curriculum calls for teachers who invite students to explore and expand their own private and public linguistic powers in an atmosphere that is natural and fulfilling; the students in this setting come to think of themselves as joyful receivers and producers of stories, plays, songs, poems—all forms of worthy and useful language. Both learner and teacher pay respect to the ideas and language of each other; they never cease asking questions of each other; and in a cooperative environment, they use language and experience to generate new questions, new ideas, new experiences, and new ways of expression—to achieve personal growth.

Invitations

In preparing for their students, teachers will find it helpful to consider any plan of action as a series of invitations that learners may accept or refuse. Teacher beckons and, if the plan is considered important and worth their while, students will respond, become involved, and extend invitations of their own. To make the invitations appealing, teachers must constantly look to their students for ideas and inspiration.

The activities that follow have been accepted by many who are taking their first intrepid steps toward a process-oriented classroom. Reasons for success vary and have to do with the student, the teacher, and language. First—and this is a good rule of thumb for selecting any activity—the endeavor must involve whole language for the whole child. *Whole language* means that there is no artificial separation of language arts into instructional categories of listening, speaking, reading, and writing and that the systems of language (graphic, phonemic, morphemic, syntactic, and semantic) function as the unified process students enjoy and use. The term *whole child* acknowledges that the learner has a life outside the classroom and that the emotional as well as the cognitive life of the learner will be given consideration. A second factor contributing to the potential success of these activities is that they are *present-* rather than *future*-related. Unless long-range goals can be made relevant for a student's life as it is right now, the goals are unrealistic and deflect the learner from important and attainable ends. The last reason for the success of these activities concerns the teacher's perceptions with regard to discipline. Cautious and beginning innovators have reason to fear, stultifying as that fear is, that their classes will be scenes of uncontrolled confusion. These four activities are relatively tidy—appropriate and productive, noise notwithstanding.

Reading to Students

Reading is a manageable and natural starting point. It evokes a feeling of family in which special stories, sayings, even jokes are shared and a tradition is built. Reading to students takes the pressure off those who have trouble with print, and it allows listeners to bring their experiences to the author's experiences. Students can comfortably speculate on what will happen next based on their own background; they can discuss the messages they received from the author, noting differences in what each one gained; and they can use the experience to lead them to talk, improvise, and read and write further. A student who is comfortable only with basal-reader prose quite likely will have trouble when first confronted with the language and organization of other texts. Hearing a variety of discourse exposes students to the diverse cognitive frames of reference used by authors in all modes of prose and poetry. Reading to students—everyday without fail—sets a tone of sharing and a comfortable rhythm for students and teachers alike; it puts imaginations in motion and helps nurture a love of literature. That's a good place to start.

Students Reading

Sustained, silent reading has many advocates, and it is no longer necessary to point out that students learn to read by reading; that to become hooked on books it is essential that they regularly devote large amounts of time to reading. It does appear necessary, however, that we investigate how students become hooked on reading. Left alone in a library bursting with informative and delightful books, most children will find their way to suitable reading material. However, some students not only need to learn how to select their own books, but also would benefit from suggestions for selections from adults and other students. Dixon (1966) in *Growth through English* points out that a predetermined list of reading assignments leaves no room for individual growth and initiative, but throwing the library at the student is no real opportunity for free choice. Stage by stage, teachers can set up a framework of choice within which they help pupils find their own purposes (p. 85).

A selection procedure called "Mine, Yours, Ours" provides such a framework for the reader. Students are encouraged to have three selections available at all times: "mine," selected by the reader for whatever purpose deemed important; "yours," judged by the teacher, librarian, aide, or parent to be of interest to the student; and "ours," the selection mutually agreed on by the teacher and the student, parent and student, or student and student. Such a selection procedure allows children to consider, suggest, reject, and select reading material for themselves and others.

Improvisation

Britton (1970) indicates that dramatic play is a special form of talking-and-doing—a way of dealing with other times and other places. Britton is not talking about a scripted and staged drama but, rather, improvisation in which students make do with the tools (materials, ideas, situations) at hand. Britton warns that improvisation as some teachers organize it is no more than a story retold in action and that success is measured in terms of getting the story right, all deteriorating into trivial detail. Britton encourages "exploration in the face of a situation in which much is known; the exploration is a realization, a bringing to life" (p. 141).

Moffett (1968, p. 288-291) suggests three situations for improvisation. In the first, students can elaborate on an action that took place in their reading. The children select and recapitulate some of the action as they remember it, but at the same time they invent changes. Their improvisation can serve as an alternative to comprehension testing and critical literary analysis. Moffett's second suggestion for improvisation, a way to interest and prepare students for reading a particular book, is to abstract some key situation from it, sketch a similar situation, provide some detail, and lead the students into improvisation of the episode. This activity helps develop experience into which students can fit information and ideas as they meet similar situations in print. Finally, Moffett suggests a type of improvisation that might be described as a spontaneous discussion from which moral, social, or psychological issues can evolve. The discussions might involve a jury deliberating over a verdict, a family settling a matter of television watching or dating, or a group considering membership rules. In any case Moffett suggests that in such improvisations students become aware of how their ideas are rooted in the roles and characters they are portraying. Such improvisation leads naturally to talk with a partner, small group discussions, private writing, and possibly further group action.

Writing

At least three conditions are essential before children will write: they must feel they have something to write about that is worth the effort, they must feel they can get their thoughts on paper, and they must have the opportunity to write. The first condition requires experience both in and out of the classroom. Students should be encouraged to think of themselves as resources, experts perhaps, in areas such as making pottery, camping, football, popular dances, the solar system, the life of a historical person, gardening, or fixing flats. Through beginning-of-the-year questionnaires, attention to material read, and discussions, teachers can find out what their students are interested in and perhaps good at. The point in having children write about something they know well and are interested in is that it puts the emphasis of writing on the message rather than on the form of writing. Graves (1978) suggests that a way to emphasize the student's reason for writing rather than the form in which it appears is the process-conference approach. In this procedure several brief individual conferences of one to five minutes each are informally conducted. Graves recommends that in the first two or three conferences, the teacher ask leading questions ("How did you get interested in this subject?" "What else do the people say about sharks?" "Have there ever been shark attacks in this area?") and give encouragement ("You have a good start with what you have just told me." "Many people talk about sharks, but few have actually seen them." "You certainly have good information about sharks." "I suspect very few people know what the Coast Guard is up against."). About the fourth conference, the teacher reviews a written draft and makes suggestions about arranging ideas, sorting out useful and less pertinent information, and eliminating fuzziness. In the final conference, the student mentions any "weird spellings" and punctuation problems. Form *will* be attended to if the student feels that the writing is worth "checking out."

Final Thoughts

The goals of a process curriculum stress the students' use and enjoyment of language in all sorts of situations; it means never being at a loss for language. If this sounds too general, then it must be pointed out again that it is the process, the means, that we focus on in such a curriculum. The selection of means (activities, materials, methods, etc.) is not difficult if the notion of whole language for the whole child is kept in mind. It isn't difficult to see that keeping a journal, having a conversation, comparing feelings and reactions to a movie, writing letters and petitions, writing and singing songs, telling stories, and reading to a friend involve students and their language, totally.

There are problems with this approach. Many find it threatening to step into a new and undefined world. Even adventurous young adolescents want to cling to the past; it may be deadening, but it is familiar. In the beginning, teachers may find themselves issuing invitations that few want to accept. It falls to the teacher then to spark the imaginations of parents who don't realize that the basics they are so eager for their children to acquire must involve useful language, not dry-run activities; to educate administrators about the promise of language expansion and the strictures of reductionism; to ask their colleagues to suspend judgment about their program long enough to get a good perspective; and to beckon students to come, take a chance, explore, and discover the power and joy of language.

References

Britton, James. *Language and Learning.* Miami: University of Miami Press, 1970.

Dixon, John. *Growth through English.* Reading, England: National Association for the Teaching of English, 1966.

Goodman, Kenneth S. "The Reading Process: Theory and Practice." In *Language and Learning to Read: What Teachers Should Know about Language,* edited by R. E. Hodges and E. Hugh Rudorf. Boston: Houghton Mifflin, 1972.

Goodman, Yetta. "Kid-Watching: An Alternative to Testing." *National Elementary Principals Journal* vol. 57 (June 1978): pp. 41-45.

Graves, Donald. "Balance the Basics: Let Them Write." *Learning* vol. 6 (April 1978): pp. 30-33.

Moffett, James. *A Student-Centered Language Arts Curriculum, Grades K-13: A Handbook for Teachers.* Boston: Houghton Mifflin, 1968.

III High School

10 High School in America: Problems and Opportunities

Philip Cusick
Michigan State University

A discussion of public education in America is likely to be phrased in terms of the structure of educational institutions. When talking about teaching and learning or schooling in general, one is likely to do so with liberal references to programs, work group size, teacher specialties, testing and evaluation programs, credentialing processes, support services, administrative structures, and other organizational elements. We have elected the complex bureaucracy as the model for our schools, and it is secondary schools that are most marked by complexity and bureaucracy. For the most part, they are large, containing from a few hundred to a few thousand students, are staffed by teachers with narrowly defined specialties, and are marked by a heavy emphasis on routine, with accompanying lists of rules, regulations, and sanctions to prevent the disruption of that routine. There is also a very strong emphasis on maintaining the status of the organization. Hence, it is only fitting that when we want to talk about students and schools, especially secondary schools, we phrase our discussion in terms of organizational issues.

The School as Bureaucracy

Large bureaucracies are developed so that we may attain goals that require the sustained cooperation of many people. Because of their size, their complexity, and the extensive efforts that go into building and maintaining them, bureaucracies not only define the character of events that take place within them, but also place demands on their members that are meant to serve the maintenance of the organization rather than its formal task. So in addition to setting tasks that will assist students in attaining an education, the bureaucratic secondary school will also demand they develop behaviors and understandings that maintain and strengthen the institution. Of course, this gives substance to the criticism frequently leveled at schools that what students learn in them is how to adapt to complex organizations. But that is a shallow criticism. In any undertaking we have to learn how to adapt to our surroundings before we can attain some further goals. Yet, however shallow, the criticism does point up the central problem complex bureaucracies face: assuring that the tasks and expectations which serve the purpose of maintaining the organization complement or at least do not hinder the task for which the organization was created. So it is with the schools. They must make certain that institutional and educational tasks are complementary or at least not at cross purposes.

While schools are sufficiently large and complex to warrant the analogy with industrial or governmental bureaucracies, there is a unique feature of the schools that severely limits the analogy. In schools the students are the prime beneficiaries of the organizations and are also intimate participants in the organization's processes. Unlike other organizations where the clients are on the fringe of the processes and are mere abstractions to those involved in the central core, the students are not only physically present in the core of the school, but their active cooperation is needed if the organization is to carry out its business. In order to survive and continue their efforts, the schools have to elicit the compliance of a large number of individuals, many of whom are only marginally committed to the maintenance and goals of the institution and some of whom are antagonistic to the business of the institution.

This requirement has three serious effects on secondary schools. First, it forces those who staff the institutions to place an added emphasis on the maintenance of orderly processes. Unlike other organizations which develop a contractual relationship with those involved in the central process and thus secure some agreed upon level of compliance, schools are constantly faced with hosts of new and unsocialized individuals whom they must take in and make a part of their central processes. A second, closely related effect is the simplification of the organization's processes and the avoidance of complex and intricate questions associated with those processes. For instance, having students addressed five or six times a day by subject specialists may not be the best way to educate one or a host of people; but secondary schools do not address that issue, nor are they even free to do so. The simple way to handle large numbers of students is to group them, and move them from specialist to specialist. While this solves the organizational problem of what to do with large numbers of students, it does not answer the deeper question of whether this process is conducive to learning or even whether learning is taking place. The third effect is what is lost with the emphasis on system maintenance and the simplification of processes: the intensity that one might expect from a learning situation. Sustained and systematic attention to an academic or artistic endeavor demands intensity. Whether one is accumulating facts and figures, analyzing data, writing an essay, or engaging in an artistic endeavor, the learner must invest some intensity in the effort. In our secondary schools, as they are presently organized, that intensity is difficult to attain. Many of the students in the classroom are not committed to academic learning, but the teacher is obliged to maintain a moderate level of interest and participation among all and so must appeal to those students as well as the more committed. That detracts from the effort needed for an intense experience. As noted earlier, the organization places a heavy emphasis on its survival and maintenance. Thus, if the students attend and are reasonably compliant, if the teacher maintains order and discipline, and if other organization requirements are met, then one is not likely to ask the fundamental question: Are the students who move through the system learning very much?

The organizational context is therefore essential to an understanding of the secondary schools. The organizational structure of our secondary schools has characteristics that will affect the behavior of the people in them. The chief of those characteristics is that a school, unlike other complex bureaucracies, must take into its central processes the host of unsocialized clients it hopes to serve. The organization is thus forced to place a particularly heavy emphasis on the maintenance of the organization, to simplify some very complex questions about learning, and to minimize the intensity necessary to learn about and engage in academic or creative endeavors.

Overcoming the Organization

Students in the secondary school must make two decisions. First, they must decide how to accommodate the realities of the organization, and, second, they need to decide how and to what degree they wish to engage in a quest for an education. Unfortunately, the sets of behaviors they develop in answer to the first question are not necessarily the same as or even supportive of those needed to answer the second. With the school's heavy emphasis on main-tenance, its simplification of processes, and deintensification of the central experience, any student is free to address the first set of needs and give only nominal adherence to the second. The argu-ment is not that many students choose this, but that they are free to go to school and not learn much more than how to accommodate the demands for organizational maintenance.

There are relatively few students who fail to accommodate the demands of the school routine and its accompanying rules and regulations. Indeed, this is not terribly complicated. Students have only to comprehend some rules and the importance given to each, learn how they should behave in certain classes or in the presence of certain teachers, follow time and place demands, and maintain harmonious relations with administrators and other staff members. In fact, for all the talk about disorder in secondary schools, there are few disorderly schools.

The students' second decision, how to acquire an education, is considerably more difficult, however. It is not that students can-not learn in school or that they do not learn in school, but the net effect of the organizational emphases discussed earlier is that each student must decide whether to pursue an education and to what degree. The student, choosing to engage in the academic endeavors on a more serious level than the organization demands, will then have to overcome the organizational realities.

Overcome is a strong term, but the fact is that the students can-not depend on obtaining an education by virtue of their mere presence in the school. Similarly, parents cannot be assured that they are fulfilling their obligations to their children's education simply by sending them to school and paying their property taxes. Nor can teachers be assured that they are educating their students just because they continually show up and maintain moderate order in the classrooms. If there is any criticism to be leveled at the public secondary schools, it is not that they are large, bureau-cratic, complex, and demand considerable attention to routine. Rather, it is that they inadvertently foster the attitude that if students, teachers, and parents fulfill the obligations that serve to sustain the institution, they are also fulfilling the necessity to edu-cate and learn. That is an unfortunate and erroneous attitude. Adherence to the demands of the organization will sustain the or-ganization but result in only the barest outline of an education.

The task of education falls on each teacher and each student. It is the obligation of each teacher to overcome the interruptions, reports, notes, passes, discipline processes, bells, and other demands for attention to routine matters. Each has to make the extra effort to force students into a recognition and analysis of the richness of the subjects being taught and thus reintroduce intensity into the subjects. As with teachers, so it is with students. If students elect to gain an education, they will have to expend considerable effort to overcome the endless waiting that goes with being a member of a group of twenty-five, six times each day. They will have to maintain their interest and enthusiasm even when those around them exhibit little of either. Finally, they will have to accommodate and overcome the time demands of the informal group activities that arise because there is a great deal of time in which students are expected to do little other than be present and minimally compliant. In such a situation, students naturally pursue their out-of-school, informal associations which have little to do with the formal task of the school.

Summary

The argument in this chapter is that the most pressing problem of our secondary schools is what to do with the large numbers of people, many of whom are only marginally committed to academic endeavors. We have seen that the answer has been a strong bureaucracy whose refinement and maintenance have required a great deal of effort. But while this has solved the problem of numbers and commitment, it has thrust the real questions of education on the individual student. Largely on their own, students have to ascertain their level of interest, develop their level of endeavor and commitment, and select their rewards; moreover, they must establish and nurture the community of students and teachers in which they will pursue their goals.

Perhaps that sounds pessimistic, but it is not. While the necessity of doing those things is absent, the encouragement and opportunity are there for those willing to make the effort. The set of experiences that one internalizes into an education is intensely personal and always will be. And they will always stand outside and above our efforts to organize and standardize them.

11 Competency Paradigm: Senior High School

Ouida H. Clapp
Buffalo, New York, Public Schools

In a competencies system, whether the setting is a traditional or an elective senior high school program, every act of the teacher and the student is performance conscious. As I see it, this is the significant feature of a competencies program in the high school English classroom.

Believing that motivation problems result from the way learning is organized rather than the unwillingness of students to learn, a teacher who chooses to design a competencies model will concentrate on organizing a course into challenging tasks based on careful behavioral analyses. Obviously, preparing performance objectives for examining and evaluating a student's attitudes, feelings, and values is a complex task. However, perseverance pays off for the English teacher when writing objectives at the valuing level of the affective taxonomy rather than dealing simply with awareness or with willingness to respond, e.g., "The student is able to express ideas independent of desires to please the teacher or the class." (See Davies, 1973, p. v; Hall and Jones, 1976, p. vii; Burns and Klingstedt, 1973, pp. 52-60.)

A teacher will want to plan a competencies system that develops student creativity, encourages student initiative, and fosters student interaction, and goals that are compatible with the security of the system's step-by-step procedure. In addition, the teacher will design exact and satisfying measurements of progress. In such a program, students can appreciate the realistic view they have of their competence, for example, in reading Naomi Long Madgett's poem (in Miller, 1979), "Woman with Flower," and understanding its symbolism. Unlike the confused student who lamely asks, "What's the answer to this poem?" they will have followed a system leading to competence in reading the poem.

How does a senior high school English teacher go about setting up a competencies program? The first two steps are critical. First, the teacher must decide how to view competencies. I suggest they be seen as "base points of general language arts education." Purves (1977, p. 3) uses this description because "it is easier to think of that which an educational system should offer than to conceive of what an individual must be able to do to survive in a complex society" since this "places the onus on the school rather than on the individual and asks 'What is it that is the least we can expect our schools to provide every citizen?' "

Second, the teacher must guard against a fragmented management system where the parts obscure the whole. One way to prevent fragmentation is to tie each competency statement and performance objective to the primary goal of the senior high school English program, which is to increase effectiveness in sending and receiving messages. Odell (1976, p. 47) says it this way: "Whether we are reading a novel or play, writing an essay or a poem, talking to ourselves or a huge audience, listening to a song or a lecture, we are doing one of these things:

1. trying to understand the speaker, deciding what sort of person we are seeing/hearing *or* (if we are the author [or speaker]) deciding what sort of persons we are/wish to create;
2. thinking about a subject (whether an abstract idea, an emotion, a brief sensation), trying to get our own thoughts straight, or trying to understand someone else's thoughts;
3. understanding our audience, deciding what we can/can't assume about the people we're addressing *or* trying to see what somebody else assumes about an audience."

Odell (1976, p. 49) concludes with the assertion that "to listen, speak, read, or compose effectively," one must be able to:

1. perform certain rhetorical acts, i.e.
   a. create a persona and understand the persona that someone else (a poet, a friend, a film maker, an essayist) has created;
   b. appeal to an audience (whether through visual images, spoken language, nonverbal language, or written langauge) and understand the audience appeals other people create;
   c. think critically and imaginatively about a subject and understand others' efforts to think about a subject;
2. use the intellectual strategies described by Pike [focus, contrast, classification, location in a time sequence] in performing these activities;
3. learn to use these strategies in an increasingly decentered way [i.e., examining one's ideas from different perspectives].

In designing a sound competency-based program, the teacher

could use as its base a combination of Purves' description of competencies and Odell's description of what is essential to the English program. The program that I will discuss in this chapter attempts to apply systems efficiency to broad units of language study and includes a large variety of language activity. The program uses the Odell statements as competencies and objectives that (1) are arranged and ordered to fit the program of the teacher and (2) incorporate role descriptions for teacher and student. The remaining components are (3) preassessments and post-assessments for each competency, with criteria and levels of competency stated for each; (4) units of study containing learning tasks to meet each objective, with options that fit various learning styles; and (5) performance plans for the teacher and the student.

Understanding the System

The record keeping required by this approach is demanding for both teacher and student, but it allows students to perceive their needs and progress. At the beginning of the term, the teacher presents the program in careful detail to the students, having them refer to the following items which they keep on file in folders:

1. The systems chart (see Figure 1) and chart of performance plans (see Figure 2)
2. Statements of the general competencies and objectives (see Figures 3–6)
3. Preassessment criteria for each objective
4. Student activity chart or daily log

The teacher should give the class a thorough understanding of the program and its procedures. Having the students rank-order the three general competencies might be a helpful activity; students ask themselves whether they have most success in:

1. Understanding a speaker or writer, deciding what that person is like or (if they themselves are the writer or speaker) deciding what they are like or want to project to others.
    Example. Students listen to a presidential address on conserving energy. How does the student sustain interest in the speech? How does the student identify key words, phrases, or ideas? How does the student feel about the president and

how will this affect an understanding of the speech? The student is to report to the class on the speech. In preparing the report, does the student consider the attitudes and interests of the class members? Will they want to hear about the speech? Will they respect the student? What can the student write to encourage them to listen receptively?

2. Thinking about a subject, trying to get their own thoughts straight, or trying to understand someone else's thoughts.

    Example. The student has been assigned an essay on the life of Amelia Earhart, a person unfamiliar to the class. How does the student approach the research? What questions does the student ask to assist understanding during the research? Does the student attempt to relate the information to personal experience? Does the student ask why or anticipate how while reading? Is the student discouraged by technical vocabulary or new words? Does the student have techniques for tackling such language?

3. Understanding their audience, deciding what they can and cannot assume about the people they are addressing, or trying to understand what someone else assumes about an audience.

    Example. The student is writing a summary of material from the *Linguistic Atlas* about several usage items. The student is to read the summary to a small group that is preparing a class project on dialects. Does the student know how personal perception of the small group members can be used to assist with the style of the summary? How will the student decide on the tone, depth of detail, and length of the summary?

In small groups students can compare their rankings and share examples of the strengths and weaknesses they perceive in themselves. (See Davies, 1973, p. 131, on the effectiveness of small group work.) Prepared with some understanding of themselves in relation to the business of the course, students are now ready for the self-preassessment of competency in the three general areas listed by Odell, using criteria the teacher or teacher team has developed. Self-assessment should be careful and unhurried, lasting several class periods, with the teacher standing by for explanation when needed. The teacher keeps a copy of the assessment, and each student files the original in the folder.

The statements of course objectives should be based on both the teacher's knowledge of the needs and interests of the enrolled students and those the teacher sees as typical of students in that grade. The criteria accompanying the objectives should be based on the language experience units in the course. One level of criteria is the presence or absence of a behavior; a second level is the standards to which a behavior should conform.

Figures 3 and 4 illustrate the assessment procedure discussed above. In each figure, one of Odell's competencies is stated above a sample objective for one aspect of language activity: listening, speaking, reading, or writing. (In practice all four language activities would be included under each competency, and each activity would have several objectives.) The charts that apply to each objective specify only a few of the criteria a teacher might employ in the classroom.

Assessment and the Learning Task

A classroom operating on the basis of a competencies model like the one proposed here would appear to an observer to be a learning situation employing a wide variety of settings for the activity of the students. The difference between this classroom and one using another curriculum model would become apparent during the assessments before and after a unit of activity, such as the *Our Town* plan discussed below. With the teacher's assistance, students consult their own preassessment to decide which of the unit's tasks, contracts, modules, or assignments would best serve their individual needs. After the unit, the students complete the post-assessment, which the teacher monitors; any further work that seems called for is then planned by the teacher and student. The work needed might take the form of small tasks designed to develop a subskill. Students might work on these tasks individually, in teams, or in small groups. If a student and teacher thought it advisable, a student might continue work on a particular objective in various learning situations in the next unit. The number of objectives on which a student concentrated would vary with the student's ability and the nature of the unit task.

The unit itself has a language development process that generates many products. For example, appraisals, critiques, interpretations, and summaries, written and spoken, listened to and responded to in writing and in speech, are likely to be included in a unit. When the unit is completed and the students move into a post-assessment period, recall of the process along with examination of the products available in the folders will assist students and the teacher in the assessment.

Student Activity Chart or Daily Log

Accompanying the student's written work or projects in the folder should be the activity chart or daily log. The student might make daily activity entries like the ones in the following example. The record for a year's course would run about ten pages.

1st Week	Unit: "The Community: A Force That Shapes Human Lives"
Mon.	Listened to local newscast; worked in small group to classify news.
Tues.	Read description of fictional community; worked in small group to identify elements.
Wed.	Continued small group work; developed classification lists for people and forces in community.
Thurs.	Made report to class for my small group; participated in class discussion about reports.
Fri.	Browsed in library and among materials on classroom resource table; made notes on special interests.

The teacher would help the student develop skill in keeping the log. This kind of personal account could be a source of motivation to the students, since it charts the student's participation and progress through a unit. During conferences throughout the year, and in assessment weeks, the teacher and student would use the log as reference.

The Learning Task: Traditional Program

In a traditionally organized curriculum, the tenth-grade program might emphasize poetry and drama, such writing tasks as reportage, business correspondence, and diary entries, and listening and speaking work that includes readers theatre, panel discussions, and formal speaking to the class.

Suppose that the teacher began the year with a unit on the play *Our Town*. Each unit activity would develop one or more of Odell's (1976) general competencies and would be tied to specific assessment criteria and performance levels. For example:

The teacher intends that every student read the play. (Develops Competency 1a, 1b, 1c)

Every student would participate in small group, teacher-structured discussions about their reading (Competency 2) and small group oral reading of the play (Competency 1a, 1b, 1c).

The teacher might read portions of the play to the class, play a recording, have the class view the play on television, or have the class see a stage production of the play (Competency 1a, 1b, 1c).

Some students would participate in a reading of the play or parts of the play to the whole class (Competencies 1a, 1b, 1c, 2).

Some students would read other works by Wilder and participate in a panel discussion about their discoveries or observations (Competencies 1a, 1b, 1c, 2, 3).

Some students would give formal speeches intended to inform classmates about their reading of a related assignment, e.g., portraits of small-town people in *Spoon River Anthology*, or to persuade them of a viewpoint developed in the small group, e.g., Emily should not have died (Competencies 1a, 1b, 1c, 2, 3).

During the unit, every student would do some writing. The speeches, of course, would be outlined and perhaps written out before they were delivered. Various writing assignments would be made which would allow for a variety of modes and student interests. Students might write chapter summaries, character sketches, or articles for the Grover's Corners *Sentinel*. They might write a defense of Simon Stimson's philosophy of life or a comparison between Stimson's philosophy and Mrs. Gibbs's idea: "Simon Stimson, that ain't the whole truth and you know it." They might write and read to the small group the diary entries that Simon Stimson might have made each of the seven days before his death.

Throughout the *Our Town* unit, the activities would range from simple to more demanding levels of performance and require varying degrees of competence. In the system's assessment statements, the teacher or teacher team would include criteria and levels of performance that apply to this unit in each language arts area. Figure 5 is a sample of assessment lists for speaking and reading that might be used in a literature unit. Equipped with such assessment criteria, a competencies system can accommodate whatever unit activity the teacher chooses for development of language competence.

The Learning Task: Elective Organization

Suppose that the school follows an elective organization for grades ten through twelve and that one of the elective courses is "The Community: A Force That Shapes Human Lives." Each learning activity would develop one or more of the system's general competencies, as follows, and would be tied to specific assessment criteria and performance levels:

> Students might develop a community resource list and bibliography (Competencies 1c, 2, 3).
>
> Students might share their lists with small groups and develop one list for the group (Competencies 1c, 2, 3).
>
> Students might plan visits with various individuals and to political, economic, and social agencies. This would involve telephoning, writing letters, etc. (Competencies 1a, 1b, 1c, 2, 3).
>
> Students might read books, periodicals, maps, studies, etc., pertinent to their tasks. Included might be a Hardy or a Faulkner novel, a history of the local community, a demographic study, the play *Our Town*, etc. (Competencies 1c, 2, 3). Sharing of these materials would take such forms as written and oral group and individual reports, critiques, panel discussions, role playing, formal speeches, reports prepared on slides and film.
>
> Students might write journals, newspaper reports, essays; they might write and participate in group presentations for school and community assembly programs; and so on (Competencies 1a, 1b, 1c, 2, 3).

As with the *Our Town* unit, the elective unit is analyzed by students and the teacher in terms of the assessment criteria and performance levels. Two examples of assessment lists for writing that might be assigned during the "Community" elective unit are shown in Figure 6.

Conclusion

Readers of the *English Journal* in the 1970s will remember that its pages reflected the response of the profession as it confronted systems thinking and behavioral objectives. In March 1974 Liveritte

(1974), planning consultant for the Idaho State Department of Education, articulated the theme of many of the *EJ* articles. He discussed the meaning of the term *objective* and argued that "the concept of *objective* cannot be forced to do the job which has been imagined for it by technologically minded educators. . . . The doctrine of the behavioral objective is less science than scientism" (p. 48, 52). Among those articles one can find the opinions of Edmund J. Farrell, Hans P. Guth, Henry B. Maloney, John Maxwell, Alan C. Purves, Anthony Tovatt, and Robert Zoellner. (See Barth, 1976, for a thorough bibliography of the literature). While these authors and numerous others continue to weigh the pros and cons of systems approaches to learning and teaching, the need for thoughtful competencies systems that are the products of pragmatism, not scientism, is real. There is an undeniable demand for such systems, and the competencies model in this chapter is a constructive response to this demand. Further, the competencies that the model establishes as basic may encourage instruction and learning that lead to success "unexpected in common hours."

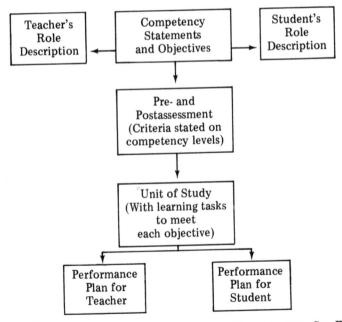

Fig. 1. Schematic of a competency-based instructional system. See Figure 2 for a schematic representation of the performance plans.

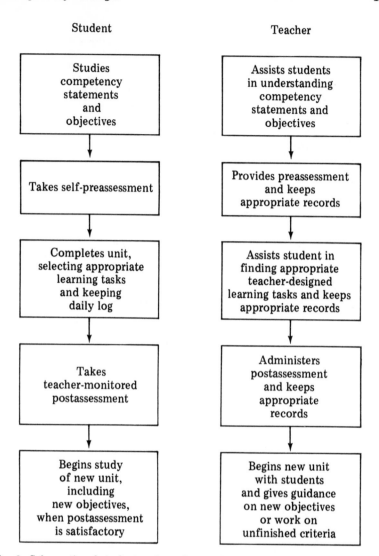

Fig. 2. Schematic of student and teacher performance plans in a competency-based instructional system.

Sample Criteria	Evaluation			
	Yes	*No*	*Little Work Needed*	*Much Work Needed*
Discriminates between similar sounds				
Explains the effect of intonation on meaning				
Recognizes the rhythmic patterns of speech				

Competency: The student is able to create a persona and (1) understand the persona that someone else has created, (2) appeal to an audience and understand the audience appeals other people create, and (3) think critically and imaginatively about a subject.

Listening Objective: The student listens effectively and responsibly to spoken English.

Fig. 3. Sample Assessment. From the Curriculum Development Center, 1970–72, pp. 52, 54, 57.

Sample Tasks	Evaluation			
	Yes	*No*	*Little Work Needed*	*Much Work Needed*
Writes a letter to the editor summarizing his or her research				
Writes a letter to grandmother, describing the research				
Writes a short speech, based on the research, for a school assembly				
Writes a letter that explains the findings to a cousin of the same age as writer who lives in another city				

Competency: The student uses the intellectual strategies in increasingly de-centered ways, examining ideas from different perspectives.

Writing Objective: The student examines ideas by addressing a single point of view to different audiences. For instance, after writing a research paper that explores the pros and cons of an issue, the student shows apt sense of audience and grasp of subject in the tasks listed.

Fig. 4. Sample Assessment.

Sample Criteria	Evaluation			
	Yes	No	Little Work Needed	Much Work Needed
Participates effectively in a variety of speaking situations				
Makes effective use of body control, movement, and gesture				
Establishes good eye contact				
Recognizes and uses appropriate tone				
Understands and uses correct articulation and pronunciation				
Makes effective use of delivery aids				
Recognizes and uses a main idea and a central theme				
Uses clear, exact, and vivid language				
Utilizes patterns of organization				
Uses various supporting materials				

Competency: The student is able to (1) focus, contrast, classify, change, and locate (facts, ideas, or persons) in a time sequence as he or she creates a persona or understands a persona; (2) appeal to an audience or understand the audience appeals others create; and (3) think critically and imaginatively about a subject or understand others' efforts to do so.

Speaking Objective: The student controls and directs speech in oral communication situations.

Fig. 5A. Sample Assessment. From the Curriculum Development Center, 1970-72, pp. 69-78, 87-97, 107-116.

Sample Criteria	Evaluation			
	Yes	*No*	*Little Work Needed*	*Much Work Needed*
Recognizes that there may be several themes that make up the meaning of a selection				
Recognizes ways the author reveals theme and purpose				
Determines what view of life or what comment on life is represented in the meaning of a selection				

Reading Objective: The student understands theme and purpose in a selection.

Fig. 5B. Sample Assessment. From the Curriculum Development Center, 1970-72, pp. 109, 135.

Sample Criteria	Evaluation			
	Yes	No	*Little Work Needed*	*Much Work Needed*
Writes a memoir, "The Community of My Childhood"				
Writes a monologue in the voice of George Gibbs or Emily Webb on "The Community of My Childhood"				
Writes a television news report, assuming the role of the reporter and interviewing various members of the community about their reactions to plans for rapid transit being proposed for the area				
Writes a haiku entitled "Home Town"				
Writes a character sketch of George Gibbs from the point of view of Emily Webb or George's father				

Competency: The student uses intellectual strategies (e.g., focus classification) in increasingly decentered ways, examining his or her ideas from different perspectives.

Writing Objective: The student examines his or her ideas by changing their form according to the point of view.

Fig. 6A. Sample Assessment.

Sample Criteria	Evaluation			
	Yes	*No*	*Little Work Needed*	*Much Work Needed*
Shows understanding of assignment				
Demonstrates awareness of the particular audience being addressed				
Follows an orderly sequence				
Holds a consistent point of view				
Demonstrates coherence and clarity of thought				
Makes smooth transitions				
Uses apt, fresh words and expressions				
Demonstrates syntactic maturity				
Employs appropriate usage and mechanics				

Writing Objective: The student writes an effective character sketch.

Fig. 6B. Sample Assessment.

References

Barth, Rodney. "ERIC/RCS Report: Behavioral Objectives in the English Language Arts." *English Journal*, vol. 65, no. 2 (February, 1976): 89-93.

Burns, Richard W., and Klingstedt, Joe Lars, eds., *Competency-Based Education: An Introduction*. Englewood Cliffs, N.J.: Educational Technology Publications, 1973.

Curriculum Development Center. *English Language Arts: Listening and Speaking, Reading, Language, Literature, Composition*. Albany: New York State Education Department, 1970-72.

Davies, Ivor K. *Competency-Based Learning: Technology, Management, and Design*. New York: McGraw-Hill, 1973.

Hall, Gene E., and Jones, Howard L. *Competency-Based Education: A Process for the Improvement of Education*. Englewood Cliffs, N.J.: Prentice-Hall, 1976.

Liveritte, Rudy H. "Getting Clear about Behavioral Objectives." *English Journal*, vol. 63, no. 3 (March 1974): 46-52.

Odell, Lee. "Basics: A Re-definition." *Arizona English Bulletin* (February 1976): 45-51.

Purves, Alan, et al. *Report on the Urbana Conference on Competency in English*. Urbana, Ill.: National Council of Teachers of English, 1977.

Miller, James E., et al. *Question and Form in Literature*. Glenview, Ill.: Scott, Foresman, 1979.

12 A Literary Heritage Paradigm for Secondary English

Ronald LaConte
University of Connecticut

Sometime in the late 1960s, the term *literary heritage* became a dirty word to many English teachers, myself among them. The term symbolized all that was wrong with the teaching of English, the dead hand of tradition that held us back from confronting the central and "relevant" issues of our times. It represented our commitment to an alien past and the neglect of an ailing present. I remember, specifically, applauding at the 1970 NCTE Convention as Neil Postman mockingly introduced the word *bullshit* into, in his own words, "the company of such exalted terms as the *topic sentence* and *our literary heritage.*"

Now, after almost a decade of championing open education and the place of futurism in the teaching of English, I find myself asked to develop a paradigm for an English curriculum based on the concept of literary heritage. Surprisingly, I find myself eager to comply, not because I find the old-time tunes coming from the "back to basics" bandwagon now rolling by to be appealing (I don't) or because I've seen the error of my ways (I haven't, at least not entirely), but because I now see possibilities in this concept for a curriculum that could be particularly appropriate for the years ahead. These possibilities depend upon a broadened and reordered definition of literary heritage. It's not enough merely to revive the term and affirm its value. We have to rethink what it means, or might mean, in 1980, as we try to teach English to kids who will be living most of their lives in the twenty-first century.

It's neither possible nor desirable to return to the "good old curriculum" of the "good old days." A lot of educational atrocities were committed in the name of teaching the literary heritage in the past, and approaches that were ineffective at best and inhumane at worst have not improved with age. The traditional concept of literary heritage, the one which has dominated the teaching of

English during this century, is seriously deficient in several respects, and a quick review of these deficiencies might serve as a useful introduction to a redefinition.

Back in the '50s when I first began teaching high school English, I was imbued with the graduate student's zeal to steep my students in the best of the Anglo-American literary tradition. No marginal stuff for my kids—only the best—and the best taught *honestly* (the way it was being taught in my graduate courses). Before long, however, I became aware that something wasn't right. I kept thinking of parties where someone told a joke and everyone laughed except the guy standing next to me. "I don't get it," he'd say. And I'd explain. Then he'd chuckle a bit and say, "Oh, yeah." And we'd both feel unsatisfied. It became clear to me that as an English teacher I had become a professional explainer of jokes. First I'd assign the literature; then, when they didn't get it, I'd explain what it was all about; and finally I'd test them to be sure they knew what they were supposed to have laughed at. It may have been instructive, but it sure as hell wasn't much fun. But then, these were the greatest jokes of all time, and everyone should know them, even if they couldn't appreciate them now.

The problem, of course, is that I was viewing the literary heritage as a body of *works*, classic pieces of literature to be studied and mastered. It's a view that continues to be very popular. One of the glaring ironies of most courses in the humanities is that they have so little to do with humans. They tend to be concerned with the form, style, historical sequence, and even a bit with the content of the *works*, but seldom do students experience a genuine feeling of identification, of sharing with other humans a "shock of recognition."

Another deficiency of the traditional concept of our literary heritage is its narrow ethnic focus. We have had a long-standing but seldom noted disparity between the concepts of cultural heritage as taught in social studies classes and literary heritage as taught in English classes. While social studies teachers and textbooks made much of the pluralistic character of the American nation, the English teacher and literature anthologies recognized only our British lineage. As a young boy growing up in a "Little Italy" in New Jersey, I was well aware that my Christmas traditions had little in common with those about which Dickens wrote. But it wasn't until I got to college that I read a word of Dante or learned of the enormous debt British literature owes to the Italian.

Finally, literary heritage has too often been used as a synonym for literary history, with whole courses devoted to a parade of author biographies interspersed with some representative works. In this context literature has been reduced to artifact and the study of English to the equivalent of a museum tour.

Entrapment in the Present

The end result of this narrow view of literary heritage too often has been dull, mechanistic teaching that trivialized literature and rendered English meaningless to most students. It was at this kind of teaching that most of the attacks of the late '60s and early '70s were aimed. But the fact remains that we do have a literary heritage, that there is an accumulation of literature that is ours, and in disregarding or discarding this heritage, we run the risk of compounding one of the more serious contemporary problems—our constriction of time sense.

Throughout the twentieth century and more particularly over the past three decades, Americans have become increasingly present oriented. One of the symptoms of future shock seems to be that the faster things change, the more intently we focus on the present, with an occasional nostalgic glance backward to "the good old days." Commenting on this phenomenon, Boulding (1978) notes that some experiments she has conducted over a twenty-five year period indicate that college students and young parents are unable to imagine what the world may be like fifteen to twenty years in the future. My own casual surveys of teachers and high school students confirm this inability to imagine any condition other than the present. Well over 90 percent of those I surveyed see life in the year 2000 as virtually identical with that of today. Yet all express a belief that we are living in a period of rapid social and technological change. Evidently this myopia (if it can be called that) derives not from a lack of information, but from a failure of imagination. Many adults are simply "image poor" when they try to think about the future. The only pictures they have been exposed to are those of far off space-time travel movies, Sunday supplement descriptions of the home of the future, or the latest forecast of the next swing in the economic cycle. As a result, they remain suspended somewhere between the *Wall Street Journal* and *Star Wars*.

While trying to imagine what the future *will* be like is an activity best left to fortunetellers and psychics, the inability to imagine what any future might be like is a serious limitation. Without the capability of seeing contemporary events and issues as part of a historical flow leading to imaginable future consequences, the individual's ability to respond to these events and issues is severely restricted. For example, unless one seriously tries to imagine life in a polluted world—eating, sleeping, going to work, socializing, and all the specifics of an ordinary day—then talk of increasing pollution can do little more than evoke vague anxiety about a coming time when "things will be bad." In order to deal with present realities, the individual must have pictures of future possibilities.

Redefining Heritage: Past as Prelude

This brings me back to our literary heritage and the English curriculum. It is somewhat ironic that the more one contemplates the future, the more important the past becomes. Certainly this has been true for me personally, and both Boulding and Polak (1961) before her have demonstrated that societies, and presumably individuals, with a strong historical sense have a strong sense of futurity also. Therefore, if we can increase a student's historical sense through a heightened awareness of a connection to a literary heritage, we may also begin to expand that student's time sense into the future.

Does this suggest a return to literary history and the parade of masterworks? Quite the contrary, it suggests, indeed demands, that we view our literary heritage as a good deal more than a mere collection of great works by great writers. Our accumulated literature is a body of continuing artistic commentary on the human condition, commentary containing deeply imbedded values and powerful recurrent themes, commentary that not only records the history of human thought, but also shapes it. It is this view of our literary heritage that can serve as the basis for a curriculum model for our time.

Such a view can neither dismiss the contemporary as ephemeral nor reject the old as irrelevant. Instead it demands that we view past and present as points on a continuum that stretches from antiquity to futurity. It insists that we treat the procession of literature as a procession of persistent human concerns reflected in works of art, concerns that continue to demand attention. While these concerns are not unique to any one age, each era has interpreted, modified, and responded to them in unique ways. The cumulative weight of these responses and interpretations over the centuries bears heavily on our own individual and collective attempts to deal with the issues of our own times.

In this sense our literary heritage can be compared to a material inheritance. In the case of a material inheritance, a detailed analysis of the estate is necessary and valuable. It is important for the heirs to know what they have and what it's worth. But the accountants' ledgers and the experts' appraisals tell only part of the story. Included in the legacy are the family attitudes toward wealth and how it should be spent, generations of postures and prejudices, and a vast assortment of other values and beliefs. Added to these is the equally important influence the very knowledge of the inheritance has had in shaping the attitudes of the heirs. In short, it is not just what the heirs *have* that they owe to the past, but what they *are*.

Without pushing this analogy too far or becoming excessively deterministic, it would not be too much to say that we make decisions about the future, or decisions that impact heavily upon the future, out of a value system that has been shaped to a large extent by the literature of the past. As today's students struggle with today's problems, personal or societal, they do so in a context shaped in part by Sophocles and Shakespeare and Milton and Dickens—whether or not they have ever read a word written by any of them.

Consider the illustration provided by Barzini (1965) in *The Italians.* Commenting on the fact that most of the moral aspects of feudalism were never incorporated into Italian culture or literature, he notes that

> the contemporary capitalistic world is still almost incomprehensible to most Italians, who admire, envy, and imitate, often very successfully, its outward aspect, its power, its practical products, but miss its moral character. They even doubt if it exists at all. Many current rules of fair conduct strike the Italians as pure nonsense. Take the English saying "never kick a man when he is down." They do not believe anybody really obeyed it. They know a man should not be kicked if he is old, if he is strong and can immediately kick back, if he can later avenge himself, if he has powerful friends or relatives, if he could be useful some day in any way, or if a policeman is watching. But why not "when he is down"? When else, if you please, should one kick a man more advantageously? When more safely and effectively? A famous handbook on how to play *scopa*, the most common Italian card game, written in Naples by a Monsignor Chitarella, begins: "Rule Number One: always try to see your opponent's cards." It is a good concrete practical rule. (p. 191)

And just as an Italian's perception of the contemporary world has been influenced by the absence of the chivalric code in Italian literature, so has the American's been influenced by its inclusion. Over and over again as we address today's issues—social injustices, environmental destruction, shifting international balances, human rights, nuclear proliferation, and on and on—we are influenced by all the voices of the past telling how we should, or shouldn't, behave. Any curriculum that ignores these voices, that focuses entirely on the contemporary, cheats the students. For just as study of the past without concern for the present and future is knowledge without purpose, so study of the present and future without concern for the past is purpose without knowledge. Knowledge of our literary heritage, defined as the literary history of ideas and values, is hardly a mere adjunct or ornamental addition to a student's education; it is as essential as self-knowledge, for, indeed, it *is* self-knowledge.

Features of the Heritage Curriculum

An English curriculum based on this view of literary heritage will have two basic elements: it will be thematic in nature, and it will consider the themes of the literature of the past as inextricably connected to those of the literature of the present. Additionally, it can and should span the entire six years of secondary education, and it need not be confined to courses surveying American, English, or world literature. It will incorporate all aspects of English into an integrated program: language, literary, and media skills. And it will include serious consideration of the future as continuation of the past and present.

Thematic organization is hardly a new concept and needs no elaborate description or justification here. However, a few words about how the concept is employed in this paradigm are probably in order. From an instructional standpoint, thematic organization can be either of two basic types: demonstrative or exploratory (corresponding roughly to deductive and inductive styles of teaching). Demonstrative organization uses literature to exemplify the theme under consideration: "This story shows courage in battle." Exploratory organization employs literature as a means to examine the theme: "Is this behavior in battle courageous?" Obviously, it is not the literature that makes the difference, but the approach to the literature (although vastly different selections can result from employing one method instead of the other).

For instance, a teacher using the demonstrative approach might introduce *Macbeth* as "a play that shows how a great man is destroyed by his own ambition," proceeding to point out, act by act and scene by scene, how this destruction takes place, asking students to "find passages that show Macbeth's ambition," comparing Macbeth to contemporary "ambitious" leaders, assigning a paper on "Lady Macbeth—A Goad to Ambition," and ending with a unit test in which students are asked to show how several characters from the play either support or thwart Macbeth's ambition. Another teacher using the exploratory approach might introduce the same play as one "in which many critics claim ambition plays a central role," proceeding to examine Macbeth's actions to determine if he is, indeed, motivated by ambition, and what form or forms this ambition might take, asking students to use passages from the play as evidence in debates on Macbeth's motivation, comparing the meaning of *ambition* in a stratified Elizabethan society and an open modern one, assigning a paper on "The Many Faces of Ambition," and ending with a unit test in which students are asked to explain Macbeth's motivation, however they interpret it, by examining his relationship to other characters in the play.

While demonstrative organization lends itself to a tighter structure and control, exploratory organization affords far richer teaching opportunities. The demonstrative approach can too easily become moral indoctrination, using both literature and theme as object lessons in a particular point of view. The exploratory approach, on the other hand, can degenerate into totally uncontrolled bull sessions with both literature and theme being lost in verbal meandering.

Thematic Polarity and Thematic Question

A sensible compromise is to adopt the exploratory approach, but to provide a focusing purpose for the exploration. Any search is more effective if it is orderly and controlled. Two simple and useful devices for providing a framework for exploration without overly restricting either the selection of literature or the student's responses to it are the *thematic polarity* and the *thematic question*.

A thematic polarity is simply a pair of words or terms that attempt to delineate a range of human behavior that has been of literary concern through the ages. Because human acts occur in a human context, they must be examined in a human context. As we consider human behavior, we invariably place a given act on a continuum between polar opposites. An obvious example is our description of an act as good or evil. As we examine the act, we attempt to place it somewhere on the scale ranging from ultimate good to absolute evil by comparing it with other acts which we or society have already classified. Because the number and kind of such polar opposites is as large and various as humankind, the usefulness of the device depends upon selecting pairs that are not so abstract as to be all-inclusive (e.g., good and evil), but which still define a broad range of human behavior (e.g., loyalty and treachery).

Within the broad range of the thematic polarity, we can then pose more specific thematic questions that serve as the focus of student exploration and analysis (e.g., "How much obedience does loyalty require?"). These questions should not suggest precise, certain answers, but should instead represent the kind of doubt that has prompted the writing and reading of literature throughout history. Obviously both the thematic questions and the thematic polarities should be framed with consideration given to the experiential, reading, and conceptual levels of the students. Polarities and questions appropriate for twelfth-grade advanced placement classes would be of an entirely different order than those selected for poor-reading seventh graders. However, a curriculum for any age or ability level can be organized in this manner.

Having established the polarity and posed some (not all, for others should come from the students) of the thematic questions, we can begin to identify appropriate literature. Obviously, we want pieces that deal with the thematic question, but these pieces should also reflect historically different responses to the question and be within the ability-interest range of the students. We will want to have available for use literature that shows how this question has been addressed at different times in the past as well as modern selections. A simple organizing technique is to create a three-tiered structure of past, present, and future, and cluster the literature accordingly. For example, using the loyalty-treachery polarity, we could examine the concept of loyalty as it exists in the plays of ancient Greece, in medieval epics, in the poems and plays of the Renaissance, and in the literature of the seventeenth, eighteenth, and nineteenth centuries. We could then select a similar body of modern literature dealing with the topic and finally a cluster of selections treating some possible future aspects of the question. How did this concept change as civilization moved from classical antiquity through the Middle Ages and feudalism into powerful monarchies and then into the era of democratic governments? How has it evolved during the twentieth century? How do modern writers treat the individual's obedience to government, corporate authority, and the like? What have been the changing views of a wife's loyalty to her husband and vice-versa? And as we face the twenty-first century, how do we deal with questions involving the loyalty of intelligent machines, obedience and chemical and electrical mind control, and so on? The list of possible questions is virtually endless, the only restrictions being the ability level of the students and the imagination of the teacher. (For a more thorough discussion of the questions, see LaConte, 1974).

Thus we have an organizational structure that provides a conceptual framework for a controlled exploration of literature. Yet the framework is flexible enough to keep the control from becoming overly restrictive. As students pursue the questions raised at the outset, they will undoubtedly raise additional, related questions of their own. And while we begin with clusters of teacher-selected literature, there is nothing to prevent additional pieces from being added along the way. In the selection of contemporary materials, particularly, the opportunity for expansion is virtually unlimited. Students can explore the whole range of popular literature for continuing commentary on the theme: newspapers, magazines, cartoons, films, television, as well as more traditional literary forms. Because each thematic question is deliberately open-ended, it can be explored for as long as students and teacher desire.

Writing and Oral Activities

We can incorporate into the unit provision for written and oral activities aimed at improving student language proficiency. Again, the thematic polarity and thematic questions provide a framework and focus, and the literature itself supplies springboards, but the range of activities is again almost limitless. They can include both traditional expository writing assignments, such as analysis of given works, comment on a particular viewpoint, or comparison and contrast, and more novel assignments such as describing "Loyalty Day" ceremonies in King Arthur's court, writing Macduff's diary entry in which he questions how much loyalty he owes Macbeth and how much to Scotland, or writing a "loyalty creed" for school athletes. Students can perform dramatic improvisations (a roving reporter in hell interviews all the conspirators in Caesar's assassination), engage in debate ("Loyalty to the family is more important than loyalty to friends"), tape, film, create slide shows—all related to the theme in question. Once more, the only limitations are student interest and ability.

A distinct advantage of this kind of organization is the built-in continuity. Once the theme has been introduced and the exploration of it begun, it becomes unnecessary to "warm up" the students for each assignment. Part of the background for each assignment comes from yesterday's discussion or activity. Activities tend to build on each other to produce a continuing stimulation for students.

Plainly, this approach provides enormous opportunity for student-generated language, which, in turn, can be used as the basis for instruction in spelling, punctuation, organization, clarity of expression, or whatever skills seem to warrant attention. Once we have a sizeable chunk of student-produced language with which to work, we can start to put together individual skills-improvement programs for each student. Unlike hit-or-miss grammar handbook exercises that may or may not address themselves to the needs of a given student, this approach insures that the teacher's efforts will be aimed directly at a student's problems. Thus, skills instruction is both individualized and integrated with the literature exploration.

For example, once we have collected several pieces of student writing, they can be analyzed to determine specific patterns of error in spelling (consistent *ant-ent* confusion, *ie-ei* reversal, phonetic difficulties). These can then be ranked in order of seriousness or frequency. Similarly, problems in punctuation, sentence structure, and the like can be identified and ranked. (Obviously, not all of a student's weaknesses will show up in a few papers, but there should be enough to work with.) These problems can then be arranged on a student profile sheet which can be used both as a guide to assigning remedial work and as a record of student progress. This approach gives both teacher and student a clear plan of attack. The teacher can also use the profile sheets to cluster students with similar problems for group instruction. At the same time, once the teacher has a "feel" for student problem areas, the literature can be used more effectively to illustrate how things look when they are working properly (e.g., examples of subordination and coordination, use of punctuation).

A Year's Plan

While it would be theoretically possible to build an entire year's work around a single thematic polarity and its related thematic questions, this would probably represent a drastic overkill for most students. Generally four to nine polarities or units constitute a reasonable year's work, with six being a typical number. Fewer than four units poses the risk of student boredom. Nine weeks of "loyalty" or "success" are probably more than most students can tolerate, particularly younger ones. On the other hand, more than nine units almost guarantees superficiality. If there is going to be a genuine exploration of the thematic questions, past, present and future, at least four weeks will be required.

Assuming six polarities for the year, these will each be subdivided according to the number of thematic questions selected. The clustering of literature according to time periods affords still another opportunity for division. The danger, then, is not so much that the units will be large, amorphous blocks of time, but that they will become so divided and fragmented that the integrity and continuity will be lost. Given a six-week unit, six thematic questions seem to be maximum, with three or four a more reasonable number.

In addition to the written and oral exercises incorporated into the unit, separate unit-ending activities are a good idea. These can be a particularly effective way of focusing student vision on the future. As the exploration of the theme draws to a close, it is appropriate for students to address themselves to the question of what lies ahead. What does it all mean? How will the changes that are taking place or are expected to take place bring new dimensions to the question? These final activities can be introspective, but they should be supported by some student research into the social, political, and technological changes that are likely to occur. To continue the example begun earlier: What effect will new lifestyles have on concepts such as family loyalty? How might increasing fragmentation of society alter our concepts of allegiance? Questions such as these could provide the focus for a wide variety of written or oral unit-ending activities.

Some Additional Curriculum Considerations

This approach to the English curriculum lends itself well to the construction of an articulated six-year secondary sequence. By carefully framing polarities and thematic questions to take into account the maturity and interest of the students, we could fashion a program of "developmental exploration" in which students confront more sophisticated and intellectually challenging questions at each grade level. For example, within our loyalty-treachery polarity, the student might start in the seventh grade by exploring the question "How are animals loyal to humans?" and end in the twelfth grade by examining the question "How can the state betray the individual?" (This is not to suggest that the same polarities be used at each grade level, although they could be if desired, but

merely to illustrate the maturity range of thematic questions.)
Additionally, by selecting literature of the past carefully over the
six-year span, we can introduce the student developmentally to
the best of older British, American, and world literature, a far
more sensible procedure than the crash survey courses commonly
taught in the last years of high school.

A six-year sequence may also include a developmental program
of literary skills. Because the variety of literature in such a program
is so great and because the old is included with the new at each
grade level, structured consideration may be given to such matters
as style, form, and techniques. A primary emphasis on ideas and
the exploration of thematic questions are no reason to ignore the
development of literary skills.

Despite these advantages, however, it is not necessary to organize
a full six-year sequence in order to implement such an approach.
For instance, elective programs would still be possible, but there
would be less room or reason for the purely contemporary elective
("Modern Fiction," "Women in Modern Literature"). The concerns
of these courses could be incorporated into other, broader-based
electives that contain past, present, and future dimensions. Other
"skill development" electives ("Film Making," "Creative Writing")
obviously fall outside this paradigm, since they are in reality supplementary and not basic. However, the number of possibilities
offered by six thematic polarities a year is large enough that there
seems little genuine need for electives other than the skill-develop-
ment type. Each polarity, indeed each thematic question, presents
most of the same opportunities an elective does without requiring
extensive counseling or elaborate scheduling.

Finally, this method of organization provides more opportunity for cooperation with other subject areas than most systems
currently in use. At every grade level, there are numerous possibilities for cooperation with social studies departments and science
departments.

Implementation

The two most serious difficulties one faces in implementing this
paradigm are the lack of readily available materials and the insecurity of teachers faced with a new approach. While these difficulties
are not insurmountable, they can be real problems at the outset.

Because no literature series currently marketed is based on this
concept of literary heritage, it is necessary to patch together the required materials from existing sources. This means "mining" books

for appropriate selections, which could lead to a lot of juggling and swapping of books among teachers, with all the logistical headaches involved.

The flexibility and open-endedness of the approach can impose heavy demands on teachers who are used to a more rigidly structured organization. Compared to the read-the-story-answer-the-questions-grammar-on-Wednesday-vocabulary-on-Friday approach, it can seem intimidating. But while the work is admittedly harder, the rewards, for both teacher and student, are much greater.

Summary

Despite all the abuse it has received in recent years, the concept of a literary heritage can and should be an effective basis for structuring the English curriculum. If we understand this heritage to be a legacy of ideas, values, and commentary on the human condition, a legacy which continues to influence our decisions and shape our future, then we can use it as a means of giving our students the Janus-like ability to see where they are going while looking at where they have been.

References

Barzini, Luigi. *The Italians.* New York: Bantam Books, 1965.

Boulding, Elise. "The Dynamics of Imaging Futures." *World Future Society Bulletin*, September–October, 1978.

LaConte, Ronald. *Teaching Tomorrow Today.* New York: Bantam Books, 1974.

Polak, Fred. *The Image of the Future.* Translated by Elise Boulding. New York: Oceana Press, 1961.

13 Process Curriculum for High School Students

Barbara Stanford

Gene Stanford
Children's Hospital, Buffalo, New York

The college supervisor sat in the back of the tenth-grade classroom observing a student teacher. The situation was depressing, but all too common. The class droned through *Julius Caesar*, reading the dialogue aloud with an occasional pause for the definition of an Elizabethan term. Brutus and Cassius argued over the fate of Rome with as much enthusiasm as they might have devoted to a 1950 stock market report. When the shuffling of feet became louder than the monotonous reading, the student teacher spoke sharply: "You know we have to get through this today."

In the conference that followed, they all acknowledged that something was wrong. The student teacher was near tears because "they just don't seem interested." The cooperating teacher shuddered as he recognized in the student teacher's behavior a precise imitation of himself, down to the idiosyncratic gestures, lacking only the life and warmth that he at least hoped he possessed. But both were puzzled and frustrated about what was going wrong with the class.

When the supervisor asked the simple question, "What was going on in the students' minds?" both looked up with a gleam of recognition. The cooperating teacher, while employing a rather unimaginative teaching strategy, at least had a strong empathy for the students and an intuitive sense of what they were thinking and how they were reacting. But the student teacher at this point in her practice did not, and even when she tried to use more innovative methods or to organize her curriculum according to sound theoretical principles, her classes were still hollow and dull. She had not yet developed the awareness of *process* that often distinguishes good teachers from mediocre ones.

138

Principles of Process Teaching

Process teaching begins with a concern for the thoughts and feelings of the student and a recognition that these are as important to the learning process as the curriculum. By this definition, almost all good teachers, regardless of their philosophical position, are process teachers. But the process curriculum develops this concern further and uses an analysis of the thoughts and feelings of the student as the basis for the selection of objectives, materials, and methods of teaching. (See Borton, 1970; Brown, 1971; Postman and Weingartner, 1969; Romainville, Blankenship, and Stanford, 1977; Stanford and Roark, 1975; Weinstein and Eantini, 1970.)

The process teacher places the student, rather than the content, at the center of the curriculum and usually operates on three important philosophical principles. First, the curriculum must be concerned with the whole person. The cognitive domain is so interrelated with the affective and psychomotor domains that none can be studied or developed effectively in isolation. For example, a person's evaluation of the literary quality of a novel is not a purely rational experience. The reader's sensitivity to the effects of literary devices may be either enhanced or dulled by an emotional state, developmental concerns, or even the contents of one's stomach. An eighteen year old who has just fallen in love in early spring may be thrilled by the vivid images of Edna St. Vincent Millay's "Renascence," while a fifty year old, overwhelmed by paperwork and suffering from a backache, may criticize the trite rhyme scheme and sing-song rhythm.

Furthermore, problems in one area are often manifested in another area. Emotional difficulties in elementary school children are often manifested as reading problems; and in adolescents social adjustment problems often serve to mask serious reading difficulties. So the process educator is concerned with fostering growth in both the cognitive and affective areas, and sometimes also in the psychomotor area. Even when the focus is heavily on one area or the other, as in the study of grammar, the teacher is always alert to implications and influences from the other areas.

In addition to focusing on the "whole person," the process curriculum is based on a recognition of the natural processes of human development. Developmental psychology, as well as more specific research in the development of language arts skills, provides a theoretical background for the formulation of a process curriculum.

Finally, the process curriculum tends to value the internal judgments about growth made by the individual learner more than external standards established by society. A boy who grew from an outcast to an accepted member of the group in the eighth grade could be considered successful, even if he shows only six months of growth on a standardized reading test. A girl who selected a career as an auto mechanic and mastered the workings of the internal combustion engine during the eleventh grade could also be considered successful, even if she did not master algebra. The failure would be a student who commits suicide or is institutionalized because of an inability to cope with a complex society.

For most humanistic educators, an ideal process curriculum would be much like that described by Rogers in *On Becoming a Person* (pp. 273–314) and later elaborated on in *Freedom to Learn.* With the encouragement and assistance of the instructor, students define or discover their own goals and their own methods of reaching those goals. The teacher acts as facilitator and resource provider, helping students identify and choose things they want to learn by assisting self-analysis and by making available to them a wide range of possibilities. The teacher's role includes both content and affective assistance. The teacher must know the subject well enough to assist students in a wide variety of quests. Within one classroom several students might be reading *Macbeth*, others might be looking for sources of modern black culture in African folk tales, an individual student might be attempting to write a novel, while someone else attempts to overcome a serious reading disability. In addition, the teacher provides a growth-promoting climate through what Rogers calls the "facilitative conditions": empathic understanding, acceptance, and genuineness. Empathic understanding, the ability to understand and feel with another, is essential to helping another person make personal decisions. Acceptance, caring for another person regardless of achievements, provides a climate in which people are willing to take risks, for they know that failure will not cause them to lose the respect and caring of others. Genuineness, dealing with students as real persons, not just a role, is essential for the development of judgment.

The Problems of Process Teaching

If any of the teacher qualities just discussed are lacking, a completely process-based classroom will probably fail. A teacher who lacks empathy will not be able to facilitate students' making their own decisions, but will probably subtly manipulate them into one particular preference. The teacher who is unable to show acceptance will seem phony to students: "She tells us to make our own decision, but she gets mad if we don't do what she wants." And a teacher who is unable to be genuine will have a class with no standards and therefore with little achievement. The purely process-oriented curriculum, therefore, evolves as the teacher provides conditions for student growth and requires a teacher who is a highly skilled facilitator as well as a person with a great wealth and depth of knowledge. Teaching with this approach requires a much higher degree of skill than most other approaches, a degree of skill obtained by very few teachers.

Furthermore, even a highly skilled teacher is likely to encounter serious obstacles in implementing a completely process-oriented classroom in a secondary school, for there is a deep conflict between the innate, developmental needs of adolescents and the desires of society about the skills they should master. In both elementary school and in college-level career preparation, the relationship between individual developmental needs and society's expectations is much closer. Early elementary school children, at least those from a middle-class environment, are fascinated by the magic and power of words, books, and numbers and will readily choose to spend time with reading and number activities. The older elementary child's developmental needs for mastery of the environment can easily be steered into activities quite closely related to traditional science and social studies curricula. But the developmental concerns of adolescence are so different from, in fact, almost antagonistic to, the goals and expectations of society and the traditional curriculum that few attempts to set up a completely process-oriented high school have lasted more than three years before the community has rebelled.

In a curriculum based on the developmental concerns of adolescents, English, along with history, mathematics, and science, would definitely be considered "frills" that one might elect during free time on alternate Fridays if the essential tasks of peer relations, identity development, sex-role definition, and relationships with the opposite sex were being achieved satisfactorily. The community, on the other hand, considers these concerns to be not only a waste of time, but something bordering on immorality. Recently, for example, our local school board once again expressed its strong opposition to an elective course in "family life education" and, of course, would not be happy to see this course emerge in a process-oriented classroom. The traditional school suppresses this conflict between adolescents' needs and community goals, coerces or entices students into accepting the community's curriculum, and is resigned to the grudging, sullen, minimal quality of work done by most adolescents in high school.

A Balancing of Needs

Since most teachers lack the skills needed to develop a truly process-oriented classroom and since the community would probably not accept it if they did, most successful process teachers attempt to combine the needs of adolescents and those of the community. The first step in doing so is usually to examine carefully the developmental characteristics of adolescents and their relationships to the goals of the community. While process curriculum development should be based ultimately on the unique needs of an individual class, research in human development and learning theory can be very helpful in giving a teacher clues to look for. The following brief survey of some of that research may suggest areas in which further study may be helpful.

Cognitively, according to Piaget, adolescents should be developing the skills of formal operations. A description of the skills of formal operations is very similar to a list of the skills needed for literary analysis or for advanced composition: ability to separate form from content, to visualize possibilities, to predict consequences, to devise and follow a procedure for testing hypotheses, and to form conclusions from data. So a process curriculum should focus on promoting the development of these skills.

However, the process of developing these abilities is much slower and more painful than many adults recall. For example, the adolescent beginning to develop the ability to see possibilities beyond the real and present is likely to spend an inordinate amount of time in unrealistic fantasies. Fantastic career goals and infatuation with remote people and exotic clothing are all part of the developing ability to see alternatives, an ability which, much to the despair of adults, appears to predate the ability to evaluate the consequences of choices.

In the affective domain, adolescents are developing a wide range of new and powerful feelings and emotions and are learning to sort out and judge values and attitudes. At the same time, their expression of feelings and attitudes and the workings of their imagination are becoming more internal, verbal, and subconscious instead of external and physical. For example, research has shown that after reading or viewing a disturbing, violent work, young children may spend several hours engaging in play with a high content of violence. Adolescents, on the other hand, may cope with the emotions by sitting moodily, listening to loud music, or dancing to it. Adolescents engage in a lot of seemingly purposeless activity that can be disturbing to teachers in the classroom. But when one recognizes that they are now doing in their minds all of the exploration and imagining that younger children do in their play and manipulative projects and that they do not yet have the skill to do this kind of thinking while they are washing dishes or driving a car, their disturbing habits become more understandable and it becomes possible to develop teaching techniques that utilize their style.

Development of a process curriculum also requires knowledge of the content young people need to learn. The basic concerns of adolescence tend to be personal and interpersonal growth. Erickson defines the central task of adolescence as the achievement of a personal identity, a task which includes becoming emotionally independent first of their parents, then the peer group; developing a set of values through personal, rational analysis rather than through simple acceptance; finding one's own unique skills and competences; accepting one's weaknesses and disabilities; and finding one's own niche in society. Closely related to the development of a personal identity is the development of much more sophisticated skills for relating to other people. Children enter adolescence with interaction skills limited to a very few people in a very few situations. While the early adolescent seems to talk constantly, the majority of that talk is with a few close friends and family members, and it is limited to a few topics and situations. By the end of adolescence, the young adult needs to be able to converse with a stranger from any background in situations ranging from business to romance. Since communication skills are central to the needs of adolescents and also to the traditional English curriculum, they are a good place to begin curriculum development.

A Process Approach to Communication Skills

To develop a curriculum that teaches communications skills, the teacher must begin by analyzing the level of skill possessed by the students. Many adults are incredulous at the suggestion that teenagers may need help with communication skills, but while most teenagers talk a lot and many talk loudly, it does not take very detailed observation to begin to see the limits of their skills.

First, many adolescents have very limited ability to talk to anyone besides friends and family. A popular communication exercise is to assign all class members randomly to partners and ask them to talk

for five minutes on an assigned topic. Unfortunately, a large percentage of high school students are totally unable to do this the first
time and will need encouragement and guidance—and additional
practice. Second, adolescents are often not fully aware of the emotional content and the connotations of their messages. Cooperative
early adolescents, when asked to try to involve quiet members of
the group in a discussion, will often respond with comments such
as "Hey, stupid, don't you have anything to say?" and will be
genuinely frustrated when the silent members remain silent. Finally,
many adolescents lack the ability to develop or elaborate on an idea
or to enhance a story or a description with lively details. Their
monosyllabic or one-word answers in class are often a result of this
lack of skill. The student who cannot think of anything to say
about Macbeth besides "He was pretty mean" may show more enthusiasm, but not much more skill, as she gushes to a friend, "Oh,
John is so cute. Don't you think he's cute? Oh, he's just SOOOO
cute. I can't stand it he's so cute."

After identifying the current level of student skills, the teacher
needs to design activities to move students to the next level. While
there is no definite list of skills that should be developed, it is often
helpful to have a list and sequence of skills that will give one clues
of what to look for. The following is a sampling of the skill areas
and general sequences of skills within each area that are important
for learning communication skills during adolescence:

Area I: Ability to talk to different people in different situations
  A. Different people
    Level 1: Student is able to talk freely with friends
    Level 2: Student is able to talk freely with classmates
            from other social groups
    Level 3: Student is able to talk freely with people of
            other ages from the same social-cultural group
    Level 4: Student is able to talk freely with people from
            other social-cultural groups
  B. Different situations
    Level 1: Student is able to take part in a discussion in a
            small group
    Level 2: Student is able to take part in a discussion in a
            whole class
    Level 3: Student is able to make a formal presentation
            to a whole class
Area II: Ability to listen effectively
    Level 1: Student is able to recall main ideas from another
            student's comments

Level 2: Student is able to recall and relate ideas from two or more speakers

Level 3: Student is able to recall a previous speaker's ideas and relate them to those of the other speaker

Level 4: Student is able to identify main ideas and relationships that have emerged in an extended discussion

Level 5: Student is able to identify consensus or areas in which consensus is lacking in an extended discussion

Area III: Ability to recognize emotional content and connotations of a message

Level 1: Student can separate emotional content or connotations from denotative meaning

Level 2: Student can recognize response to emotional content or connotations

Level 3: Student can identify and describe the connotations responded to

Level 4: Student can recognize when someone else is responding to connotations

Level 5: Student communicates the intended emotional messages as well as denotative meanings

Area IV: Ability to develop or elaborate on an idea

Level 1: Student can describe an event or person so that all of the essential features are included

Level 2: Student can describe an event or person with enough detail that the listener can picture it

Level 3: Student can describe an event or person with an exciting enough style that listeners enjoy hearing it

Teaching techniques for helping students develop these skills begin with the communication that takes place within the classroom itself, for the classroom is not something that is set apart from the real world. The messages communicated by the positions of the desks, the language of the teacher's assignments, the process by which ideas develop in a discussion, and the words students use to speak to one another—all are potential subjects for analysis and discussion. While topics and lessons are usually planned in advance, a concern or interest that arises from the group can always supercede the teacher's plan. "Teachable moments," examples of communication principles that arise naturally in the course of a class, are seized and discussed.

The communication process is learned primarily through communication. In *A Student-Centered Language Arts Curriculum, Grades K-13,* one of the earliest and still one of the best attempts to build a complete process curriculum, Moffett states, "School should be a place where children talk at least as much as outside, for fostering speech is the business of the language classroom. Too often there is the hidden inscription above the door which says, 'Abandon all speech ye who enter here' " (p. 45). Teaching methods that foster student-to-student interaction are therefore encouraged. But small groups or whole class discussions are not just allowed to happen by chance. The skills of holding an effective discussion are seen as part of the curriculum, and the oral language production of the class is analyzed and developed as thoroughly as the written language.

Communication skills are central to the concerns of adolescents. Other aspects of the traditional English curriculum may not emerge quickly in adolescents' analyses of their needs, but a teacher who is willing to consider their needs seriously and carefully can usually help them to see ways in which the traditional English curriculum can play a very important role in helping them learn the skills they want. The following sections show some of the ways in which traditional curriculum areas interact with perceived needs of adolescents, some of the developmental sequences for those skills, and a sample sequence of activities to develop those skills. It is important to keep in mind, however, that these are only possibilities; the real process curriculum must emerge from the concerns of actual students in a particular class.

Language Study

A process curriculum tends to look at quite different aspects of language than the traditional curriculum. Discussions are more likely to focus on the impact of a sentence on the listener and the reasons for that impact than on labeling the elements of syntax. When grammar and usage are studied, the concern for authenticity and honest reactions in a process curriculum cause a headlong confrontation with issues that traditional teachers try desperately to sweep under the table. First, students recognize the absurdity and inaccuracy of many rules of traditional grammar and the triviality of much of modern linguistics, at least in relation to their own goals and interests. Students who have been taught to communicate openly, express their opinions effectively, and organize skillfully are likely to revolt if a teacher attempts to impose grammar exercises on them.

Second, and more significant, students who are sensitive to the communication process can become conscious of the way in which one's language is deeply interwoven with one's culture and identity.

Therefore, the process teacher is aware of the tremendous, though perhaps subconscious, emotional conflict that may be caused by a simple exercise requiring that *I ain't* be replaced with *I'm not.* For many children it is the equivalent of a renunciation of their family and a declaration of allegiance to white, middle-class America. The process teacher does not regard a child as stupid just because the child cannot learn to eliminate double negatives in twelve years of writing instruction. The conflicts caused by the study of grammar should not cause a process teacher to eliminate it from the curriculum, however. In fact, the process educator recognizes that conflict often leads to growth and tries to design a curriculum that will enable students to cope with the conflicts in productive ways.

In attempting to foster growth in language skill and facility in the use of standard English, a process teacher tries to identify both the affective and the cognitive levels of the student and might focus on specific objectives such as the following:

1. Students will recognize the importance of dialect in creating identity.
2. Students will recognize the dialect and level of language needed for the vocations they might want to enter.
3. Students will learn to write and speak the level of standard English needed for potential vocational choices.

A unit on grammar and usage designed to meet these objectives might include lessons such as the following:

1. Have students listen to tapes or records of a number of different people speaking different dialects and employing different levels of usage. Have students discuss their impressions of the characters from the way they talk, perhaps rating them on scales according to several different variables (intelligence, likability, etc.). A lesson on stereotyping should follow. Point out that the process students have used was to classify a person into a particular group by dialect and then to ascribe certain characteristics to that group. Point out that these judgments are often quite inaccurate, but that there are often reasons why these stereotypes develop.
2. Read selections from works of literature in which the author uses dialect or language level to develop a character. Discuss

the impressions of the character one gets from the level of language. Point out that our stereotypes are widely held by society. By speaking a certain way, one will be categorized into a certain group.

3. Have students analyze their own identity and the way they talk. Exercises in classifying one's own dialect by identifying which expressions one does and does not use could be employed. Have students discuss their language patterns, and what they tell others about them.

4. Discuss the relationship of language to careers. Investigate the kinds of careers that students might be interested in, and discuss the level of language and kind of dialect required in that career. For students who are planning to go to college, a comparison of the grammatical-syntactical structure of a college term paper with that of a high school term paper could be quite interesting and motivating.

5. Based on the previous lessons, set goals with the students for appropriate grammar and usage skills for them to develop. Use any of a variety of approaches to learning language skills, including drills. Whenever possible, however, incorporate the drill into activities relating to their original purpose. For example, to practice past tense of verbs, students could be divided into groups of three with two people carrying on a dialogue that would require them to use specified forms of verbs, while the third person checks verb usage. For instance, one person could be explaining to another why it was necessary to return a pair of shoes ("The heel *broke*, and the leather *wore* out. I only *bought* them two days ago.")

Composition

Writing skills are important to adolescents for a variety of reasons. First, of course, writing skills are essential in most vocations, although some students may need a different vocational emphasis than that of traditional composition programs. Second, writing is a useful way of improving thinking skills. A major task of adolescence is the development of mature thinking skills; in fact, in many schools training in composition is almost the only assistance many students get in developing formal operations skills. Writing is also a useful means of self-expression and thus is a means for coping with the tensions and conflicts that are an inevitable part of adolescence (see Hawley, Simon, and Britton, 1973).

A teacher committed to a process curriculum recognizes that writing needs and interests change at different ages. Many adolescents, for example, go through a very romantic period when they love to write flowery poetry filled with clichés and commonplace adjectives. It is important to realize that the adolescent poet is developing a sensitivity to language and its possibilities for expressing feelings. All too often, the work is judged against adult standards as an inferior creation. The clichés are pointed out and ridiculed, and the student's growing appreciation of language and literature is stifled. By contrast, a process teacher uses the student's natural interest—in this case, a desire to express love and affection in words—and enjoys the creations that are shared by students, while also using the opportunity to show students more possibilities, other ways of expressing ideas. For example, poetic devices could be taught as ways of expressing romantic feelings: "Let's brainstorm some metaphors for love." "Can you personify love?"

The sequence of composition skill development in a process curriculum is fairly similar to that of the traditional curriculum: students need to learn to distinguish general from specific, they need to learn to support generalizations with supporting details, and they then need to perceive and communicate relationships between ideas. The process curriculum departs from the traditional approach to composition, however, by developing these skills differently. In traditional instruction students are given a prescription: "A paragraph should have a topic sentence followed by three to five sentences containing examples, an incident, reasons, or details." Research on the process of writing reveals that many of these prescriptions are highly inaccurate descriptions of the writing process. Emig, in concluding *The Composing Processes of Twelfth Graders*, points out:

> Partially because they have no direct experience of composing, teachers of English err in important ways. They underconceptualize and oversimplify the process of composing. Planning degenerates into outlining; reformulating becomes the correction of minor infelicities.
>
> They truncate the process of composing. From the accounts of the twelfth-grade writers in this sample one can see that in self-sponsored writing, students engage in prewriting activities that last as long as two years. (p. 98)

The teaching of thinking and writing in a process curriculum is primarily inductive. Students examine their own and each other's writing, analyzing the effectiveness of communication. For models students may be provided with outstanding papers by students a year or two older than themselves, students who have mastered the skills they are currently working on, but who have not developed such complex styles that beginning writers become confused.

The writing teacher must also be a writer. How can a person who has not written anything more complex than a friendly letter for fifteen years convey empathy and genuineness to student writers? A teacher may find that writing in front of the class is a useful exercise. The class can assign a topic and the teacher, thinking aloud and writing on a blank transparency on an overhead projector, writes the composition in front of them. The class may then critique the finished product.

Literature

Literature, of course, can relate to many adolescent concerns. First, the teacher can attempt to encourage the students' naturally developing literary interests and aesthetic sense. Second, literature can be used to teach the identity and interpersonal skills needed for mature adulthood.

During adolescence there is a natural development of aesthetic values. The typical adolescent is devoted to music, is extremely sensitive to personal attractiveness, and is often fascinated by poetry, romantic fiction, and adventure. Unfortunately, in aesthetics as in many other areas of their lives, adolescent tastes tend to differ drastically from adult tastes. Because in numerous ways teenagers have started to resemble them, many adults fail to recognize that there are many ways in which teenagers are not yet adults and fail to respect teenagers' real level of development. Adults usually acknowledge that young children's tastes differ from theirs and don't hesitate to encourage their fascination with garish colors, sing-song poetry, and repetitious stories. But these same adults often see adolescent literature, art, and music simply as inferior versions of adult art rather than as the outgrowth of a normal developmental stage. To many English teachers, for instance, a junior novel is just a short, shallow novel.

During adolescence most young people are only slowly developing the intellectual skills that Piaget calls formal operations. Adolescents slowly develop the ability to separate form from content, to unravel multiple causes, and to understand abstract symbols and ideas. Attempting to teach a young person to interpret symbolism or to do a formal literary analysis can lead to confusion, resentment, and efforts to figure out the teacher instead of the literary work. The result is a tenth-grader who explains how one analyzes a literary work in this way: "First, you find a character who has either a *J* or *C* in his initials and you label him a Christ figure. Next, you find any recurring object and describe it as a sex symbol." This is a student who has been fed literary analysis before developing the cognitive structures necessary for formal operations.

In a process curriculum, by contrast, the teacher listens carefully to students' own honest responses to literature and builds from there. The teacher attempts to discover the level that the student is presently operating on, accepts and affirms that level, and then slowly introduces experiences to help develop more mature intellectual skills. If the student does not understand on a literal level, the teacher may be used as a guide in how to read a work of literature. If the student reacts negatively to a literary work, the teacher accepts that reaction and encourages the student to analyze the reasons for disliking the work. As much as possible, the students should be encouraged to read and enjoy the works they respond to at that age. Often young people will respond to romantic novels and poetry with an intensity that they will never feel in later life. If properly nurtured, this response can lead to enthusiasm for reading other forms of literature and a lifelong interest in reading.

Not only is literature enjoyed for itself in the process curriculum, but it is also used to help young people achieve many of the developmental tasks of adolescence. Through literature they can explore options in sex roles, life styles, and vocations. They can learn about the choices other persons have made in terms of values and questions of ethics. They can gain insight into themselves and their own identities through discussion of the characters they encounter in their reading. Probably no better single vehicle exists for promoting achievement of adolescent developmental tasks than works of literature, particularly novels and biography.

In order to learn human relations and self-analysis skills from literature, students must first recognize literature as vicarious experience. They must identify with characters, follow the sequence of events, and feel the excitement or suspense of the story. While most children develop these skills at a young age through the literature that is read to them, some adolescents are so lacking in basic reading skills that they cannot become involved in literature. For these students dramatic readings of exciting and suspenseful literature may help them to become engaged. And, of course, remedying skill deficiencies needs to occur alongside the development of response capabilities.

As they develop a capacity to respond to literature, students need to learn to feel empathy with literary characters and to learn to generalize that empathy to other people. Most people empathize more easily with people who are somewhat similar to themselves and who have similar problems; therefore, it is useful to begin developing this skill with books whose characters are similar to the students reading them. For example, a black, urban student will probably find it easier to feel empathy with Muffin in *A Teacup Full of Roses* than with Ken in *My Friend Flicka*. But the development of empathy should not stop with people who are similar to the reader. Once students have begun to develop a capacity for empathy, they should be exposed to works about people from widely different backgrounds, of all ages, and from all parts of the world.

In addition to learning empathy from literature, students can learn alternative ways of behaving and can see the relationship between choices and consequences. A useful technique is to have students role play a scene as it is described in the book. After the role playing, the teacher can interview the students who played the characters about the choices they made and any reasons they may have for being dissatisfied with them. The teacher can then ask the class to brainstorm other ways they could have behaved and replay the scene trying out the alternative behaviors. Advanced students can use literature to examine values and philosophies of life and their implications. Students can analyze the values that characters in a novel profess or live by. This type of discussion can lead into an examination of student values and the way these values have affected the students' lives.

Organizing the Process Curriculum

While a process curriculum includes all of the traditional elements of the language arts, it is often organized into integrated units relating to the developmental tasks of adolescence. Thematic units derived from the tasks seem to be more helpful to students than units focusing on isolated skills such as composition, vocabulary development, or public speaking. There are two reasons for this. First of all, students can more readily see the relationship between the instructional unit and their own concerns. For example, a unit on "Coping with Parents" that includes reading assignments, instruction in communication and conflict reduction skills, writing assignments, practice in group discussion, and other language arts skills, is far more likely to arouse interest and commitment than a unit on "The Novel" or "Expository Writing." Even if the average adolescent cannot name the developmental tasks or doesn't even understand the concept of developmental tasks, it is known intuitively what matters at this stage of development. Second, the integrated teaching of the various language arts skills is far more sound pedagogically than attempting to teach them in isolation. Since, for example, oral reports and expository essays both require similar forms of organization, they can readily and effectively be taught together. Many reading skills (e.g., finding the main idea) and writing skills (e.g., constructing a topic sentence that summarizes a group of details) are very similar, and these too should be taught in conjunction with one another. The thematic unit, then, offers the ideal framework for capitalizing on the concerns of adolescents and for integrating the various skills and subskills of the language arts.

The first unit of the year needs to provide the teacher with an opportunity to get to know the students and to assess their skills and needs; it also should provide students with an opportunity to get to know one another and to review skills they may have learned previously. An ideal focus for the first unit is thus interpersonal relationships ("You and Others" or "Interaction"). The unit might begin with getting acquainted and name-learning activities. A good early activity is the group interview, which gives students practice in oral communication skills while they learn more about each other. After some brief instruction in conversation skills (particularly on the need for giving "free information" and for listening actively), students should practice in pairs, ultimately remaining with one partner long enough to learn enough to write a character sketch.

This unit is also the best time to teach students the basic skills of working toegther effectively in small groups, sharing ideas in discussion, and arriving at decisions that take all group members into account. At the conclusion of a unit of this type, students should have not only become more comfortable with other members of the classroom group and better able to work with them, but also have learned many specific communication skills that they need for success in future school work and other life activities.

Subsequent thematic units could focus on topics such as identity, woman and man, dealing with conflicts, death, communication, generations, values, loneliness, love, and planning for the future. The teacher can choose those topics which seem to be of most concern to a particular group of students, using the developmental tasks as a starting point, but focusing on the specific aspects that seem most relevant; or students can be given a chance to determine the topics they want to focus on, with the teacher supplying the materials and the learning experiences suggested by the student choices. As with all aspects of the process curriculum, neither teacher domination nor total freedom for students is ideal. Cooperative planning is far more likely to be successful.

References

Borton, Terry. *Reach, Touch, and Teach: Student Concerns and Process Education.* New York: McGraw-Hill, 1970.

Brown, George Isaac. *Human Teaching for Human Learning: An Introduction to Confluent Education.* New York: Viking Press, 1971.

Emig, Janet. *The Composing Processes of Twelfth Graders.* Research Report No. 13. Urbana, Ill.: National Council of Teachers of English, 1971.

Hawley, Robert C., Simon, Sidney B., and Britton, D. D. *Composition for Personal Growth: Values Clarification through Writing.* New York: Hart Publishing, 1973.

Moffett, James. *A Student-Centered Language Arts Curriculum, Grades K–13: A Handbook for Teachers.* Boston: Houghton Mifflin, 1968.

Postman, Neil, and Weingartner, Charles. *Teaching as a Subversive Activity.* New York: Dell Publishing, 1969.

Rogers, Carl. *Freedom to Learn.* Columbus, Ohio: Charles E. Merrill, 1969.

Rogers, Carl. *On Becoming a Person.* Boston: Houghton Mifflin, 1961.

Romainville, Martha, Blankenship, Cynthia, and Stanford, Barbara. *Designs for English: A Humanistic Program of Skill and Experience.* New York: Bantam Books, 1977.

Stanford, Gene, and Roark, Albert E. *Human Interaction in Education.* Reading, Mass.: Allyn and Bacon, 1975.

Weinstein, Gerald, and Eantini, Mario D. *Toward Humanistic Education: A Curriculum of Affect.* New York: Praeger Publishers, 1970.

IV Community College

14 An Overview of Community Colleges

Lucille G. Shandloff
Prince George's Community College, Largo, Maryland

In 1972 in Florida I had to predict the financial future of higher education. It will be dim, I prophesied. Hard-pressed legislatures will cut funds for public institutions, and soaring tuition will combine with low public confidence to threaten enrollments at all but the most prestigious private institutions. As enrollment shrinks, overextended institutions, locked into programs taught by tenured faculty, will divide fewer dollars among a constant number of departments. In less than ten years, I wrote, they will all exist at bare subsistence level, competing among themselves both for dollars shrunken by inflation and for fewer and fewer students.

When I moved to New York City a year later and saw how money was allocated and spent, I remarked to colleagues at Hunter College that we were headed for serious trouble. "Nonsense, Lucille," said my department chair, smiling and reassuringly patting my hand. "The whole city of New York would have to go bankrupt first."

With a record like that, it is with some caution that I write about what will shape curricula of the future in community colleges.

My predictions in the early '70s took no ability as a seer, since the evidence upon which they were based was readily available to everyone. They did require, however, something that is difficult for everyone, the recognition that we may have to believe and act upon predictions we do not want to hear. Indeed, had Freud explored this pervasive human trait, today we would all study the Cassandra Complex.

The determinism underlying what Freud did explore pervades the major influences upon community college curricula today and will for the foreseeable future. Many of us do not want to hear this because it implies that our professional fates are largely beyond our control, but the facts suggest that neither faculty nor administrators can dictate the directions community college curricula will take. We can, at best, only modify their destinations, but only if we recognize and act upon the facts.

Factors Influencing the Curriculum

As professionals we want community college programs to be based upon educational concepts. Nonetheless, unpalatable as the fact may be, curriculum follows money more closely than it follows educational ideals. The allocation of money is in turn influenced by three factors external to the community college. Students and their perceptions of which courses are "useful" are the strongest direct influence. Outside funding sources influence both directly and indirectly where the money and the curricula go. Finally, the requirements of major four-year transfer institutions have a strong effect upon community college students' choices.

The two primary sources of money for community colleges are public funds and tuition. Most of the public money is allocated on a sustaining, annual basis by state and local governments, the latter usually being the county and, sometimes, municipality. The major portion of these funds is allocated according to an institution's total credit hours, or full-time student equivalents. So the number of courses for which students register determines the financial base of colleges. Federal funds, though they support a few specific programs, afford their major support through tuition, in the form of direct grants and loans to students. Consequently, both of the major sources of a community college's financial support are directly determined by how many students take which courses. And that shapes curriculum, because, in a time of falling enrollments and strong competition for students, only those colleges that attract a sufficient number of students can maintain their faculties, their buildings, and their support facilities.

While student preference has always had some influence upon curriculum, it has become a major factor in recent years, partly as a result of the public's demand that professors pay attention to undergraduates and that colleges respond to students' concerns. Public attitudes are reflected not only in the distribution of money to students rather than to institutions, but also in the current jargon that refers to students as "consumers" of education, with its implication that they "purchase" courses from educational "supermarkets."

These attitudes have a direct effect on which courses "sell." Both younger and older students, recognizing the credentialing function of a college education, approach higher education largely as job training, following Royall Tyler's centuries-old admonition to "mind the main chance." And although fairly affluent young people may have the option to bypass college for a time, when they must become self-supporting, they too return to college for the credential. Consequently, to the majority of community college students, education is at best a secondary concern in their schooling. In these circumstances the characteristics of community college students are even more important now than they were in the past, because they illuminate the kinds of courses students select. Characteristics vary, of course, from school to school, but general demographic features of students are discernible.

A Profile of the Community College Student

Established homes, jobs, and families limit most adults who return to college to the closest and, frequently, least expensive college available, usually the local community college. Moreover, veterans still make up a large proportion of the student body on many campuses. Thus, the average age of students in community colleges now ranges from mid- or late twenties to mid-thirties.

Both older students and recent high school graduates reflect the ethnic and economic range of the local community. In-town campuses may be largely black; campuses in suburbs may be mostly white. But in most community colleges, students from affluent homes sit next to students on welfare rolls, and their goals cover an equally wide spectrum. First-generation college students often are there solely to gain access to jobs, prompting a pragmatic attitude toward their choice of college courses. Most hope to transfer to a senior institution when they complete their Associate of Arts degree. Students with college-educated parents, who grew up with the expectation of a college career, are equally pragmatic in their course selections, viewing the community college primarily as a way station on the road to a four-year college or university.

These broad characteristics illuminate today's enrollment patterns, and the influences they will exert upon tomorrow's curriculum. Older students are frequently part-timers whose selections at the "supermarket" are determined either by job preparation and advancement requirements or by a desire for intellectual stimulation. They are practical about their education, however, generally limiting their enrollment in courses they consider stimulating, or "fulfilling," to those that also "count" toward degree requirements. Younger students, who also frequently hold jobs whether they enroll for a full- or part-time credit load, generally exhibit a "What-do-I-have-to-have?" attitude at registration, too often taking courses as if they were medicine, only because they are prescribed or because they fulfill transfer requirements. For upwardly mobile, job-oriented students, this means they see as important only those courses that have a direct bearing on their specific job objectives. Courses which may fulfill degree requirements but do not have obvious significance for job training are not perceived as important. One student wanted to know, "Why do I have to take humanities? I'm going to be a doctor." When he acknowledged that his future patients would be humans, his attitude was chastened but unchanged.

The extent of this job orientation is in interesting contrast to attitudes of a decade or two ago. In the mid-'60s the majority of community college students enrolled in liberal arts transfer programs. One Southern state, in an effort to improve the status of community college career programs, insisted that new two-year schools be established first as technical schools and allowed them to add some liberal arts courses only after enrollment in the technical two-year degree area was acceptable in order to prevent the dominance of the more popular and prestigious transfer programs. Books and articles about community colleges regularly bemoaned the problems this dominance created. For example, in 1965, before the Community College of Philadelphia opened its doors, its planners consulted with local industries, such as Philco, and tailored its technical curriculum to meet the hiring needs of local employers. The college opened with 1,000 places each in technical and liberal arts areas. After intensive recruiting, 800 students enrolled in the technical program; liberal arts enrolled the full 1,000 and turned away many more.

At the end of the '70s, the pendulum had swung. Although technical programs may still trail in total enrollment, in part because they may not be acceptable for transfer credit, business, allied health, and similarly "practical" areas are growing. Furthermore, within liberal arts programs, courses the public perceives as "basic" or "practical," such as grammar, usage, and technical writing, are in great demand, while enrollment in "impractical" courses such as literature continues to shrink.

Among students enrolled in the first two years of a degree program, the same very practical economy in course selection prevails. A few of the more sophisticated students planning to transfer to senior institutions may not even seek associate degrees, but instead may just take courses that meet requirements at the four-year school where they will complete bachelor degrees. If community college course, even those as standard as freshman composition, do not specifically fulfill the senior college's requirements, the more knowledgeable students do not enroll in them.

Indirect Influences on the Curriculum

Student attitudes and enrollment patterns that result from them also affect college curricula in other, less direct ways. For example, the much discussed public loss of confidence in higher education has had little verifiable effect upon total undergraduate enrollment. Other factors, such as the number of eighteen year olds in the general population, the end of the Vietnam war, and general economic conditions, have had more apparent effect upon whether students enroll and upon the number of credits they take.

The loss of public confidence in higher education occurred, in large part, because college degrees failed to meet public expectations of guaranteeing graduates affluence and job security. These expectations had been raised largely as a result of government-sponsored promotions. In reaction to the 1957 Russian launching of Sputnik I, the United States undertook to offset Russian technological superiority by stimulating the production of highly trained scientists and technicians. To meet these goals, it launched a promotion campaign that advertized the statistical fact that the more formal education a person completed was directly related to higher lifetime earnings. College graduates, many of them with advanced degrees, eventually saturated the job market until, in a slowing economy, it could not absorb their vast numbers. Ironically, the success of this years-long campaign was a major factor in destroying both the correlation supporting it and the public confidence that colleges and universitites had long enjoyed. Higher education, not the faulty logic, became suspect. *Sic transit gloria.*

But loss of its prestige did not drive consumers out of the academic marketplace; they just changed their shopping habits. The larger the number of college-educated people, the more extensively employers applied the credentialing function of a college degree. In a catch-22 progression, they upped the ante; jobs that once required a high school diploma now demand a college degree.

Distrust of higher education, wedded to the necessity to have a degree in order to compete for jobs, fosters ambivalence and creates a combination of contempt and desire. These symptoms result in the Peripatetic Student Syndrome, a drop-in, drop-out, part-time, college-switching attendance pattern many students display. In commuter community colleges, the effects of this syndrome and students' sporadic commitment to education make course scheduling for colleges a four-times-a-year crap game, with the colleges betting and the students setting the odds. No longer can schools count on the majority of their students to enter in the fall of one year and graduate in the spring of the next or assume they will take a predictable sequence of courses. Students enroll in courses offered in their "free" time, tightly scheduling work and class time. The odds in the colleges' scheduling gamble are further affected if competing institutions within commuting distance enter similar courses in the credit-hour sweepstakes.

As a result, colleges schedule required courses, and if their guesses about numbers of students are inaccurate, open or cancel sections depending upon actual enrollment. Electives, however, are much less of a sure thing because they face the competition of other electives. This results in a reluctance to include a wide variety of such courses that tie up rooms, faculty, and students which could otherwise go to courses more likely to "float." Ultimately those that are not popular enough to fill a classroom each term are cancelled, if they are cancelled frequently enough, they are no longer scheduled, regardless of their educational value. At Prince George's Community College in metropolitan Washington, D.C., for example, most students elect American Literature to fulfill their English requirement. Other courses, such as British or World Literature, either enroll only half as many students or so few they must be cancelled. If enrollment is consistently low, they may become casualties in the curriculum gamble. One consequence, therefore, of the Peripatetic Student Syndrome is that it encourages colleges to limit courses to those required, augmented only by "popular" electives, to the detriment of curricular breadth, depth, and intellectual rigor.

Moreover, a high percentage of part-time students also increases educational expenses, but adds no additional income. For example, the costs of registering part-timers, keeping their records, and providing other services as diverse as counseling and parking space are the same as for full-time students; thus, two half-time students, whose tuition and public funding produce the same income as one full-timer, cost twice as much to process. As the Proposition Thirteen reaction to ever increasing taxes spreads across the country, producing CAP and TRIM laws that limit local taxes and expenditures to set amounts and spawning proposals for a constitutional amendment, the increased costs of processing part-time students will further limit the money available to educate them. As a consequence, only full-time students will be admitted or college curricula will be narrowed even more or both. All of these effects will diminish the quality, the flexibility, and the accessibility of higher education in open-door community colleges.

Summary

And so we come full circle. Curriculum follows money. And for those of us who are among the puritan divines (as described by Edmund Volpe in a succeeding chapter) proselytizing our "impassioned vision . . . of a liberal arts education," how can we spread the gospel in a marketplace where the main chance reigns supreme? And how can we exercise free will in a world where external forces predestine our fates?

As for Jonathan Edwards's disciples, so for us. There are no easy answers, but we should not give up hope for salvation, for ourselves or for our students. Our mission is to educate them while they earn their job credentials and to hope that when they have both, they will value the education more.

15 A Community College English Program: A Competencies Model

Karl K. Taylor
Illinois Central College

In her acclaimed *Errors and Expectations*, Shaughnessy says, "We lack developmental models for the maturation of writing skills among young, native-speaking adults and can only theorize about the adaptability of other models for the students" (p. 119). Without such a guide, many community college writing programs are often based on what is done at a nearby university: one semester of remedial grammar review for the basic writing (BW) student, a course in expository writing for typical freshmen during their first semester, and an introduction to literature study during their second semester. (*Basic writing*, or BW, is a term that was apparently satisfactory to Shaughnessy for describing these kinds of students, so I will use it in this chapter.) Likewise, community college literature offerings frequently resemble those at nearby universities: various genre, film, and survey courses. Such a model for writing and literature study may make good sense for the typical university, but it deserves close scrutiny before it is considered acceptable for the community college. The reasons for the scrutiny are quite simple: standardized test scores, prior preparation, and reading skills.

First, without admissions standards the two-year college attracts an entirely different kind of student than the typical university, as Cross has pointed out in a number of her books. As one indication of those differences, consider the American College Test (ACT), which is often utilized as a placement tool. The average English ACT score for a community college student in Illinois is 17; the same score for freshmen entering the University of Illinois is 27. Although someone is likely to say that the ten-point spread indicates community college students are hopelessly deficient (a score of 17 places them in the lower third nationally), I believe the scores simply suggest differences between the two groups of students. Among these differences are less writing experience and considerably less knowledge of grammar. These low scores should not imply, however, that the skills of the second group cannot be improved—or that using a university model will bring community college students up to a level comparable to their peers in the four-year school. Logically, then, if there are differences between these two groups of students, different programs are needed to meet their needs.

The second reason for scrutiny is closely tied to the first one. Part of the differences noted above can be attributed to prior experience with composition. For example, if students have done considerable writing in high school, their preparation should influence the type of college course to which they should be exposed. The reverse is also reasonable. If they have done very little writing previously, they should have an entirely different college course. Therefore, any sound writing program must reflect the preparation and skills of the students taking the courses.

Third, scrutiny is important because many community college students do not read as well as their counterparts at the university. Although more research needs to be conducted on this problem, a few schools have tested or are testing their students and have found that typical two-year college freshmen read at the tenth-grade level or below. Two such schools are Moraine Valley in Palos Hills, Illinois, and Illinois Central College in East Peoria, Illinois. For other studies see Anderson (1973), Zaccario et al. (1972), Bashinski (1973), Kahn (1974), and LeFevre (1973).

The low reading scores are significant for writing instruction in several ways. First, students obviously cannot read textbooks written two or more years beyond their ability; by the same token, if they are unable to read explicit expository prose without great difficulty, literature, with its subtle inferences, will be beyond their present abilities. Second, if students do not read at the twelfth-grade level or above, it is believed by many teachers that their composing skills will lag even further behind since writing is probably more difficult than reading. For these reasons—low test scores, weak prior preparation, and low reading skills—the university model does not seem particularly relevant to the needs of community college students. A curriculum especially designed for them appears appropriate and logical.

A New Model

Shaughnessy's observation that we lack a model was probably accurate. A number of short studies and a long one may contribute significantly to a potential model of an English program for the community college. None of them present a broad theory, but together they form parts of a kind of mosaic, incomplete but developing. By putting all these pieces together, we will have a much better view of a curriculum than we previously had.

Moffett's *Teaching the Universe of Discourse* (1968) was one of the first attempts to outline a systematic language curriculum from the elementary school through the early years of college. Although it was an important and influential work, Moffett had not really tested his ideas; they were merely theoretical notions. Therefore, *The Development of Writing Abilities* (Britton et al., 1975) is extremely important because it attempts to study and test many of Moffett's ideas in the classroom.

Britton and his colleagues went into the English schools and examined how writing abilities develop in children age eleven to eighteen and what assignments fostered that development. Although some teachers subscribe to the notion that students improve their writing by merely writing, Britton found that particular assignments were more successful than others. This should come as no surprise. Teachers of mathematics, for example, would not teach multiplication until addition and subtraction were mastered because success with multiplication depends on knowledge of the other two subskills. My point is that without a model language curriculum, we may be asking for students to perform tasks without the requisite subskills. I believe students in the two-year college may be found at any one of the stages of language development, and for them to move to their highest level of achievement, we must develop courses that meet their needs.

Thus, we must develop programs for eighteen year olds who may be found at the second stage, the fourth, or maybe even the first. To meet the needs of a heterogeneous student body, we need three types of writing courses: several for the BW student and perhaps two for the transfer-level student. This series of courses, which might number as many as six or eight, is unusual because it does not lump all basic writers into one category. Although these courses will be described in detail later, I believe they should be covered generally here.

Instead of emphasizing grammar and elementary organization, the basic writing classes, I believe, should focus on the development of fluency and specificity, while the initial transfer course should stress organization. The second transfer course should center on argumentation and perhaps the research paper. If my own experience is typical, I would anticipate that 30 to 50 percent of all entering freshmen would be enrolled in some kind of BW course, figures that are consistent with what Roueche and Snow (1977) have suggested.

No doubt critics will detect the absence of literature in this writing curriculum. As Tway (1976) has pointed out, no research to date has demonstrated that the study of literature will improve writing, and as Britton et al. (1975) have said, many students object to writing about what someone else has written. Therefore, Britton recommends personal experience as the principal source of ideas for composition. Some teachers may believe they must teach literature to improve student reading skills, but I believe this notion ignores the difficulty of literature and the complexity of reading instruction. For that reason, I believe reading instruction should be left to those professionally trained to deal with this highly sophisticated problem. Thus, because many community college students have so many problems in writing and the time available to help them is so limited, priority must be placed on composition.

The Development of Fluency: The Theory

Judging from my experiences, many English teachers are caught up in a kind of dubious haste; they seem to want to deemphasize the means and emphasize the ends. They give the impression of hurrying through the preliminaries so they can do something important like teach the term paper or discuss *Silas Marner*. My suspicions were reinforced by Britton's study. He and his colleagues found one chief characteristic of most writing assignments given in the British schools: teachers frequently asked students to write papers for which they were inadequately prepared. The teachers had not really attempted to develop a sequential writing program, moving from short writing assignments to longer ones, from the simple to the complex, and from the concrete to the abstract. The situation is probably little different in this country. (For example, I know of one community college where the term paper is taught in basic writing.)

The problem of sequence is particularly acute in the two-year college because of the heterogeneous student population. Perhaps 40 to 50 percent of the students have had so little previous writing experience (see Shaughnessy) that their skills lag far behind their peers at the university; moreover, within this group the range of skills is enormous. In fact, it is difficult initially to distinguish between students who have little ability and those who have had little experience. The difference is crucial. For that reason, BW students cannot simply be placed arbitrarily into one category as they so often are. To my way of thinking, BW students fall into two broad categories: those who do not write satisfactorily because they have serious learning problems and those who do not write satisfactorily because they have not written. The distinctions between the two groups are extremely important because they will suggest different ways of overcoming or reducing writing problems in the respective categories.

The development of a BW curriculum is highly complicated, requiring familiarity with the other modes of communication: listening, speaking, reading, and writing. These modes are commonly introduced at the primary and elementary levels roughly in the above sequence. This order seems not only to follow our natural language development, but also to move from the simple to the complex. As Kroll (1977) has shown, speech is the most effective way of communicating for most youngsters through at least the fourth grade. If the language skills develop at the usual rate, by approximately the sixth grade some youngsters are beginning to communicate more precisely in writing than in speaking. As the years go by, written communication should become more effective than the spoken.

For one reason or another, the first group of BW students—those with serious learning problems—has not experienced this customary development. Their writing skills still lag far behind their oral skills. Since they have done little writing previously, Shaughnessy (1977) believes many students do not grasp the differences between oral and written language.

> Unaware of the ways in which writing is different from speaking, he [the basic writer] imposes the conditions of speech upon writing. As an extension of speech, writing does, of course, draw heavily upon a writer's competencies as a speaker—his grammatical intuitions, his vocabulary, his strategies for making and ordering statements, etc., but it also demands new competencies, namely the skills of the encoding process (handwriting, spelling, punctuation) and the skill of objectifying a statement, of looking at it, changing it by additions, subtractions, substitutions, or inversions, taking the time to get as close a fit as possible between what he means and what he says on paper. (p. 79)

The Development of Fluency: The Practice

To meet the needs of the BW student at this stage of development, I believe a curriculum that initially stresses fluidity or fluency in writing must be developed. The students must learn to express themselves with reasonable ease in writing (see Moffett, 1968, and Britton et al., 1975). The long-term objective is to make them feel almost as comfortable writing as speaking.

At this point the students' writing will probably resemble talking very closely, perhaps being characterized by weak organization, questionable usage, incompleteness, colloquialisms, and an imperfect balance between detail and generality. When this talking is written down, it will usually exhibit misspellings, punctuation problems, repetition, lack of clarity, weak syntax, and a general lack of precision. Nevertheless, since the writers are simply being asked to place their words on paper and since no one needs to understand what they have written except themselves, all these "errors" should be ignored without comment for the time being (see Squire and Applebee, 1969). They should be tolerated because if teachers become concerned with correctness too early, the goal of fluidity will never be reached (see Britton et al., 1975).

The types of writing assignments that foster fluidity are generally narrative. Britton (1975) and Shaughnessy (1977) both suggest that students at this time should be assigned topics based on their own experience. The work of Macrorie (1970) and Kelly (1973, 1974) would seem especially appropriate for this stage. I have had success asking students to write seven short assignments (from 50 to 500 words) that focus on improving their self-concept; in so doing they explore their successes, achievements, accomplishments, and goals. The chief purposes of the assignments are to help students overcome their hatred or fear of writing and their inability to put words on paper. Grammar is taught on an individual basis and is subservient to actual writing.

The Development of Specificity: The Theory

In my experience with BW students over the last ten years, I have found that most are deficient because they have done little or no writing. The most glaring problem with these students is their lack of specificity. For example, if they are asked to write a description of a room, the result is often a vague list of objects and adjectives that would fit almost any room. As Hillocks (1975) has said, "Experience in teaching composition at every level from seventh grade to advanced writing courses intended for college sophomores reveals one common problem: lack of specificity. The occasional striking detail is a welcome oasis in a dry desert of generalization" (p. 1). Some teachers may think students write so generally because they lack the interest or concern for such matters. However, a body of research has begun to show us that the cause is highly complicated, involving such psychological factors as perceptual and cognitive development.

Here is a grammatically correct student example lacking details that would make it meaningful:

> The living room is large with doors opening into the kitchen, dining room, and the front porch. Along the sides of the room are various pieces of furniture—several sofas and several large arm chairs. In a corner of the room is a large book case, filled with many large hardbound books and some paperbacks. In the middle of the west wall is a fireplace with a brass trimmed glass door covering the opening of the fire box. There is carpeting on the floor.

The person who wrote this paragraph was not blind, but he did not see the details necessary for writing a specific description. Note all the necessary qualities he ignored or left out: the actual size of the room, the kinds and styles of furniture, the condition of all the contents, the colors, the kinds of books, the textures of all the materials, and the like. Many teachers might respond to the paper with the marginal comment "Be specific!"; but the problem is much more complicated and requires instruction that will develop the perceptual skills, the sensory powers of discrimination. Vernon (see 1937, 1952, 1957, 1966, 1971) and Gibson (see 1969), two of the principal psychologists who have studied perceptual development, have pointed out that human beings *learn* to see, hear, and taste specifically; hence, perceptual or sensory awareness is not an automatic process.

Another cause of too much generality is cognitive egocentricism, which was originally defined by Piaget (1955) and has been refined more recently by other researchers. The term means "a cognitive state in which the cognizer sees the world from a single point of view only—his own—but without knowledge of the existence of viewpoints or perspectives and . . . without awareness that he is the prisoner of his own" (Flavell, 1963, p. 60). Through practice talking with others, by age eight children have overcome part or most of this problem of egocentricism in speech. However, when children begin writing, this same difficulty with egocentricism appears in written communication. Research on the role of egocentricism in composition is uncommon, but Kroll (1977) completed a major study on fourth graders and Taylor (1972) reported on the same difficulty in adults taking basic English. Chronological age appears to have little to do with egocentricism; it appears to be a problem for most fourth graders as well as for some BW students in college. (For instance, the student example given earlier is typical of a writer who is egocentric, who sees little need for addressing an audience.)

Complicating the problem of egocentricism is the difficulty some students have bridging the gap between oral and written communication. As Shaughnessy (1977) has said, many beginning writers, regardless of age or year in school, visualize writing as the process of recording speech on paper. Yet, in order to write well, people must do without particular habits of oral language (such as the use of gestures to indicate various persons or objects) and acquire the new skills (such as the precise use of nouns and pronouns) needed to address an audience effectively. Shaughnessy did some pioneering work on the differences between oral and written language, and solid study has since been done by Rubin (1978) and Schallert et al. (1977). To overcome the problems of egocentricism, perceptual development, and the gulf between oral and written language, new exercises and assignments must be created for that large group of students who are unable to write clearly and specifically.

The Development of Specificity: The Practice

Specificity is a skill worthy of concentration, unimpeded by conflicting goals such as correct spelling or punctuation. To overcome problems of vagueness and inadequate perceptual development, descriptive assignments are very helpful, but the number and type have to be carefully selected and controlled because complete freedom in the selection of topics invites potential trouble. For example, descriptive papers of a very general nature, such as what it's like to be a college freshman or what a whole town looks like, are a mistake. Depending on their experience, students seem to need five to eight or more descriptive assignments that range from the simple to the complex, the short to the long, and the concrete to the abstract. For instance, with my weakest BW students, I ask them to write papers describing geometric diagrams (see Taylor, 1972). These assignments are narrow in scope and quite specific because the students write about a given geometric figure that we both can see. We both can look at the figure, compare it to the written description, and determine if the writer has been complete and specific. The diagrams are also limited because they involve only a series of one-dimensional lines, angles, and curves; students thus are not faced with describing several dimensions, color, hue, and other such features. This descriptive assignment is further limited because sight is the only sense that is employed and the student does not have to select some material to include and some to delete. The latter is particularly important because the process of learning what should be included and what excluded is difficult; that process should be stressed after a student has learned to perceive everything there is to describe in a given assignment. (Hillocks [1975] has compiled a number of comparable assignments that assist in overcoming egocentricism, fostering perceptual development, and bridging the gap between oral and written language.)

Some BW students are capable of dealing with considerably broader assignments that gradually incorporate all the senses and lead to more precise and thorough compositions. For them I recommend more elaborate kinds of tasks: describing a small object, a place, a person; describing how people talk; writing a profile; narrating a personal experience; and, finally, writing a process or summary paper (see Taylor, 1973). These assignments, which constitute one entire course, must be carefully selected so they are sequential—the length of compositions is carefully controlled so the students write less at the beginning and more at the end, ranging from 250 to 1,000 words, and the content moves from simple to complex and concrete to abstract.

For example, when describing an object small enough that exclusion is not a problem, the students must look carefully enough to find all the details necessary to describe it. In the second task the students discover that describing a place is more than listing everything in that place. They learn that good description involves selection of key features using all the senses and emphasis on the important facets of the place. This assignment shows students how to extract a few key elements from a multitude of potential characteristics. Other assignments involve the selection of even more abstract qualities in subjects. This concentration on description and the development of perception may seem excessive, but the development of writing skills is a long-term proposition and attempts to reduce the amount of time required are likely to end in failure or partial success. Without the means, there can be no satisfactory end product.

A Moment on Grammar

Many experienced BW teachers may question the conspicuous absence of grammar instruction in this program. The reason for this is twofold: I have never been successful in teaching formal grammar, and the research indicates little correlation between increased knowledge of grammar and improved writing. (For further information, see Meckel, 1963, Braddock et al., 1963, Moffett, 1968, and Elley et al., 1976.) Moffett (1968) clearly and distinctly points out the meaning of the research data:

> What has been rather definitely proven so far . . . is that parsing and diagraming of sentences, memorizing the nomenclature and definitions of parts of speech, and otherwise learning the concepts of traditional, classificatory grammar do not reduce errors. When correctness is the goal, these studies show an incidental and individual approach to errors is more effective. In other words, the preoccupation that inspired the bulk of this research—correctness—is precisely that aspect of composition to which grammar study has nothing to contribute. (p. 164)

Like most teachers, I am concerned about faulty grammar, but I believe placing too much emphasis on grammar instruction will consume precious time that can be more profitably spent on other activities and assignments. In addition I am convinced that the traditional workbook method of teaching some aspects of grammar is needlessly abstract for many students. I believe such an approach is not meaningful because grammar problems often stem from habit and from oral language. Students make such errors as dropped endings in writing because the people with whom they associate often do not use these endings in their speech. To overcome this problem, an approach that teaches students to hear the endings before they are expected to use them in writing seems most useful.

To confront the problem of proper endings, the student is given three similar sentences typed on a sheet:

We walk across the street.
We walks across the street.
We walked across the street.

Then on a tape recorder the student hears one of the three sentences (the third) being read and is asked to indicate which of the three sentences was read. Experience has shown that students with basic writing problems often cannot *hear* correct endings or other basic features of English grammar. For example, a colleague and I have found many students who could not select the correct sentence from the three listed above because they could not hear the *-s* or *-ed* endings. This suggests that faulty grammar may be more an auditory or oral problem than a writing problem. Therefore, changing grammatical patterns and habits may be handled more efficiently and effectively with a tape program than with a traditional grammar book or workbook.

The Development of Organization Skills: Theory and Practice

I would reserve the teaching of organization for first-semester transfer English, and I would concentrate on these rhetorical types in this order: process, comparison-contrast, classification, definition, summary, and cause-effect. (Because description and narration were emphasized in the previous courses, I would not cover them in this course and would suggest them as prerequisites for transfer English.) This order for the rhetorical types allows the students to deal with abstractions last, after they have had some experience writing and some concentration on specific, concrete topics. I would teach the rhetorical types, not because they represent various ways of organizing written material, but because they help the students develop their ability to think.

I have found that students have basically two problems with the rhetorical types. First, a few have such confused thinking that they are unable to grasp the significance of organization; as a result, their writing lacks structure. Second, large numbers of students are able to understand the rhetorical types, but they are only able to use the modes in the most superficial ways. When I began investigating these two problems several years ago (see Taylor, 1978), I initially believed the students either could not organize or their ideas and experiences were too synthetic, mundane, or immature. I viewed weak student achievement, then, as a writing, not a cognitive, problem.

A Cognitive-Developmental Approach to the Modes

After studying Piaget, I began to realize that English teachers, when dealing with the rhetorical types, were making an assumption about their students' cognitive development. They assumed students knew how to perform the mental operations of comparison, definition, and classification, but they needed to learn how to write comparison, definition, and classification papers. However, it seemed possible that some students had trouble with the rhetorical types because they did not know how to compare, define, or classify or could do so only at the simplest level.

Piaget and others have pointed out that an individual seems to progress cognitively through four stages, from the sensory-motor and preoperational to the concrete and the formal level of operations. To simplify somewhat, one could say that a person at the third stage, the concrete, learns a concept or acquires a skill best while actually manipulating concrete objects. For example, the concept of comparison-contrast is best taught to students at the concrete level by using two objects that can be handled or examined closely; and, indeed, this approach is common during the first years of elementary school. Once students have reached the formal level of operations, however, they can grasp the concept of comparison in an abstract manner. Instruction can then take place without reference to concrete objects, as it usually does beginning with the junior high school years or earlier.

Despite Piaget's hypothesis that seventeen or eighteen year olds should have arrived at the formal level, I concluded that many of my students might not have fully reached that point. If so, my instruction, geared to the formal, was directed at minds unable to understand what I was trying to teach. In other words, a writing problem might be a manifestation of a much more basic problem in cognitive development. Research conducted by science educators supports this view. It shows that many young adults have not reached the formal level of operations; instead, they operate at the concrete or at a transitional point somewhere between the concrete and formal levels. Representative of these studies are Campbell (1977), Dunlap and Fazio (1976), Griffiths (1976), and McKinnon and Renner (1971). Although these studies were encouraging, they focused on various Piagetian experiments such as conservation of number or volume; that is, they measured whether students could grasp scientific phenomena. None directly investigated the rhetorical modes or types that seemed as fundamental as some of Piaget's tasks.

To test my notions, I developed a course that dealt with the rhetorical types but started at a much lower level than usual. Unlike other such courses, I assumed students were at the concrete or transitional levels and therefore needed basic "hands-on" instruction in order to learn how to write papers using the rhetorical patterns. For example, when teaching classification, I began by asking the students to perform several types of classificatory tasks.

First, they were given a set of blocks which they were to group in as many logical ways as possible. Later I gave them pictures and figures to classify, and eventually I asked them to group a set of letters to the editor. As far as possible, I tried to arrange the exercises in an ascending order of difficulty, moving from the perceptual and concrete to the abstract and formal.

While I cannot report my findings in detail (see Taylor, 1978), I will make a few observations. In the case of the blocks, the mean score was six out of a possible thirteen ways of classifying them. When I questioned several students privately, I found they had rather confused notions about this mode; most realize the material had to be grouped, but they did not understand that the categories must be related. Thus, they classified data without regard for the relationship between the categories. I obtained similar findings for the other modes.

What do these experiments mean for the classroom teacher? First, I believe we must be careful about casually dealing with the rhetorical types. Students obviously need instruction in them, but our customary methods of instruction may not be particularly effective with students in the community college. Second, while I did not find students completely ignorant of the modes, I did find evidence indicating their knowledge is far less than we have suspected or assumed. And third, I found that beginning with the concrete and moving toward the formal, rather than beginning with the formal, produced better, more substantial papers.

The Development of Argumentation and Research Skills: Theory and Practice

As one can see, the program I have recommended for the community college is cumulative, with each course concentrating on a specific skill. Once the basic skills of fluidity, specificity, and organization are intact, we can consider teaching argumentation and research. In this last course in transfer English, the students need facility in those basic skills because each is essential to more sophisticated skills.

For instance, if the students are not fully grounded in comparison-contrast and classification, they will have much more difficulty with logic and the various forms of reasoning. Moreover, the research paper requires a great deal of knowledge of summary. If students cannot summarize what someone else has written, they will unintentionally (or intentionally) plagiarize or use entirely too much quotation in their research papers. These are crucial issues that are more easily solved when studying summary than when discussing research. If they are not clarified earlier, the teacher needlessly complicates the instruction by having to deal with summary, footnotes, bibliographies, note cards, and outlines all at the same time. As Bruner has said, these skills can be taught successfully, even to community college students, if the instruction is broken down into small segments that the students can grasp. We fail when we overwhelm them with too much to learn in too short a time.

Literature in the English Program

Once students have mastered fluidity, specificity, organization, and argumentation, they are ready to apply them in literature courses. Once the skills are intact, literature can be an exciting, pleasant experience; without them, literature study can be extremely difficult. Literature plays a significant role in humanizing our students, but I suspect that a new approach to teaching it is needed—breaking the instruction down into small pieces, beginning at the concrete level, and carefully selecting writing that is not too difficult. Once again, I suspect the university model has blinded us to the significant ways in which we can bring community college students to an appreciation of literature.

Summary

In this chapter I have explained my vision of an English program for the community college. The proposal was stimulated by the fact that the student attracted to the two-year college is quite different from the one who attends a university: those in the community college often have lower test scores, less preparation in writing, and weaker reading skills than their peers at the university. To meet the needs of this heterogeneous group, I have suggested a sequential program of courses that stresses basic cognitive and writing skills. The program is tempered by the realization that a major share of the instruction will be rather basic, that we cannot teach everything at once, and that improving writing skills takes a great deal of time. Once these skills are raised to an adequate level, the traditional study of literature becomes possible and desirable.

References

Anderson, Clarence. "A Study of Accountability in the Community College Reading Program." In *Programs and Practices for College Reading*, vol. 2, edited by Phil L. Nacke, pp. 7-11. Boone, N.C.: National Reading Conference, 1973.

Bashinski, Marion C. "The Reading Laboratory: An Integral Part of the English Program." In *Programs and Practices for College Reading*, vol. 2, edited by Phil L. Nacke, pp. 12-18. Boone, N.C.: The National Reading Conference, 1973.

Braddock, Richard, Lloyd-Jones, Richard, and Schoer, Lowell. *Research in Written Composition*. Urbana, Ill.: National Council of Teachers of English, 1963.

Britton, James, et al. *The Development of Writing Abilities (11-18)*. London: Macmillan Education, 1975.

Campbell, Thomas. "An Evaluation of a Learning Cycle Intervention Strategy for Enhancing the Use of Formal Operational Thought by Beginning College Physics Students." Ph.D. dissertation, University of Nebraska, 1977.

Dunlop, David L., and Fazio, Frank. "Piagetian Theory and Abstract Preferences of College Science Students." *Journal of College Science Teaching* 5 (May 1976): 297-300.

Elley, W. B., Barham, I. H., Lamb, H., and Wyllie, M. "The Role of Grammar in a Secondary School English Curriculum." *Research in the Teaching of English*, 10 (Spring 1976): 5-21.

Flavell, John H. *The Developmental Psychology of Jean Piaget*. Princeton, N.J.: D. Van Nostrand, 1963.

Gibson, Eleanor J. *The Principles of Perceptual Learning and Development*. New York: Appleton-Century-Crofts, 1969.

Griffiths, David H. "Physics Teaching: Does It Hinder Intellectual Development?" *American Journal of Physics* 44 (January 1976): 81-85.

Hillocks, George, Jr. *Observing and Writing*. Urbana, Ill.: ERIC Clearinghouse on Reading and Communication Skills and National Council of Teachers of English, 1975.

Kahn, Gloria B. "Expectations of Open-Enrollment Students in the Community College Reading Program." In *Interaction: Research and Practice for College-Adult Reading*, vol. 1, edited by Phil L. Nacke, pp. 268-271. Clemson, S.C.: The National Reading Conference, 1974.

Kelly, Lou. "Is Competent Copyreading a Violation of the Students' Right to Their Own Language?" *College Composition and Communication*, vol. xxv, no. 4 (October 1974): 254-258.

Kelly, Lou. "Toward Competence and Creativity in an Open Classroom." *College English*, vol. 34, no. 5 (February 1973): 644-660.

Kroll, Barry M. "Cognitive Egocentricism and Written Discourse." Ph.D. dissertation, University of Michigan, 1977.

LeFevre, Helen E. "Writing and Testing Activities in a Junior College Remedial Reading Course." In *Programs and Practices for College Reading*, vol. 2, edited by Phil L. Nacke, pp. 57-61. Boone, N.C.: The National Reading Conference, 1973.

Macrorie, Ken. *Uptaught.* New York: Hayden Book Company, 1970.

McKinnon, Joe W., and Renner, John W. "Are Colleges Concerned with Intellectual Development?" *American Journal of Physics*, 39 (September 1971): 1047-1052.

Meckel, Henry C. "Research on Teaching Composition and Literature." In *Handbook of Research on Teaching*, edited by Nathaniel L. Gage, pp. 966-1006. Chicago: Rand McNally, 1963.

Moffett, James. *Teaching the Universe of Discourse.* Boston: Houghton Mifflin, 1968.

Piaget, Jean. *The Language and Thought of the Child.* Translated by Marjorie Gabain. New York: New American Library, 1955.

Roueche, John E., and Snow, J. J. *Overcoming Learning Problems.* San Francisco: Jossey-Bass, 1977.

Rubin, Ann D. "A Theoretical Taxonomy of the Differences between Oral and Written Language." Champaign, Ill.: Center for the Study of Reading, 1978.

Schallert, D. L., Kleiman, G. M., and Rubin, A. D. "Analysis of Differences between Oral and Written Language." Champaign, Ill.: Center for the Study of Reading, 1977.

Shaughnessy, Mina P. *Errors and Expectations: A Guide for the Teacher of Basic Writing.* New York: Oxford University Press, 1977.

Squire, James R., and Applebee, Roger K. *Teaching English in the United Kingdom.* Champaign, Ill.: National Council of Teachers of English, 1969.

Taylor, Karl K. "If Not Grammar, What?" Ph.D. dissertation, University of Illinois, 1978.

Taylor, Karl K. "PERCOG: A Progress Report." *Community College Frontiers*, Winter 1972, pp. 5-10.

Taylor, Karl K. *Stages in Writing.* New York: McGraw-Hill, 1973.

Tway, Eileen. "The Interrelationship of Literature and Composition." In *Help for the Teacher of Written Composition: New Directions in Research*, edited by Sara W. Lundsteen, pp. 44-51. Urbana, Ill.: National Conference on Research in English and ERIC Clearinghouse on Reading and Communication Skills, 1976.

Vernon, M. D. *Backwardness in Reading.* Cambridge: At the University Press, 1957.

Vernon, M. D. *A Further Study of Visual Perception.* Cambridge: At the University Press, 1952.

Vernon, M. D. "Perception in Relation to Cognition." In *Perceptual Development in Children*, edited by Aline H. Kidd and Jeanne L. Rivoire, pp. 391-406. New York: International Universities Press, 1966.

Vernon, M. D. *Reading and Its Difficulties: A Psychological Study.* New York: Cambridge University Press, 1971.

Vernon, M. D. *Visual Perception.* Cambridge: At the University Press, 1937.

Zaccaria, Lucy, et al. "Disadvantaged Students in the Traditional University Reading Improvement Program." *Journal of Reading Behavior*, vol. 4, no. 4 (1971-72): 12-17.

16 Approaches to Cultural Studies at the Two-Year College: Perspectives and Prescriptions

George L. Groman
Fiorello H. LaGuardia Community College,
Long Island City, New York

At the community college, perhaps more so than at other kinds of institutions, justification for supporting the humanities, indeed for supporting all of the liberal arts, is a continuing necessity. Students come to the community college specifically for training leading to careers, for work in basic or developmental skills when it has not been obtained elsewhere, or for enough in the way of college credits to transfer to a senior college. "Liberal arts" majors are most often those students who have not yet decided on a specific career direction. The more traditional and general purpose of the liberal arts, that of educating the whole person for long-range life experience, is simply not of interest to many students, though, of course, strenuous faculty efforts can alter the situation—sometimes in striking and dramatic ways.

In tentatively offering some general objectives for the humanities at the community college, and perhaps elsewhere, I would suggest that we begin with the student's primary concern, that of career preparation. In fact there are solid precedents for such an approach. As Olson (1977) points out, the study of the trivium and the quadrivium in medieval times was directly related to the preparation of students for careers in the Church and State; only later, in the nineteenth century, did the Aristotelian conception of *eudaemonia*—happiness derived from, among other activities, "leisure which looks on the nature of things"—take hold (pp. 5-6). However, modern-day students, perhaps unlike their faculty counterparts, need no such reassurance from out of the past. They know well enough that economic survival may depend on appropriate career choices and that status in their world can be vitally affected by such choices. The concern is and must be a central one.

180

Purposes of the Liberal Arts

It is worth noting that the arts do provide for careers of varying sorts, either directly or indirectly. Training in language arts (writing *and* speaking) can be essential for careers in management that require writing or oral ability, for work in some health-related fields, and, of course, for positions in the media. Foreign language training can lead to careers in, for instance, import-export firms as well as in government. Training in the visual arts can be useful in newly developing hospital and nursing home therapy programs as well as in publishing. And training in music can lead to work in music publishing, in retailing, and in musical instrument repair as well as in performance. Where students decide on a business major and a liberal arts minor or the reverse, the combination may well be enough for an entry-level position that can lead, eventually, to unusual and challenging career choices. Those colleges that actively seek to build links between the classroom and the world of work, by way of cooperative education programs and curricular reform, can contribute to the immediate survival and ultimate strengthening of the liberal arts in any number of areas.

Such emphasis on work is certainly not meant to obscure other necessary purposes. It is still important, as Reagor (1978) suggests, "to prepare free men for citizenship," a "general ideal of the humanities [which] has not altered much in the past 2,500 years" (p. 148). Where students are adequately prepared for the reading, Sophocles' *Antigone* can still be "relevant" in suggesting the necessity for the responsible use of authority, Shakespeare's *Henry IV* can still speak to us about the nature of workaday politics, and Kafka's *The Castle* can still recreate all too clearly the terror experienced by individuals who are subject to a remote and unpredictable authority.

Finally, it seems to me, the humanities must provide a framework for interpreting creative experience. It is often a good idea, as I have suggested elsewhere (1973), to introduce the student to a particular humanities discipline by means of a series of hands-on activities. But whatever the approach used, the student should eventually come to a greater awareness of human experience and the possibilities for creative invention used to describe it.

In the case of language arts, there are any number of possibilities. Students who are studying plays in an introductory course may find it helpful to view dramatic conflict first in a life setting. I once took some students to visit a nearby courthouse where litigants were involved in bitter disputes. Later some members of the class sought to reproduce in playlets of their own not only the sense of the arguments, but also the underlying tensions. Students who tried the exercise learned a good deal about observational techniques, some important distinctions between life and art, and artistic judgment.

Students studying poetry often complain that the poems they read are remote or boring; a good solution to the problem is to attempt an immediate in-class rewrite. Such poems as Wordsworth's "I Wandered Lonely as a Cloud" and Keats's "Ode on a Grecian Urn" are particularly useful because they deal directly with the creative act and the responses to it as well as with metaphoric usage. In attempting to rewrite the poems, most students will come to see why the poets have selected the particular words in the poem and even why such selections are indicative of superior insight and imagination.

Still another approach is to create modern or local versions of literary works under discussion. The adaptations can be fascinating, but perhaps more important ultimately is the recognition of archetypal patterns. The causes and effects of violence in Camus' *The Stranger* have wide application as do the withdrawals in Melville's "Bartleby" or the betrayals in such folk ballads as "Barbara Allen" and "Lord Randal." As in the approaches cited earlier, the exercise of personal imagination comes first, with the student moving from a personal knowledge and realities to those of the work.

To be sure, the community college student, even one committed primarily to the liberal arts, will in all probability not go much beyond introductory-level work, but such an individual may have made a significant beginning in learning. Moreover, the quality of the involvement can also be important. When Socrates asserted that the unexamined life is not worth living, he undoubtedly believed that a meaningful search would lead to overt and beneficial results, but he also had in mind the satisfaction and joy a life of learning can bring. The student who is so affected will be on the way to education in its best sense. However, to accomplish such extensive goals is a very large order indeed. The faculty and students who seek to achieve them should provide living proof that the humanities still have a meaning for our time.

Ideas for an Arts Curriculum

In a discussion of cultural studies at the two-year college, it would be helpful, as well as psychologically satisfying, to be able to recommend a specific body of work for inclusion in the curricula of various humanities departments. A common heritage might conceivably provide a center of gravity, a philosophical or religious orientation, some social identifications, a set of aesthetic criteria, and an appropriate historical framework. Where such programs have been launched (most notably at Harvard and the University of Chicago), students presumably are given a basis for reflection and continuing dialogue. The concept has much to recommend it, but it has limited application at the community college, where basic skills problems are great and where large variations in the ethnic and racial backgrounds of students sometimes can make selections of material difficult.

Although more traditional materials cannot always be used to good effect, it does not necessarily follow that humanities programs of substance must be abandoned along with the purposes for which they were created. The first step may well be an emphasis on the commonality of human experience; what has been widely shared can represent at least a beginning point for discussion. Only after there is some common base for group awareness can the idea of diversity be attractive. Oscar Handlin's classic study of immigration, *The Uprooted*, emphasized such commonality and showed again and again how immigrants of differing ethnic and racial backgrounds faced many of the same fears and difficulties, and responded, at least some of the time, in the same ways. Curriculum builders in the humanities might well consider the literature of immigration as a source for beginning cultural studies along with such popular forms as the folk song, the poster, and the political cartoon.

The shared experience is usually most identifiable in a contemporary setting, and it is probably a good idea to begin discussions by using what is most familiar. Although it is easier to develop a survey course moving from the beginnings to the present or to some other fixed point than it is to begin with the present and work backwards, the latter has an advantage that may outweigh the difficulties: the student knows the present and is interested in it. If the past is shown to have some bearing on contemporary concerns, then it will be important. In a literature course, for example, when an instructor is attempting to show that a journey or trip can represent a symbolic quest of large dimensions, it is useful to begin with a form as familiar as the detective story. An aging television hero like Kojak knows all too well about the dangers as well as the excitement of venturing into unfamiliar territory, he understands the lure of sweet temptation, and he comprehends the penalties for transgression. For those who can be saved, he points the way home to the comforts and moral worth of family life that can be enjoyed *after* a time of testing. With such a review of the familiar, it is possible for students to look at a work like the *Odyssey* and begin to make some sense out of it.

In addition to the use of contemporary settings, it is also sound practice to focus on large issues. Indeed, much has been written over the last several years about the importance of using broad themes set in an interdisciplinary framework (see Cohen, 1975). The idea continues to be a good one, although administrative obstacles can be formidable. Students will be interested in issues that currently do or will involve them—family institutions, physical and social environment, jobs, economic management, and health. In designing programs that focus on such themes, planners should give the "clusters" of courses forming the basis of interdisciplinary study a clearly articulated rationale that will be offered to students at the beginning of a term. Clusters should also be designed and identified as introductory or advanced and may possibly be linked either to specific disciplinary studies or to career programs.

At LaGuardia Community College of the City University of New York, we have experimented with a number of combinations. One cluster has included Basic Composition, Oral Communications, and Philosophy. All three courses have focused on the concept of freedom (viewed in historical as well as conceptual terms) and have stressed the need to combine analysis with communication techniques. Another cluster, Work, Labor, and Business, dealt with the rise of American capitalism, with cooperating areas including English, Social Sciences, and Mathematics. Still another cluster, Ideal Societies, focused on various attempts at social reorganization in the United States and elsewhere. This effort, sponsored by English and Social Sciences, introduced students to a variety of utopian concepts. Later, guest speakers from local government agencies, private rehabilitation facilities, and even a commune were invited to participate in a series of seminars.

Since most faculty have been trained in a particular discipline, team teaching is an obvious and useful answer for interdisciplinary study; however, there must be a good deal of advanced preparation, or the effort will be unsuccessful. Members of the team need to be familiar with the approaches used in each of the classes, with all materials assigned for study, and with the timing of various presentations. Joint sessions can cover crucial points, stimulate discussion or generate controversy, or provide the opportunity for an overview.

The Glossary as an Approach to Basic Skills

This chapter is not directly concerned with basic skills, but it is obvious that what happens in remedial programs has a large general impact. While responsibility for basic skills instruction can be divided in many ways, there is one area where faculty throughout the college can make a contribution to basic skills *and* to the strengthening of student work in their own fields. I refer to the systematic development of vocabulary lists in the form of glossaries focusing primarily on key concepts in one or more disciplines. Once assembled, a glossary can be sent to the Basic Skills Department for review, for comments, and for possible use at the remedial level. Later the amended glossary may be circulated among subject-area departments to lay the basis for reinforcement and possible cross disciplinary teaching.

Though word lists will obviously vary, it may be useful to begin with some basic sequences related to general problem solving as well as to the interpretation of art. The *fact-inference-judgment* sequence (used as a primary point of reference in many oral communication courses) is a good possibility. It is important to emphasize that facts are demonstrable. Inference may indeed have a factual basis, but in addition may involve various forms of speculation. Judgment also makes use of speculation, but the emphasis may be placed on diverse ethical, social, cultural, and political assumptions. For instance, in a classroom exercise, one might begin with the fact that a student can type thirty-five words per minute without error. The inference, which, unlike the fact, may or may not be demonstrably true, is that the student has studied or taken a course in typing. The judgment, which expresses approval or disapproval, may be that the student is an efficient typist. Going to a broader field such as the women's movement, one might cite as a fact the passage of the constitutional amendment giving women the right to vote. The inference would be that women have become more powerful politically. The judgment could be either that "it's a good thing women have the right to vote" or "it's important for women to concern themselves with home, not politics."

A similar approach makes use of the terms *description, interpretation,* and *evaluation.* Here, essential descriptive elements lead to an interpretation which may or may not be illustrative of an author's (or artist's or composer's) intention. Evaluation, the last step, is, like judgment, a complex term and obviously moves beyond the perception of language, object, or sound to an examination of varying attitudes and values. *Content* and *structure* can also be important basic terms for a glossary. Although an instructor would probably not attempt to provide a high level of sophistication, it is still important to suggest that content and structure are intimately connected and that structure (as well as style) affects our understanding and the level of our responses. Seemingly familiar terms like *classical* and *romantic* clearly form an underpinning for all of the arts and might well provide a good beginning for wide-ranging discussion. Classification by genre can be of use as can historical labeling. Whatever the terms employed, students need finally to come to an understanding of the importance of conceptualization and of the uses to which it can be put.

The assembling of a glossary should also stimulate much discussion in departments about what is crucial in a particular course and why it is of prime importance. For instance, an introductory course may be so designed that it lays the foundation for upper-level courses, seeks to meet the requirements for some form of professional work, and includes components for "appreciation" aimed at the student who plans to take only one course in a discipline (Little, 1974, p. 100). But for the student with basic skills problems, such a large number of goals may be overwhelming. A solution may lie in the refocusing or narrowing of objectives.

The skillful organization of a glossary can also be tied to the structured development of a course outline, at least at the introductory level. Such careful structuring can be beneficial, especially for students who have difficulty in understanding, organizing, and relating ideas. Where subject-area departments are willing to cooperate, key concepts can be discussed from different vantage points in class at prearranged times in order to gain maximum advantage. If the Basic Skills Department has done some work previously or does so during the same period that other departments are stressing the same ideas, the student will have a very good chance to learn in a significant way.

The Importance of the Instructor

Whatever the methods employed, the teacher is central to the success or failure of any course or program. In addition to knowing the subject matter and caring about it, an instructor must understand individual students' needs and expectations. The teacher must have such personal qualities as patience and sympathy and the ability to draw students out in useful ways. Beyond personal rapport, the instructor must be the advocate of some rather old-fashioned ideas—that hard work can lead to tangible success, that excellence is worth striving for, that true learning offers pleasure.

Very often, such views run counter to the lifestyles of students. Yet as heritage teachers we know these ideas are essential. The instructor who cares will, of course, persist in experimenting with motivational devices providing immediate stimulation, such as classroom psychodrama or the impressionistic journal. However, in the long run, students need to move on to those essential processes that make sustained, serious effort possible—in-depth research, synthesis, evaluation, and logical communication. Such standard tools as the essay examination and the term paper provide substantial training, and students who make the transition to these difficult forms successfully will have mastered skills and approaches that should have lifelong significance.

Summary

There can be no question that the work of great minds and great imaginations continues to deserve our attention and our energies, though, to be sure, the controversies over what is to be selected and how it is to be treated will continue to be intense. But if our sense of what is important in literature, art, and music keeps changing, so do our views of ourselves and of the times in which we live. The benefits of continued reflection and effort can be as large as our conception of them. We owe it to our students and ourselves to grow, to meet challenges as they arise, and to accept nothing less than the large fulfillments that will be a heritage in times to come.

References

Cohen, Arthur M., ed. *The Humanities in the Two-Year College: Reviewing Curriculum and Instruction.* Los Angeles: Center for the Study of Community Colleges and ERIC Clearinghouse for Junior Colleges, 1975.

Groman, George L. "Goals for a Core Program in the Humanities." *ADE Bulletin* 38 (September 1973): 44–48.

Little, D. Richard. "Beyond Careerism: The Revival of General Education." *The Journal of General Education*, vol. 26, no. 2 (Summer 1974): 100.

Olson, Paul A. *Concepts of Career and General Education.* ERIC/Higher Education Research Report No. 8. Washington, D.C.: American Association for Higher Education, 1977.

Reagor, A. Simone. "The State of the Humanities." *Educational Record*, vol. 59, no. 2 (Spring 1978): 148–155.

17 Language Arts in the Community College: A Process Model

Elisabeth McPherson

The community college English Department described here is a composite, based on several departments that believe in a student-centered, process approach to English teaching. Although the description does not give a totally accurate picture of what goes on in any one school, it is more convenient and useful to talk about a single department.

The class schedule of the department looks much like that in any other two-year college: some literature courses (but not very many); some reading courses, divided into three kinds; and a lot of writing courses, split into two levels, developmental and transfer. The schedule also shows the hours of a language-learning laboratory, which students can use without formal registration and without extra tuition.

The English teachers are not proud of the schedule. They know that most students come with a strong native language ability, despite little practice in reading and writing and an ability that cannot be measured in conventional ways. Most members of the department would like to run a completely open program, with all students working together, growing at their own rate, freed from labels, grades, and penalties. However, the time limits of a semester, the institutional insistence on letter grades, and the government demand for a rigid pattern of progress from students receiving grants all prohibit such freedom. Since grades must be given at an arbitrary time, it is obviously unfair to place adults who read and write at what is assumed to be fourth-grade level in the same class with others working at an assumed tenth-grade level and expect everybody to read and write with the same competence at the end of four months. Thus, for the students' sake, some sectioning must occur.

Diagnosis and Placement

Using standardized tests for placement is out of the question. The department refuses to categorize students according to impersonal percentiles that ignore differences in background, experience, and dialect. Even if the tests did not discriminate against the majority of students, they still measure only the most superficial aspects of writing skill—spelling, punctuation, usage, terminology. They are tests of editing, not writing. What the department needs to know, if students are to be placed where they have the greatest chance of success, is how successfully they can express their own ideas. Thus, recommendations have to be based on a writing sample.

Because of time and the large number of students, the sample has to be brief. The assigned topic must be something with which everybody has had some experience, it must be structured enough that students are not left floundering, and it must involve some choice. "What I like (or don't like) about the neighborhood I live in" meets these criteria fairly well. It forces students to take a position, and it invites specific details. Students are told to write as much as they can in twenty minutes and advised to save a few minutes at the end for reading over what they have written and making whatever changes they think would improve it. At least two writing teachers read every paper and make a quick holistic judgment; if they disagree, a third teacher also reads the paper. Little attention is given to mechanics unless the spelling, punctuation, and sentence structure are so bizarre that teachers can't understand what the writer is saying, but considerable weight is given to how much the student has written. Two or three painfully achieved lines show an obvious need for developmental work, but two or three pages of repetitive generalizations, without examples or support, can show the same need. Occasionally a paper is almost gibberish; when that occurs, the department tries to provide individual professional diagnosis of learning disability—vision, hearing, dyslexia, and the like—and to recommend the specialized help the college cannot give.

The department's placement is not compulsory. As students register, counselors urge them to take the writing class the department thinks would help them most, and the majority do, even though the choice remains theirs. This sectioning system is admittedly rough. The brevity of the tests and the haste with which the judgments are made inevitably lead to some misplacement. So that students won't waste time in a class too elementary or too advanced for their needs, they can shift from one level to another any time during the semester, whenever a teacher recommends the change. People who move from a developmental to a transfer class are pleased with what they consider a promotion; they willingly meet with the teacher to catch up on what their new class has been doing. Asking students to move from transfer composition to a developmental section is more difficult. It requires a tactful explanation of why more practice in writing is essential, not just for English classes, but for all the other courses the student will be taking. Tact is sometimes not enough, and students who insist on their right to remain where they were originally placed are allowed to take the chance.

The Writing Courses

The main difference between the two writing courses is in emphasis. Developmental English (sometimes called "basic," but never "remedial") moves more slowly, expects less, and provides the extra writing experience students need as a background for transfer composition. Neither class asks people to memorize rules, fill in the blanks, or punctuate sentences somebody else has written. Both classes work for fluency. Many community college students have been so thoroughly conditioned to believe they are "no good in English" that they are afraid to write at all. They have a notion that writing exists only so somebody can mark it "wrong." One way of shaking them loose to write is to spend five or ten minutes of the class period on free writing. Students are told to write whatever comes into their heads without lifting their pens from the paper; if they get stuck, they write "I can't think of anything to say" over and over until the process bores them. The aim is not coherence but quantity, and the student who writes the most gets the most praise.

Regular journal writing, however, is a more effective way of convincing students that they can write something other people will want to read. They are required to write for at least twenty minutes, at least three times a week, on anything that interests them—childhood experiences, frustrations, reactions to what they have read, comments on what happens in class, poetry, short stories—anything except the conventional diary entry that reads,

"I got up and ate breakfast, then I missed the bus, after school I went to a party, it was very nice. . . ." Students are warned that their journals will be collected every two or three weeks, but they are also promised that nothing they write will be graded and nothing will be "corrected" unless they specifically request it. Instead, the teacher will respond to what they have written in much the way a friend might, by asking questions, making comments, or requesting more details. When the journals are turned in, students choose the entry they like best and their selections are typed—usually by the teacher, since there is seldom enough secretarial help—and reproduced in a class magazine for everybody to read and discuss. If the writers' names are not included, students feel freer to comment on what other people have written, even though the anonymity is seldom maintained very long. Some time during the discussion, the writer will say indignantly, "But that isn't what I meant!"

Discussions of writing begin with students saying what they like about a paper. Then the teacher encourages them to analyze why they liked it and what made it effective. As the comments become more critical, the class talks about the way a writer's purpose affects what's said; about what readers have a right to expect; and about why some people seem more disturbed by unconventional spelling than by unconventional ideas. Although teachers try hard to keep their own opinions and values out of the discussion, they do exert enough guidance to insure that the students are talking about what has been written rather than wandering off to a general bull session on the same topic.

Language Study

Very early in the semester these discussions lead to a consideration of the nature of language: how people learn it, how their language habits are bound up with their sense of identity, what is involved in changing deeply ingrained language patterns, and why people react emotionally to attacks on their language choices. Students are told that "dialect" is not a pejorative term; everybody speaks a dialect, and so-called "standard English" is no more logical or inherently right than any other set of choices. In speech no single standard exists for all educated people, and in writing the standard is merely a dialect that has evolved over the last two or three centuries and is still slowly but inevitably changing.

Certain topics and activities help advance the discussion of language. Students enjoy finding vocabulary variations among members of the class. They enjoy making guesses as to where people in the class grew up, based on the way they pronounce their words. They enjoy listing new words that have entered the language in the last decade and interviewing elderly relatives for words that have disappeared. They enjoy comparing speeches, Kennedy's with Johnson's, Johnson's with Carter's. They enjoy examining the judgments they make about other people's syntactic choices. There are five or six ways of saying "I'm broke"; why are listeners' emotional responses to the alternatives different even though they understand them all equally well? Once students see that the problem with "I don't have no money" is not the double negative—no rational listener supposes that statement means the speaker has at least a dollar or two—but rather the impression it creates, they are more willing to adapt to the conventions of the classroom. Choosing what's appropriate is less damaging to their self-respect than being told what sounds comfortable is always wrong. Role playing in different situations—applying for a job; gossiping in the coffee shop; explaining a change in plan to a six year old, a parent, a close friend, and a professor—emphasizes the importance of audience and reassures students that they can, and do, vary their language choices to fit the occasion.

Although accurate information about how language works is an important part of the course, nobody sets aside two or three weeks for an intensive survey. Without turning the composition course into a lecture on the history of English or a seminar on linguistics, teachers introduce this information whenever the question of "correctness" comes up. Erratic spellers are helped by knowing something about the development of the English spelling system, and people who have been clobbered for comma splices are helped by realizing that punctuation is a relatively recent system, existing only to make life easier for readers. Those mysterious rules are nothing but conventions; they have no legal force.

Coverage of the Writing Process

From the beginning, students have been writing, both in class and out. In developmental classes most of the writing is done during class, with a lot of help from the teacher. In transfer classes most of the assignments are written on the students' own time, but a good deal of the class period is spent on preparation. Prewriting strategies are examined and discussed, often in groups of two or three students working together. The class practices narrowing topics, identifying thesis statements, brainstorming for ideas, listing supporting details and examples, making tentative plans, and rearranging those plans. When first drafts have been written, students get more advice from other members of the class. But none of the advice is binding, even when it comes from the teacher; students can ignore it all and write whatever pleases them.

After they have produced papers they're satisfied with, they begin the editing that will make the finished copy look better. Sometimes this editing is merely a matter of checking for spelling, punctuation, and omissions; sometimes it involves rearranging sentences or finding more precise words. The class is given the usual advice about the value of a cooling-off period to gain more distance from what they have written, and they are reminded that when papers are read aloud, either in the privacy of a closed room or to a sympathetic listener, the ear can often catch an awkwardness that the eye misses. Students frequently edit each other's papers, with the teacher acting as arbitrator when the students disagree. Instead of spelling drills, the class practices using the dictionary; instead of exercises on misplaced modifiers and periodic sentences, the class plays with combinations of kernel sentences and decides which combinations seem most successful for the effect the writer wants to achieve. Even the finished papers are not graded; students can judge how well they've done from the oral comments other students make or the written comments the teacher provides.

Audience and Purpose

Members of the class are always part of the audience, but some assignments are made in such a way that students write for other readers too, either real or imaginary. They discover for themselves, for instance, that writing directions for people totally unfamiliar with a process, such as giving first aid to a heart attack victim, requires different words and different advice than explaining a new method to readers already expert in the old system. They also discover that an angry letter to a friend is quite different in tone and style from a letter to the local paper defending the educational philosophy of the college against the scurrilous attacks being made on it. And the pleasure the class takes in seeing one of their letters actually printed is quite different, and far more effective, than any A the teacher could have given.

The English Department realizes that writers cannot respond to fallacious arguments or write persuasively themselves unless they can distinguish between fact and opinion, recognize and avoid jargon, and handle common-sense logic. Class time is therefore spent on forcing judgments back to the facts on which they are based, translating educational and political jargon into ordinary language, and determining whether conclusions are logically justifiable. Students learn to recognize and partially eliminate the slant in their own work when they write two accounts of the same event, omitting none of the facts but deliberately creating two quite opposite impressions. They discover the difference between emotional appeals and rational argument, between misleading statistics and honest surveys, by analyzing advertisements and campaign speeches. They form groups, decide on a topic, write questions, conduct their own survey, and report their findings. Sometimes they set up their own doublespeak committee and present their own local awards, on the model of NCTE's committee and its annual awards. As they examine how language colors our view of reality, they create their own guidelines for avoiding sexism in the classroom, using their own educational experiences as the basis for what they decide.

Since writing teachers often have trouble convincing students that composition skills have application outside the composition class and since many freshmen have trouble coping with examinations in their other classes, some time is spent on how to take tests. For students who understand the material, succeeding in an objective test is less a matter of skillful writing than of careful reading, and practice in taking such tests probably belongs in a reading course. Writing students, however, can gain useful insights into how such tests work by creating questions on what the composition course has covered and answering questions created by other students. Practice in answering essay questions does belong in a writing class. For students who understand the material, success in an essay test often depends on interpreting the questions, budgeting their time, summarizing main points, and supporting general statements. If students bring actual essay questions that have been used in their other courses, the class can relate such terminology as *compare and contrast, discuss, define, evaluate,* and *summarize* to the kind of papers they've already been writing.

Note taking and summary writing are also easy to practice. The teacher can give a half-hour lecture on practically anything, let the students take notes, and ask them to put those notes into a brief paragraph. Better, small groups of students can compare their notes and write a composite summary that pleases all of them—good experience in the committee writing that characterizes many organizations and some jobs. However the test-taking and study skills sessions are handled, they help students see the relationship between writing a good English paper and writing a good essay test or study materials.

All these activities and assignments are a kind of exercise, designed to promote flexibility and build confidence. They don't interfere with the more personal and creative writing of the journals, where students use their writing to explore who they are, what they believe, and what they value.

Consultation and Evaluation

Most of the composition teachers plan to hold frequent conferences with everybody in their classes, talking about what the students are currently writing and making sure they understand the written comments the teachers have made. In actuality, however, the very tight schedules on which many students are operating make it hard for them to get into the office. When the conferences can be arranged, the teacher uses a series of nonthreatening questions to help students determine for themselves the changes they need to make; the aim is to guide them gradually toward becoming their own critics. When a student is having several kinds of difficulty, the teacher doesn't try to deal with them all in a single conference; instead, the discussion concentrates on one or two, and the student is praised for whatever improvement occurs. When there are more problems than can be handled in class or in conference, the teacher recommends some sessions in the language laboratory.

Neither half of the transfer course includes a traditional research paper, both because many students will never need that rather specialized academic skill and because the time required for teaching a reference paper thoroughly is time not spent on more practical and important aspects of writing. Reference work is not entirely ignored, however. English teachers know that unless they familiarize students with the college library and how to use it, some students will leave the college unaware of the resources available to them. Consequently, one class session is devoted to a library tour, and at least one assignment requires students to find some information in a book or periodical and give credit to the source. For the few students who must produce term papers in their other courses, the department provides individual help and advice, either through appointment with any English teacher or through the drop-in laboratory, whichever is more convenient for the student.

Two semesters are never time enough for what teachers want to do. Even in transfer classes, where students can be expected to accomplish more in a shorter time, some material is always left out. The most carefully planned syllabus gives way to the special direction each class takes. Writing teachers are always, and justifiably, complaining that two sections of what is supposed to be the same class cannot be "kept together." Occasionally a teacher can steer a discussion back to what has been planned for the day, but most process teachers believe that a class that's forced into a prescheduled plan is a class where immediate needs are being ignored.

Developmental teachers realize they can cover only a little of what has been outlined here. But even though developmental students spend most of their time in planning, writing, and discussing what they've written, it is especially important for them to realize that "right and wrong" in language is not the same as "right and wrong" in mathematics or ethics. Teachers are careful to avoid those terms and limit their comments to *clear* or *confusing, convincing* or *unconvincing.*

The developmental course lasts for only one semester. Students who have gained enough confidence and experience are given an S for satisfactory and encouraged to enroll in the transfer course. Students who need more practice are given P for progress and can take the course again without penalty. The transfer course lasts for two semesters. The major difference in the second semester is that fewer specific assignments are made and the students have more time for exploratory writing. They continue to share what they have done with the rest of the class, but they have become more sure of what they want to say and more secure when their writing is criticized. They understand that their final grades are not an arbitrary and incomprehensible judgment made by the teacher alone, but are instead the result of a consultation in which they have had a part. They have written a paper offering support for the grade they think would be fair, and most of them are adequate judges. On the few occasions when students have overrated their work or modestly underrated their achievement, the teacher has explained the reasons for the disagreement.

The Reading Courses

Most community college students, whether they are enrolled in developmental or transfer composition, could use some improvement in their reading skills. The department offers three reading courses: one on an elementary level, where students who are almost nonreaders get help in translating the symbols of print into the symbols of speech; one on comprehension, for students who can make the literal translation without difficulty, but who need help with vocabulary and interpretation; and one on increasing speed, for students whose understanding is adequate, but whose rate is slow. It's often difficult, however, to get students to enroll for these classes. While most experts agree that reading and writing skills are closely related and most community college instructors in all departments know that a lot of their students cannot read well enough or fast enough to keep up with the assignments, a course in reading is not required for graduation from the two-year college, and most four-year colleges will not accept reading courses for transfer credit. Students who feel the pressures of outside jobs and family responsibilities, who are anxious to complete their career requirements as fast as possible, are reluctant to spend the time and tuition necessary for reading improvement. Sometimes it takes a semester's experience to convince them that the effort is worthwhile.

And sometimes it isn't. Their success when they do enroll depends on factors beyond their own motivation. Perhaps the most important is the teacher's skill. Not much is known about teaching adults to read, and few English teachers have any formal preparation for the task or much comprehension of what is involved. Most English teachers have read so easily and so much ever since they can remember that it's hard for them to understand why all intelligent adults can't read as well as the teachers themselves do. It may be true that some very perceptive and successful reading teachers have taught themselves to teach, just as they taught themselves to read, but it's also true that randomly assigning literature teachers to elementary adult reading sections is deadening for the teachers and damaging to the students.

Another essential factor for success is the content of the reading selections. Material written for young adolescents is demeaning for students whose ages average twenty-seven, and material that deals exclusively with middle-class white concerns has little interest for working-class and minority students. Even when the material is suitable, classes must do more than plod through a ready-made workbook, reading paragraphs, answering multiple-choice questions, and adding up scores based on a mechanical count of "right" answers. Successful reading teachers expect to spend as much time on discussion and explanation as on the reading itself. They are prepared to analyze individual difficulties; discover when conjunctions, qualifiers, or inverted sentence structure is creating the stumbling block; and answer the same questions over and over without any sign of impatience. These reading teachers encourage reading for fun at any appropriate level; they show no scorn for comic books, sex magazines, or cheap westerns. They are flexible enough to shift from editorials in the local paper, which they recognize as an excellent practice source, to an electronics text. They are satisfied with some progress, however slight it seems, and they do not expect miracles.

But even if all the students who could benefit from a reading class did enroll, the reading teachers could not do the job alone. The department urges all college instructors to select texts at the simplest reading level that does not oversimplify content, and the department provides help in determining approximately what the reading level of a proposed text is. Reading teachers also offer in-service seminars for instructors who know that students have difficulty reading the specialized subject matter of their disciplines, but don't know what to do about it. In these seminars the reading teachers point out how much students are helped when the instructor isolates definitions, emphasizes main ideas, points out relationships, and organizes the lecture material in outline form. They remind instructors that students who are having great trouble should be referred to the reading laboratory early in the semester.

The Literature Courses

That many community college students arrive with a lack of reading experience and a lack of confidence in their own reading ability partially explains the continuing decrease in literature enrollments, a decrease that has been reported nationwide for more than ten years. But there are other reasons for the decline that are hard for the English Department to combat. Most career programs are so tightly organized they leave room for only one elective a year, and the advisors for those programs, who endured rather than enjoyed the courses they were forced to take, seldom suggest literature to their students. The college administration is unsympathetic; as one influential dean said, "What does a plumber need with Chaucer?" It's apparent that the English Department has a public relations problem. Teachers who believe that literature lets us out of ourselves into a larger world and deepens our understanding of the world we actually inhabit need to persuade deans and counselors, students and secretaries, that the literature taught at the community college is neither esoteric nor inaccessible to ordinary people, that it does relate to the frustrations they face and makes them more bearable.

The Issue of Relevance

Teachers make sure that the literature is made accessible for those students who do make their way to the classes. The cliché that the content of introductory literature courses should have some connection with the students' own lives is not bothersome to literature teachers. They assume that if the stories, poems, or novels they introduce can gain the students' interest, the contrast between their own lives and values and lives and values about which they read can be made exciting. The students can discover the universals for themselves; sometimes they will maintain, with reason, that the emotions and conflicts in some of what they are asked to read are too trivial to be worth their while. Rather than insisting on an artificial appreciation, teachers urge the students to speculate on why the selection has been included. Most students can, when their judgment is respected, distinguish the shoddy from the meaningful, even though the criteria they use are not the same as the teacher's.

Although so-called relevance may be unimportant, variety is not. Texts which pretend that everything worth reading was produced by white Americans and that almost no women have written anything worthwhile create a false picture that perceptive students resent. English teachers know that black literature courses belong in the curriculum and that those offerings attract students who shun more traditionally titled courses; but they also strongly believe that black writers, in more than token numbers, must be included in every general and American literature course. Teachers know that some black students are already experts on the black experience in America; the majority of nonblack students, however, know little about Black, Chicano, Puerto Rican, or Native American experience and even less about the writers who have transformed those experiences into literature. Students find satisfaction in reading what they can identify with, but they grow by empathizing with the unfamiliar.

In the same way, the department is careful not to confine writing by and about women to women's literature courses, where enrollment is almost exclusively female. Rather, women's concerns, which are actually human concerns, become an integral part of all introductory courses. When texts with a wide representation of minority and women writers are unavailable, imaginative teachers work within the copyright law to duplicate their own selections.

Another way to keep prose and poetry accessible is for teachers to treat literature as a normal, natural human product, not something that must be regarded with distant admiration and awe.

Teachers take it for granted that once a poem has been published, it belongs to everybody who can enjoy it. To enjoy a poem, students don't need to be told that critics consider it influential or important; the students do need to discover its importance to them. Teachers encourage students to argue about their own interpretations; the teachers occasionally ask questions, but they don't kill the discussion by insisting on the authorized version. They will, of course, give their own opinions if they are asked, but they don't pretend that what they think is gospel. Inevitably, some students want to be told what a poem "really means." Then the teacher reminds them that nobody except the author can answer the "really means" question with absolute assurance, and even authors can only say what they were trying to do or what they thought they meant.

The terms used in literary criticism are introduced casually, with little emphasis placed on them. Beginning students are confused and repelled by undue attention to symbolism, imagery, and metrics; a teacher who wants the class to consider how a poem works is more likely to ask why Reed shifted back and forth from the parts of a gun to the weather outside than to talk about controlling metaphor. The teacher is careful not to destroy the students' pleasure in a poem by too much close textual examination.

Teachers also realize that requiring students to produce detailed written analyses is more likely to produce plagiarism than appreciation. Teachers ask for journals in which students are encouraged to record their honest responses. Journal writing leads students to think about what they have read instead of waiting for the teacher to tell them what they ought to think. "I didn't like it" is just as valuable as "I liked it," provided that in both cases the student says why.

Beyond the Basic Course

If students are comfortable in an introductory course, many of them willingly take more specialized courses. The farther back in time a survey literature course reaches, the more important it is to make earlier writers seem real and alive. Lots of devices are available: teachers show films of the Canterbury pilgrims and the Elizabethan theatre; play records on which the poetry of Milton, Herrick, or Browning is read effectively; encourage informal dramatizations of *Everyman* or Marlowe; explain archaic vocabulary and syntax before anybody asks for the explanation; and find a comparison of the supernatural exploits of Beowulf and Superman more welcome than a derivative paper on kennings. Their tests, if they give them, emphasize values rather than dates and details. They spend more time on why Melville matters, or doesn't matter, to twentieth-century readers than on his prose style.

If none of the scheduled literature offerings are attractive to students, the department is willing to teach any specialized kind of literature that fifteen students want to try. If there aren't enough students to make a course economically feasible, most teachers will undertake an independent study overload for the handful of students who want to start with detective stories, the poetry of rock, Utopian fiction, or even soap operas. Students whose schedules or inclinations don't allow for a separate literature course are encouraged to take integrated humanities, team-taught by music, art, and literature teachers. There the writing produced in any given period is seen in its relationship to the historical events and philosophical attitudes that prevailed at the time. Such team-taught courses are especially enlightening, and enlivened, when students hear unrehearsed discussions and disagreements between two of the instructors teaching the course. But whatever a literature course covers, the department remembers that helping students read for pleasure and personal profit is more important than a pedantic insistence on traditional attitudes.

The Demands and Rewards of the Approach

Student-centered, process teaching makes great demands on teachers who pursue it wholeheartedly. It requires a genuine respect for all students as potential learners rather than a concealed condescension for their present shortcomings. It requires some knowledge of psycho- and sociolinguistics or, more frequently, a willingness to acquire that knowledge on the teacher's own time, since almost no advanced degree work in English includes such courses. It requires more than a superficial understanding of how difficult it is to change language habits; what the underlying basis for so-called "errors" is; and the rate at which changes can be expected to occur. It requires teachers who see themselves as participants in learning rather than authorities who make pronouncements, teachers willing to write with their writing classes and explore unsanctified ideas with their reading classes, whether the reading class is elementary comprehension or world literature. Above all, it requires knowing that process teaching never means an unstructured situation in which "anything goes"; instead, such teaching always places stringent demands for growth in clarity, precision, organization, imagination, and originality on both students and teachers.

Nonprescriptive teaching costs more in creativity, effort, and time than more conventional methods. It takes longer to respond individually and thoughtfully to what students have written than it takes to circle mistakes and assign grades. Finding suitable selections and isolating individual problems is more time-consuming than marking a workbook or running a reading machine. Making literature come alive, duplicating student journals, and holding student conferences can extend a teacher's work week by so many hours that a cot in the office sometimes seems a necessity of existence.

Conclusion: The Courage of One's Convictions

And it takes courage to withstand the increasing pressures from administrators, communities, and legislatures for a return to what they mistakenly consider "the basics." Very little research exists to demonstrate that the process approach to teaching adults produces, in the long run, better readers and writers; tests are not designed to measure the growth that has taken place. Community college teachers who believe that student-centered classes help a greater number of students to master skills more important than the ability to achieve high test scores must fall back on conviction and common sense. They sympathize with Emig's (1979) view that we must "fight the current retreat—no, rout—into the élitist irresponsibility of earlier decades, where once again we agree to teach only those who can learn without our active and imaginative efforts," for "unless, as a community, we reverse ourselves and the direction that our schools, colleges, and universities are currently taking, this country [will be] truly no longer morally habitable."

That statement may seem too strong. Certainly English departments that take other approaches are equally convinced that their methods meet the needs of their students. Traditional and competency-based programs, however, are not under attack. It is the process approach that is at risk, and its survival may depend on the vigor with which its practitioners support it.

Reference

Emig, Janet. "Mina Pendo Shaughnessy." *College Composition and Communication*, vol. xxx, no. 1 (February 1979): 36.

V The Four-Year College

18 Modern Higher Education

Edmund Volpe
College of Staten Island

From 1964 to 1970, I was chairperson of the Department of English at the City College of New York. When I left the chair, I published an article, entitled "Confessions of a Fallen Man," in which I suggested that we English professors were trained to become high priests of literature. We used our classrooms to proselytize, and our greatest satisfaction came from creating mirror images of ourselves who would go on to graduate school, enter the priesthood, and carry the faith into the next generation.

I was expressing in that article some of the frustrations I had known during the tumultuous period of the '60s when the expanding and changing student population demanded an ever-increasing attention to basic writing skills that the priesthood was neither trained nor inclined to give. During those years the departmental Jeremiahs dominated our meetings with impassioned declamations on the ineptness of the central administration for admitting students who could not write a decent sentence, on the general corruption of higher education and the decline of the liberal arts, and on the power of literature to liberate and elevate the human soul. The oratory, which I am sure continues to resound in our English departments throughout the nation, was filled with stimulating metaphors and rich allusions, but it did not resolve the problem: we needed teachers of writing, and we were professors of literature.

Now, after four years as a college president, I realize that I was a bit harsh on my colleagues in English. The problem, I am sorry to say, is institutional, not departmental. I would have much preferred to have left the problem to English departments to resolve than have it follow me, magnified, into my present role. English professors are not, as I then thought, a breed apart. They belong to a whole fraternity: liberal arts professors, as a group, are direct descendants of Jonathan Edwards, educational puritan divined with an impassioned vision of the moral sanctity of a liberal arts education.

My quarrel with my brethren is not so much with their vision as with their absolutism and their rigidity. Their unwillingness to adapt themselves and the curriculum they control to the changing environment of higher education has made them and their values an endangered species. Indeed, this intransigence may place the liberal arts themselves in some danger.

The Decline of the Liberal Arts

The history of higher education in this country records a continuing struggle between the proponents of career education and liberal arts educators. The very structure of our larger colleges and universities documents the battle lines, the uneasy truces, the strategies of encroachment and resistance. At one time, normal schools prepared the nation's teachers; technical schools trained the technicians required by an increasingly industrialized society; colleges of agriculture were established in most of the states to train individuals for what would become "agribusiness"; and whatever passed for pure liberal arts education was the province of the four-year colleges. Had all these schools providing career education been elevated, as were medicine and law, to post graduate status, there would have been no problem.

Instead career education sought baccalaureate status when education became the vehicle for economic and social mobility in a society that cherished the dream of mobility. The penetration of the colleges by career education was vigorously opposed from within, but behind it were the irresistible forces of a changing, democratic society. The liberal arts purists therefore chose to retreat up the hill of Carcassonne to the fortified citadel at the very top. The institutional result can be seen in the current structure of our larger universities: a liberal arts college surrounded by satellite schools of engineering and business, education and nursing, each with its own faculty and its own curriculum.

Defeat strengthened the citadel of the liberal arts—for a time. Because of their traditional prestige and the service courses they offered the satellite schools, the departments were able to grow. During the heady period of expansion in the '50s and '60s, the liberal arts faculty was able to maintain the posture of educational purists. The job market for Ph.D.'s was wide open, and it was easy to persuade students to major in literature or history. But when that market collapsed, the majors disappeared, and our liberal arts departments turned into service departments, satellites of the satellites. And with ever more students demanding career education, the liberal arts have become a serious economic problem for their institutions. Faculty positions that are desperately needed in career programs are occupied by tenured liberal arts professors with few students to teach.

Perhaps economic reality will induce the flexibility and adaptability necessary to survival, but there is little in our history that holds out much hope. Our response, for example, to the student revolution in the late '60s was typical of the way we have dealt with any encroachment of reality. The students informed us with searing slogans that we had become too isolated from society, that what we were teaching had little to do with their lives, their needs, the boiling social issues which they were facing. To a great extent, they were telling us the truth. We were educators only incidentally; our real career was our discipline, and our training had made us narrow specialists. We wanted to teach our dissertations, and we turned our undergraduate electives into duplicates of graduate courses. Our response to the student demand for relevance in the curriculum was to replace sophomore survey courses, in the name of freedom and reform, with a myriad of courses that allowed every specialist to teach that particular small piece of the discipline to sophomores and freshmen.

During the past few years, there has been a growing recognition by everyone involved in undergraduate education that the core curriculum, the basic exposure to the liberal arts, is in desperate need of revision. It is generally agreed that in the liberal arts program, the core curriculum lacks a rationale and coherence and in the career programs, the proportion of liberal arts should be increased.

Despite the satellite structure of our institutions and shrinking budgets, the urgency of reform might produce some surprising flexibility. English departments might finally get around to designing a basic curriculum that deals realistically with the severe writing problems of our undergraduates and that offers a sensible, exciting means of introducing students to literature. Even the social scientists might, through some miracle, get together and agree upon a group of courses that would provide a solid general introduction to the social sciences. But how, at this stage of our history, do we persuade professors in engineering and business that they should eliminate professional courses to make room for the liberal arts? Though most would readily acknowledge that their students require more exposure to the liberal arts, they would certainly not agree that over the years their curriculum has become too specialized, especially when substituting liberal arts might mean a loss of faculty positions. Liberal arts professors, too, may be ready to acknowledge that some subjects are more important than others in the core curriculum, but they are also painfully aware that a more rational distribution of requirements than now exists means a redistribution of the institution's limited resources.

The Growing Need for Basic Skills Instruction

But it is not merely a lopsided, incoherent curriculum that has resulted from the satellite structure of our institutions. In the same way that the four-year liberal arts colleges responded to career education, they also responded to the massive expansion of the student population following World War II, and with comparable results. In part the expansion was dealt with by establishing many new four-year liberal arts colleges, modeled, for status, upon the older colleges. But it was not the four-year colleges alone that undertook the challenges of mass higher education. A new type of school, the community college, became necessary to absorb the new students seeking higher education.

The demarcations of educational responsibility that the community colleges represent are based upon the illusion of maintaining educational quality in the four-year liberal arts colleges. Had the demarcations held, we might not be facing the serious problems that we do. But they have not held. The high attrition of students in the first two years of college has made most four-year colleges more and more dependent upon transfers to maintain upper-division enrollment. The majority of those transfers are graduates of the community colleges, whose transfer programs generally accept students who do not qualify for admission to four-year colleges. Many other students who do not fit the traditional mold are also in the liberal arts colleges. A drop in the national literacy norms and a relaxation of requirements at the secondary level have made high school averages an uncertain indicator of academic skills. Even our most selective four-year colleges are reporting that training in basic academic skills is increasingly necessary. Social pressures, exerted by minority groups throughout the nation, have forced many four-year colleges to admit students who, too often, require remedial work in basic academic skills.

Some Suggestions for Curriculum Reform

These are the realities for most of our four-year liberal arts colleges, realities that the curriculum must address. Fortunately curriculum is the responsibility of the faculty, and I can take refuge in my administrative role to sidestep being specific. But, as one who has worried about the fate of the liberal arts in American higher education, I should like to make some general suggestions.

An essential first step for those concerned with the liberal arts is an honest assessment of the realities of higher education today and the role of the liberal arts. Despite the fervent proclamations by our orators and essayists that a liberal arts education is a good unto itself, most Americans view higher education as a means of achieving the credentials necessary to pursue a career. The liberal arts disciplines that are attracting large numbers of majors today are those, like psychology or sociology, that may lead to human service jobs after graduation. With those few exceptions, if medical, law, and graduate schools did not require liberal arts degrees, the undergraduate liberal arts programs would be mainly populated by students who had not yet decided upon a career. And had the current job situation in higher education been similar when those who are now professors went to college, many probably would have opted for a career program.

We can, of course, continue to tilt at windmills and teach sixteenth-century prosody to seven students, or we can begin to deal with the facts and launch a campaign to restore the liberal arts to a central position in higher education.

That campaign will require not merely a scrutiny of the curriculum, but a penetration of the community colleges by opening up a real dialogue about the goals of higher education. There will be resistance, but there will also be a greater receptivity than our decades of snobbery deserve. Since the four-year colleges are dependent upon community colleges for upper-division students, it might make sense as a starting point to exchange professors with local two-year colleges to discover the problems and the nature of the programs that are so interdependent.

The goal of curricular reform must be the greatest possible exposure to the liberal arts for students intent upon gaining the necessary credentials for a career. Aside from the current movement to increase distribution requirements, there are other curricular problems that should be addressed. The liberal arts curriculum functions at three levels: basic academic skills, introduction to the discipline, and electives. We have no problem in convincing our colleagues in the career programs of the importance of reading, writing, and mathematics. Our problems at this level are our own. Most of these derive from our reluctance to teach skills courses, but in terms of curriculum, our courses are not sufficiently responsive to the heterogeneity of our student population. Each course should constitute a challenge, a real opportunity to improve skills. Too often, for reasons of economy or sentimentality, these courses are designed to accommodate large groups of students rather than to challenge students at the level of their skills.

At the introductory level, we are, I believe too tightly locked into our disciplines. It might well be that a general course in the humanities or the social sciences that could be taught by professors from several departments might offer a better exposure to the liberal arts for engineering or business students than a course in short fiction or sociology. And finally, if we are to integrate liberal arts into upper-division study, we shall have to make our elective-level courses, or at least some of them, less forbidding to the nonmajor.

Spending our time and energy lamenting the decline of the liberal arts may be good catharsis, but it is not helping to break down the barriers that our satellite structure and community college system have created in American higher education. If we are to develop the kind of curriculum that will provide a sound education for all our students, it is clear to me that the initial steps must be undertaken by the liberal arts faculty. Only by acknowledging the realities of what we have wrought by our intransigence and dealing with the realities of modern higher education will we begin the process of upgrading the role of liberal arts in undergraduate education.

19 Teaching Stylistic Competence

Louis T. Milic
Cleveland State University

As best I can determine, *competency* implies a testable recall of knowledge or possession of skill. A competent student is one who can recount on a test what took place in class; that is, a competent student is one who is able to perform a task deriving from the instruction received. Needless to say, the task must be more complicated than simply opening the book and reading the assignment, though some instructors would happily settle for that much.

The competencies approach can be contrasted with two others: the "process" or "student-centered" and the "heritage" or "text and culture" approaches. The process approach emphasizes the student's development in the grasp of the subject matter. Such an approach would appear to be best suited to the acquisition of a skill rather than a body of knowledge, since its main feature must certainly be the absence of any ordinary criterion of achievement. The student, that is, is rated according to personal progress, regardless of that of others in the class or of any standardized expectations. The heritage system appears to be nothing more than the standard method of presenting a text and facts about it and later asking questions that test retention and understanding of the text. If these definitions are correct, then the competencies paradigm must include a standard external to the student and the student's ability to perform a task rather than reveal or recall knowledge.

Each paradigm is thus best suited for a special task. The teacher of reading or composition may readily prefer a process approach, while the teacher of literature probably practices the heritage approach. If English consists of reading, writing, and literature, what then is left for the competencies approach? To answer this question, I must give some personal background.

The Stylistics Approach

Although I have taught English for many years, I have only
gradually come to realize that (almost) regardless of the title of
the course I am teaching, I always teach the same thing or the
same way. In literature courses I always find myself more interested in the language of the text and in the writer's style than in
the interpretation of the works. In linguistics courses I find that I
place more stress on the resources of the language than on the
linguistic system itself. In composition courses I devote more time
to the options available to the writer for achieving an effective
statement than to expressiveness, subject matter, or organization.
In other words my preoccupation is with "stylistics"—a recent
name for an old phenomenon—which entails the ability to *do*
something rather than merely to *know* it in an abstract or theoretical sense. I am aware, of course, that this admission convicts
me of a perhaps fatally idiosyncratic approach to teaching, but I
am resigned to it because it has at least the virtue of unity. Eclecticism of method in the instruction of English derives from a
fundamental uncertainty about both the value and the usefulness
of the activity (to say nothing of our ability to succeed in whatever our purpose may be). The approach I use has a limited aim
and a perhaps greater chance of success. I shall illustrate its func-
tioning by reference to its application in courses in literature.

Stylistics and Literature

Since the literature we study is in the student's native language,
how can we bend the student to the task of reading it with the
intensity displayed by the student trying to translate Euripides
or Cicero? Or how do we prevent the student from skimming
Areopagitica, the essays of Addison, or Burke's or Carlyle's works
on the French Revolution with a lack of concern for a complete
understanding of the syntax and a sense of the relations of its
parts? In other words the difficulty at the outset is clearly one of
reading, a problem that has concerned the schools as well as the
developmental reading clinics in colleges. I approach this problem
with a single but fundamental bit of theory.

The premise that aligns reading with understanding is that
writers, in setting down their thoughts, have available to them
certain choices, which are realized either deliberately or uncon-
sciously. The existence of these choices signifies that a writer
could choose any of a large number of forms for each sentence of

text. And, therefore, it means that the reader may rephrase any sentence of the text in a different way. Unless students can be made to understand this truth in the most practical of ways—by framing an alternative—they cannot be said truly to comprehend or be able to interpret the sentence or the text.

Let us consider a passage from a past remote enough to offer an illustration of the difficulties normal in any reading assignment. The prose of John Dryden is often described as the first modern prose in English and does not offer complexities like those of John Milton, Robert Burton, Thomas Browne, or the earlier Elizabethans. The passage of Dryden reads "No man is capable of translating poetry, who besides a genius to that art, is not a master both of his author's language, and of his own." The general sense of this utterance can be apprehended by any modern reader, though the use of *genius* will be puzzling. The average student, however, given the assignment of reducing the text sentence to a simpler form, will not know how to proceed. For the use of this student, I have invented a pedagogical device, called "Propositional Reduction," a method of proceeding systematically to simplify a text sentence. The principles of this method include the elimination of nonessential modifiers, reordering of the basic syntactic elements, substitution of plain for fancy lexical items or figurative language, and dropping of connectives (Milic, 1967, and Chisholm and Milic, 1974). Thus the reduced sentence (or "base") might read "The translator of poetry must have talent and know both languages."

By reducing the twenty-seven words of the original to the eleven of the "base," I have probably gone too far, but I wished to dramatize the possibilities of the method. Leaving aside for the moment the question whether the base is really synonymous with the text, it may be noticed what changes were made in the process. The double negative, the relative structure interrupted by the parenthetical *beside* phrase, the lexical items *genius* and *art*, and the parallelism at the end have all been discarded. Needless to say, there is not the slightest implication that the "base" version is superior to Dryden's original. Rather, Dryden's language and the habits of his style have been removed in the interests of comprehension of the text, understanding of the language of the text, and a glimpse into Dryden's own style.

These three benefits, the first of which was also offered by the traditional French *explication de texte*, I think are indispensable preliminary to any further serious work in any literature. Struggling with the vocabulary of the late seventeenth century, becoming acquainted with its idiomatic turns of phrase, and eventually noting its skepticism about the higher and more orderly rhetorical devices, along with learning about its subject matter, is a study that is both truly literary and conducive to an understanding of the times in a manner relevant to literature. Of course these benefits have different values for different students and kinds of students. Some teachers may be willing to concede that students majoring in English, foreign language, classics, linguistics, or philosophy might benefit from such a literature course, but most supporters of the present system would insist on the uselessness of a close study of the text for students choosing English courses as an elective. Our missionary duty toward them, it will be said, is to expose them to our literature in any manner at all. If they read Shakespeare or even Vonnegut, runs this argument, they will be better educated, whether or not they have any acquaintance with the mechanisms these authors use to produce their effects. This argument has a certain force, I acknowledge, though it is built upon two shaky supports: (1) departments of English must attract students with appealing (i.e., easy) courses and (2) nothing can be done anyway to raise the standard of literacy. I sympathize with the first of these, which is the unfortunate result of applying the competitive factory model to universities, but I have no patience with the second. It must surely be our objective to offer the most arduous courses of which we are capable if our purpose is to teach rather than merely fill quotas. If our students are unable to study in our institutions what they need to know in order to manage in a verbal society, they are justified if they rise up in fury against us.

Evolution of the Literature Course

In order to clarify the distinction between the sort of literature course I believe should be taught and the literature course as presently taught, it is necessary to consider briefly how the latter evolved. The literature course derives uncertainly from its predecessor, the course in classical texts. In the latter the main concern was that the text was written in a dead langauge, and the main difficulty was the discovery of its plain meaning. Thus *interpretation* signified *translation*. It was assumed that the process of extracting the plain sense from the aorists, protases, *orationes obliquae*, and the like would have sufficient impact to force comprehension. The study of modern literature in one's native language, on the other hand, offered no scope for such philological inquiry. Indeed, it seems not to have allowed any very specific sort of study at all; rather it fostered a variety of approaches leading to interpretation in the more complex sense of elucidation or explanation. Literary criticism has provided an intolerable profusion of approaches to literature: psychological, anthropological, sociological, musical, artistic, medical, mythological. . . .

Strictly from the viewpoint of interest or even of entertainment, such various fare is far from reprehensible. The disadvantage, of course, is that different groups of students who study, let us say, Romantic poetry, will not emerge with any common set of facts or ideas about the texts they have studied. Indeed, they may not even study the same texts. Unlike, for example, the student of mathematics, physics, or even the Bible, they could not survive an examination set by someone other than their own instructor. The inference that can be drawn is that the instructors are not certain what they are supposed to be teaching and are rather unclear about the purpose of the course. To say this is not to disguise the considerable difficulties in the way of a simple, coherent statement of purpose in the teaching of literature. Calculus, Sanskrit, logic, and behaviorist psychology confer on those who master these subjects the ability to *do* something. The study of literature is of a different order.

Let us revisit those students of the classics, working their way through Euripides or Cicero: What of their purpose? Students of Euripides have perhaps already read Aeschylus or Sophocles and are not therefore in need of lectures on the history of the drama in Athens. The process of translation has acquainted them with everything that might obscure the meaning of the text and impede their understanding. When they have made their translation, they understand not only what a given play of Euripides is "about," but also the differences between his vocabulary and syntax and that of others. Whether these students grasp the psychological implications of the mythology is doubtful, nor can we be certain that this knowledge would sufficiently enrich their understanding to insist that it be included in the syllabus. Similarly, students of Cicero's correspondence, rhetorical treatises, or essays could not fail to learn a great deal about Cicero, the Roman republic, and the state of letters in this period, but most of all how Cicero's use of Latin differed from the norm and how he achieved his effective-

ness. Somehow the philosophy, the history, the psychology, and
the rest all entered in the cracks of the paradigm, between the
scholia and the footnotes.

Consider now the current course in English literature, in particular the survey, because it is the prototype of the literature course.
Nearly always it requires that the student read a more or less
chronological series of texts and listen to lectures about various
aspects of the culture associated with the texts. The extremes of
the range are easily described: at one end there is the "new critical"
approach, involving primarily in-class conversation about difficulties of interpretation; at the other end, there is cultural background, which includes political and military history, current
social conditions, a survey of relevant art slides, music on records,
the reading of newspaper advertisements, and some contact with
the literary works themselves. Everything else falls between these
two extremes, and indeed many courses involve a bit of everything. Both kinds of courses can accomplish important purposes,
but it cannot be claimed that these purposes are consistent with
the study of literature.

What will students achieve by pursuing such courses? The usual
catalog description speaks of "acquainting the student with the
literature (great values, major authors)" of a period. It does not
say how intimate the acquaintance will be. The acid test, the
examination, tells a vague tale. The questions asked on final
examinations may request the student to discuss "the role of the
loyal friend in three of the works that we have read" or "the
influence of political events on the literature of the Restoration"
or to compare "the literary forms employed during the period
under discussion." These questions, the answers to which may be
important in graduate study, are hardly relevant if we wish to
discover whether students have comprehended the literature they
have (supposedly) read. Questions of this type can be successfully
negotiated without reading the works themselves, often by re-
calling lecture material or by using secondary study aids.

The standard "lit" course really conveys abstraction—abstract
concepts about the relation of literature to history and philosophy, abstract relations between a writer and his or her works,
abstractions about form and theme—but offers very little contact
with the text from which these abstractions are drawn. There is
every reason to believe that these abstractions are not retained.
Students cannot remember whether the Renaissance preceded the
Romantic movement, why either is called by its name, or what
works are related to either.

Apart from the fact that the training of teachers of literature generally does not include linguistics, stylistics, and other subjects likely to facilitate literary study and aside from the fact that teachers nearly always teach what and as they have been taught, the "lit" course itself is resistant to successful instruction. Consider, as an illustration, a course in the literature of the eighteenth century. How does the teacher choose among the myriad of works from this period? Usually the teacher does not choose, but lets Norton choose and then selects from the anthology. Assuming the use of an anthology, the teacher can present the texts in chronological sequence or group them according to genre, theme, or some other system. If the class reads all the poetry, then the fiction, and finally the plays, they abandon chronology, authorship, and history in favor of genre, form, and theme, which may be a step in the right direction, but is limited by the choice in Norton within any single period. A chronological reading leaves the student awash in abstraction. It is not clear why reading in chronological sequence is an aid to understanding in the absence of a substantial, accompanying body of historical knowledge. Reading *A Tale of a Tub*, *The Beaux' Stratagem*, *The Tatler*, and *An Essay on Criticism* in sequence will give no more insight than reading them out of sequence. The problem is really with the structure of the course itself, a bastard alloy of incompatible elements, not suited to be the only course in literature for many students in college.

The literature course I have discussed reaches only an insignificant part of its potential because of its emphasis on abstraction, its mixture of genres, its neglect of the text, and the necessarily superficial nature of its coverage. By comparison, courses given from a Marxist or a fundamentalist viewpoint have at least the virtue of a unity deriving from a purpose believed in by the teacher.

It is parity, on several levels, that the standard survey of literature course lacks most plainly. It is an axiom of any research rationally pursued that a number of variables cannot successfully be analyzed at the same time. To read a poem such as Pope's *The Dunciad* and to follow it with Gay's *The Beggar's Opera* and Swift's "A Modest Proposal" (all products of 1728-29) can lead to no sense even of what the readers of the period expected, since all three of these works are *sui generis* and were surrounded by a legion of other mediocre and worthless writings, which constituted a background against which these stood out. There is, in fact, a lack of thematic and generic parity even in writings contemporary with each other.

The influence of politics, which may be detected in all three of these works, is perhaps real enough to be noticed and to serve as a topic of discussion. But what matter if Swift's treatise on Ireland is directed at Walpole, who is also the villain of Gay's piece, if it is not understood how either work achieves its effects? It is the reduction of variables, such as genre, topic, period, and function, that leads to the sort of parity in which successful comparison can take place. Needless to say, analysis leans heavily on comparison. Unless there is a norm, deviation cannot be recognized.

Students without a literature background come equipped only with the norm provided by their own reading (whether it be trashy novels, science fiction, the poetry of McKuen, or the lyrics of Elvis Presley), according to which every text older than 1950 or heavier in substance than those mentioned will appear laced with unimaginable deviation. In other words unless students can be given a standard, they will sink in a sea of wonders, all of them incomprehensible. Today's students have a very thin layer of historical knowledge, much of it absorbed episodically from such incidental sources as film and television. For this reason the abstractness of the conventional relation between literature and history is unappealing and indigestible. They have an appetite for the dramatic, one formed and perhaps fed by the news and entertainment media. Today's students are also practical—inclined to prepare themselves for vocations and more aware of the need for competence in certain areas. They question the need to study poetry and to know about the abstract processes of language, but not the value of writing or reading with understanding. A course in literature should perhaps jettison its concern with higher literacy and exploit students' desire for practical knowledge.

A Suggested Course in Literature

Where to begin? Not, as is commonly done, with fiction, supposed to be attractive because of its story. To the average nineteen year old, reading *Roderick Random* differs not much from trying to understand *The 47 Ronin* or Lady Murasaki's *Genji-Monogatari*. The best material is the most familiar material: expository prose. The essay has a long history in English, from Francis Bacon to Art Buchwald and Russell Maloney. It is not likely to be mysterious to any newspaper reader.

Proceeding on the principle that enjoins movement from the customary to the exotic, the easy to the difficult, I would compile a list of essayists beginning with such moderns as Tom Wolfe, Joan Didion, E. B. White, and others found in modern anthologies. I would proceed back through Matthew Arnold, Mark Twain, Thomas Babington Macaulay, William Hazlitt, Charles Lamb, and perhaps Ambrose Bierce and Sydney Smith, in premodern times. The previous age is the one in which prose became the instrument we have come to rely on, visible at its best in the works of Samuel Johnson, Jonathan Swift, Edward Gibbon, Richard Steele, Joseph Addison, Oliver Goldsmith, among many others; before these are the thorny efforts of John Milton and Robert Burton, Abraham Cowley, and the rhetorical Thomas Browne and Francis Bacon. A selection of essays by the foregoing authors would offer the advantages of a single genre without being monotonous. Even within a homogeneous group of works, exclusion of variables should not be neglected. Greater parity can be achieved by careful grouping of subject matter. All essayists have certain topics in common (books, dress, life and death, the folly of their contemporaries) that furnish opportunities for comparison. Interest arises from successful analysis and the mastery of procedure. Even Milton's tracts can be full of interest to those who break his code. But a course in literature will not be better if it simply becomes a course in the essay. This is merely a good place to begin if the purpose of the study of literature is what I think it is. Letters, speeches, pamphlets, sermons, introductions, and dialogues are available from all periods and offer many of the same advantages as the essay form.

Earlier I cited a catalog description asserting that the purpose of a certain survey of literature was to "acquaint" students with certain masterpieces in their native language. I contend that such a purpose is insufficient and makes the course superfluous. Students can acquaint themselves with *Tom Jones* if they have the patience and the book. Acquaintance is an inadequate goal. I propose a more ambitious one, which offers at least the possibility of success: to distinguish between the literary use of language and all other use, which implies being able to tell literature from laundry lists and horoscopes and which is on the way to an understanding of what literature is.

Thus, let us say, one begins at the present with some simple examples of the reflective essay. Joseph Wood Krutch's nature works, L. P. Smith's *Trivia*, and Lewis Thomas's *The Lives of a Cell* are not simply expository prose, but rather a compound of fact and lyricism, which brings into focus the literary use of language. I have a favorite passage on the spring peeper by Krutch which makes an effective contrast with both an editorial on the same topic and a technical description of *hylas crucifer*. The purpose of the comparison is to discover what facts are presented, how they are arranged, what additional material, if any, makes the description literary. The answer is surprisingly simple and can easily lead to imitation, in the rhetorical sense. In the old rhetoric, analysis of the literary work provided the formula for another production on the same model, perhaps inferior to the original but recognizably related to it.

Among the shortcomings of the standard survey is the student's inability to produce anything literary. Some teachers, I know, ask students to attempt a sonnet, but it is an isolated effort. By contrast, the conversion of one form into another can be rewarding. I have asked students to convert "We Are Seven" into heroic couplets, to write a new Canterbury Tale, to make *The Rape of the Lock* into a short story. Some of the results were surprisingly good, many simply awful. But all who try it come to grips with the process of composition and are in a better position to appreciate the genius of Pope and other writers. For the same reason, I see a literature course devoted in significant part to writing, not critical essays about the works studied, but literary imitation. Without careful and detailed preparation, however, such efforts produce only wastepaper and are demoralizing to the writers.

Analysis by Comparison

The preparation I have in mind consists of analysis: the examination in detail of vocabulary and syntax of pieces commensurable in a number of particulars. I can think of seven kinds of literary material suitable for comparative analysis.

Seven Types of Comparison

1. The first is the same topic treated by two or more writers. Unfortunately, such examples are not easy to find, though certain obvious comparisons will always be available, e.g., between Gibbon's *History* and a modern one. Lyric poetry, particularly between 1570 and 1630, probably offers many examples on the popular topics of love and religion.

2. More common is the existence of variants of a text. These are more numerous for poets than for prose writers, but the latter also exist (e.g., Swift's *Gulliver's Travels*). More recently, copies of novelists' revisions have become available. A convenient collection of such examples can be found in Hildick's *Word for Word* (1966).

3. Numerous writers have altered their works substantially in later editions, sometimes completely rewriting them. Henry James and Francis Bacon come to mind at once. Bacon's aphoristic early essays contrast usefully with the Ciceronian later versions. James's reworking of his early novels (e.g., *Roderick Hudson*) is revealing, as is the contrast between his early and late styles.

4. Successive translations of the same work lend themselves to comparison. For example, there are dozens of translations of the Bible and the Homeric poems, some in very distinguished form. The diachronic aspect of a comparison of the same passage of the *Iliad*, as translated by Chapman, Pope, Butler, Rouse, or Rieu, makes the chronology of literature concrete.

5. A method of creating an artificial text for comparison is Propositional Reduction, described earlier. It has the advantage of requiring from students more than mere observation. They must actually analyze the original text, excise the superfluous, clarify the ambiguous, and, by reducing it to a base, attempt to discover and state its meaning. This kind of exercise can be done in class by individual students whose efforts can then be collated.

6. Corrupt or deceptive versions of a well-known sentence or aphorism can be presented to students with an invitation to select the authentic from the imitations. Despite the common belief that the original has an "inevitable" form (Strunk and White, from Milic, p. 249), it is surprisingly difficult to select the original unerringly. I have concocted some examples from Jonathan Swift[1] and L. P. Smith. Any teacher can do the same.

7. Analysis can be done by imitation. Imitation, in the sense of an effort to duplicate the style and organization of another writer, derives from the time of Quintilian as a rhetorical exercise. The instructor should select an essay (e.g., Addison's "Adventures of a Shilling" or "The Vision of Mirza") and before the students have read it, describe its structure and theme accurately, and then ask for an imitation of it. To be effective, this exercise must be preceded by an examination of Addison's method of developing an essay. Benjamin Franklin in his *Autobiography* describes how he became a writer by applying a version of this method to *The Spectator*.

---

[1] The following are three corrupt versions of one of Jonathan Swift's "Thoughts on Various Subjects" as well as the original, in no special order: "The power of fortune is confessed only by the miserable"; "Only by the miserable is the power of fortune confessed"; "The power of fortune: only the miserable will confess it"; "Only the miserable will confess the power of fortune."

From Competence to Traditional Study

It is unnecessary to describe in greater detail the particulars of the competency literature course I have proposed. The course is based on the belief that an understanding of literature means an understanding of the literary use of language. Therefore it begins with exercises graduated in difficulty from analysis to synthesis, which inculcate and demonstrate an understanding of literary-linguistic devices. Although I suggest proceeding from modern expository prose backward, I do not consider the method antagonistic to other genres, such as the short story, lyric poetry, and drama, though the treatment of long fiction, the epic, and stage comedy present special problems.

Students beginning a new subject may prefer to be entertained, but will profit more from substance than from background and abstraction. Once they have tried the literary use of language, they usually respond with some satisfaction at having learned to *do* something. As a result they can later deal more successfully with generalities. Competence in literature means being able to (1) say what any sentence in a work means, (2) point to the means whereby it achieves this meaning, and (3) discuss the literary nature of this effect. When students have achieved competence in these skills, they can profitably progress to the historical and religious backgrounds,[2] social conditions, and the history of genres. They will then be able to make sense of them.

References

Chisholm, William S., Jr., and Milic, Louis T. *The English Language: Form and Use.* New York: David C. McKay, 1974.
Hildick, Wallace. *Word for Word: The Rewriting of Fiction.* New York: W. W. Norton, 1966.
Milic, Louis T. *Stylists on Style.* New York: Scribner's, 1967.

---

[2] The link between literature and culture can be forged by attention to certain vocabulary items containing neglected allusions that occur especially in the occasional poetry of earlier times. Such lines of Pope as "Thieves, Supercargoes, Sharpers and Directors," "What made Directors cheat in South-Sea Year?," "South-Sea subscriptions take who please" are incomprehensible without some understanding of the curious events of the year 1720. It is out of the question to broadcast such knowledge as background, but it is not beyond imagination to suppose that students could be made to seek it if the knowledge had immediate application to a problem they were expected to solve.

20 Literary Tradition and the Talent of the Individual Student: A Heritage Paradigm

Hamida Bosmajian
Seattle University

The necessity to reflect on and to talk and write about the literary tradition of our culture no longer seems obvious to the college student. The literature teacher can no longer assume that there will be many intelligent and sensitive English majors to carry eagerly into the world the message about the depth and meaning of words in literary structures and to nurture and cultivate our language in their own use of the spoken and written word. Given our present social and economic realities, the teacher of literature must search out students who may be unaware that they have a need for the meaning in literature.

And why should we study the cultural memory of literature? Would it not be better to neglect a humanistic study of words written by people long dead and imbued with the patterns of neurotically repetitive compulsiveness that inform all art? Why not begin anew, name anew, and free ourselves from the past in a convulsive anticulture revolution?

Because it is impossible. Literary history is, in James Joyce's words, part of the "nightmare of history" from which we cannot awake. We, our world, are today what our world has been. Moreover, our languages shape and shelter us, no matter how we personally arrange our particular space within that shelter, no matter how infinitesimally our particular style may eventually alter the structure of language. The study of literature will continue to be necessary because of the forces of history and language and will remain desirable as long as we agree that the conscious and reflective human being is preferable to the unconscious and unreflective individual. As we study literary tradition, we not only rejoice over values and forms, but we also become conscious of symbolic structures and mythologies that have held us tenaciously for millenia, giving us meaning and boundaries, but also

223

imprisoning us. By becoming conscious of these structures and mythologies, we may perhaps gain limited control over their determinism and even enlist their aid in effecting imaginative breakthroughs toward new possibilities. I would say that the study of literature enables us to discover the compulsions and discontents in civilization—with the benefit of perhaps gaining some control. Literature is an especially suitable study for this because it introduces a reality principle into philosophy and puts human *praxis* in history in a contemplative perspective.

There is another reason why the study of literary tradition is a dire need. The word *love* defines that need, though almost all literature is about the failure of love. Just as an astronomer should not only observe and study but also love the stars, so the teacher of literature, no matter what techniques he or she uses to make literature accessible, should not only teach but love literature. What I mean by *love* here is the capacity for empathy that allows us to connect not only with what is like us, but also with what is quite unlike us. Like a shaman, we must learn to squeeze even into the smelly, slippery skin of the beast and thereby discover the destructive energy in us so that we can harness and channel it constructively. No other field of study allows us to develop the capacity for empathy to the extent that literature, with its polymorphously perverse evolutions, revolutions, damnations, and blissful epiphanies of the human spirit, does. The images of literature help students and teachers to discover their potential for good and evil. This search is a necessity. As Adorno (1970) argued, "Every person today . . . feels not sufficiently loved because no one can love enough. The incapacity for an empathetic identification was unquestionably the most important psychological reason that made it possible for Auschwitz to occur among relatively proper and harmless human beings" (p. 98). I am not implying that a humanistic education alone will prevent inhumanity; but I am suggesting that the history-conscious teacher can structure the student's learning so that it is not merely cumulative, but raises the student's consciousness and conscience, thereby contributing to the student's education in empathy.

I have reached the conclusion that the conventional survey of literature course neither purveys a sense of the totality of historical development nor intimates the breadth, depth, and interrelationships of several important and long-lasting symbolic systems in our culture. It is therefore necessary to develop alternatives to conventional survey courses to reach students who, while interested in humanistic studies, do not intend to become English majors. Seattle University offers those students two programs. The first is the Honors Program, and the second is the Western Cultural Traditions sequence in the university's Matteo Ricci College. I will discuss both programs at length, but will first turn briefly to two courses, Mythology and Children's Literature, which, along with the Bible as Literature (also taught in the English department), lend themselves well to an exploration of the roots of our literary tradition.

An Introduction to Literary Tradition

For several years I have been teaching Mythology and Children's Literature in an alternating sequence. Both courses are electives and have attracted students from many areas of study. Both have enabled students to overcome the "English anxiety" that is always evident at the beginning of the quarter. These two courses provide students with insights into the basic forms and meanings that generate multitudes of forms and symbolic systems. Almost all students have some experience with the content of these courses and thus are intellectually ready to recognize diachronicity and synchronicity in symbolic structures. I have designed each course in such a way that students slowly become conscious of the blending and layering of symbols and of the displacement of human fears and desires into mythological projections, which are in turn displaced into literary imitations of reality. A good text, such as Morford and Lenardon's *Classical Mythology*, supplemented with an interpretive study like Edinger's *Ego and Archetype*, and several carefully chosen examples from classical and modern literature introduce the student to at least some of the fundamental patterns that shape literature, the arts, and ourselves.

Similarly, children's literature reveals through folk tales—which I like to call "proletarian mythology"—and through tales of romance and realism fundamental patterns of human emotions and actions as well as the literary forms appropriate to them. The ultimately healing effects of romance and comedy are especially necessary to the growing person, whereas the overt and covert ironies of realism, as found in such works as *Little House on the Prairie* or *Sounder*, introduce the child to a tragic vision of life and to some recurring themes in American life and literature.

To make the student conscious of formal patterns and their psychological relevance, I assign three kinds of writing: a memory paper in which the student rediscovers that first moment of coming upon a story or image in children's literature, an analytical paper where the student shows a conscious grasp of patterns, and a creative effort where the student suppresses analytical learning and attempts to write a piece of children's literature without sentimental or moralizing impositions.

Matteo Ricci College

Much of my teaching at Seattle University is within Matteo Ricci College and the Honors Program, both of which are directed at the student who is unlikely to become an English major. Matteo Ricci College is a fully coordinated and integrated six-year program of studies, which begins with the traditional freshman year of high school and concludes with the granting of the baccalaureate degree from Seattle University. The college is divided into two parts: Form I consists of three years on the campus of a former preparatory school, and Form II consists of three years at a college within Seattle University.

The Thought Model Approach in Western Cultural Traditions

The course that I have been team teaching with my colleague James Parry, from the history department, is Western Cultural Traditions, a two-quarter course combining history, literature, and philosophy. Approximately thirty students come to us from Social Ecology where they have studied institutional change and value conflicts in the local community. They will leave us to enroll in a course that explores, compares, and contrasts the models and symbolic systems of several non-Western cultures. Along with Social Ecology and Western Cultural Traditions, the students take a series of composition classes—Modes of Reasoning, Composition in Language and the Arts, and Modes of Humanistic Inquiry.

All of these courses ought to introduce the students to conceptual models that shape and make comprehensible the *matter* of a course. In Western Cultural Traditions, we make the students conscious that we—teachers and students, as well as the thinkers, poets, and actors of history—are symbol-making animals and that we use these symbols to order our past, shape our present, and project our future. Thus in our study of the continuity, transformations, and revolutionary change in symbolic structures, we keep in mind Cassirer's (1944) statement that "in language, in religion,

in art, in science, man can do no more than build his own universe—
a symbolic universe that enables him to understand and interpret,
to articulate and organize, to synthesize and unversalize his human
experience" (p. 191). We teach students that all these patterns
have a diachronic and synchronic perspective, and we explore each
pattern in terms of its historical context and its significance to our
own experience. What evolves is students' increasing awareness
that thought models both nurture and restrict human development
and lead to conflicts between individuals and the community.

We begin with the problem of how human beings view their
collective autobiography and history and thereby establish from
the start that the study of culture is a combination of art and fact,
a selective and condensing process that reveals some truths about
human experience. Teachers and students keep in mind questions
such as: What happens to past or present human experience if
history is seen as a mere accumulation of events? How is our
reality different if we see human time teleologically? What
happens if history is interpreted in terms of "great men and
women" or through a cyclical or spiral model? What are the
consequences when human experience is projected as a dialectical
process in the sense of Hegel or Marx? How are historical action,
philosophical thought, and literary revelation affected when the
thought models are hierarchical, organic, mechanical, or evolu-
tionary? What are the results when a culture emphasizes community
or elevates an individual to be the shaper of destiny?

The thought model approach to tradition partially eliminates
the tedium of chronology for the student and compensates the
teacher for the frustration that "so much has to be left out." In a
sense one teaches a grammar with a minimum of vocabulary,
hoping that as the student's vocabulary increases, he or she will
be able to associate it with the right grammatical order and thus
think independently. My colleague and I have wondered to what
extent the seventeen-year-old student is intellectually mature
enough to perceive human experience through models and whether
she or he will not confuse the model with the "truth." Up to now
we have found that the majority of students do possess the
necessary maturity and that patterns and their relationships begin
to "click" for them, especially in the second quarter. It also
happens that they will insist on designating a particular symbolic
pattern, e. g., Marx's or Freud's, as "a mere model," especially
when they disagree with the content or feel threatened by it. On
the other hand, some antiquated models such as the Great Chain
of Being or the four humours and their elements are attractive

because they are esoteric. There is pleasure in discovering how
the Ptolemaic model applies to Dante's cosmos or how Desde-
mona's "hot and moist" hand conditions Othello's responses. And
there is surprise in the realization that the quaint model of the
humours can be related to modern psychological theories.

The Literature Program

Literature plays a very important role in the study of cultural
tradition, for literature in its depiction of human experience makes
theory ambiguous and inverts or infuses with irony established
and accepted symbolic structures. Thus it is through literature
that we frequently see how an accepted thought model is under-
mined and a new model generated. However, it is also possible
that a twentieth-century work makes us look back to the Middle
Ages and urges us to contrast and compare the transformations
of symbolic structures. In this way we discover that Dante the
pilgrim, while submitting to the hierarchy of the medieval cosmos,
is through Dante the poet more Faustian than Marlowe's Faustus.
Or the experience of Eliezer in Wiesel's *Night* shocks us into the
awareness that Dante's icy inferno of the betrayal of love is a
nightmare that antedates the historical reality of the concentration
camp.

While the literature teacher has to omit much that is cherished,
exploring literature is still an enriching experience in relation to
history and philosophy, and is delightful recognizing once more
the subversiveness of the literary imagination. Among the works
studied by the class as a whole or in small groups are Dante's
Inferno, *Everyman*, several Shakespeare plays, *Candide*, selections
from Goethe's *Faust*, Ibsen's *Peer Gynt*, Hochhuth's *The Deputy*,
Duras's *Hiroshima mon amour*, Wiesel's *Night*, Shaffer's *Equus*,
and Wells's *The Time Machine*. Hochhuth's *The Deputy* has been
used for synthesizing and questioning many of the patterns we
have studied. The play makes us rethink Dante and *Everyman*,
Rousseau's sovereignty of the people and their general will,
Nietzsche's notions of nobility, and Saint Augustine's earthly and
heavenly city. Students are profoundly shaken by the Christian
tragedy of Father Fontana in *The Deputy*, not only because most
of them are Catholic, but also because the play exposes them to
the reality of collective catastrophes.

Intellectual and emotional experience become integrated by the
end of the second quarter as the human rage for order and for
chaos are seen as competing potentials in each of us. Much of this

is personally experienced, for the emotion towards what one has studied cannot be taught; it evolves from the depth of the student's willingness to take risks. Such willingness and emotional growth, along with intellectual comprehension, are especially evident in the student's choice of topic for the integrative paper. For this the student chooses one work to concentrate on and then relates to it the subject matter we have studied. Thus one student told me that above all she had to understand the meaning of "the heart of darkness" as that image relates to the *Inferno*, to the experience of Marlow and Kurtz in Conrad's story, and to the idealist Riccardo facing the man without restraint, the Doctor, in *The Deputy*. A few quotes from her paper "Eternal Infernos" reveal how a competent and sensitive student was brought to new insights into consciousness and conscience:

> As both men travel deeper into reality, they pass a variety of lesser evils in comparison to what they find at the end. Marlow signs up with the "Company" which mainly controls trade with the natives. As he travels deeper into the continent, he must deal with the managers at the stations posted along the way. Riccardo is in a similar situation. He must deal with the church, the Pope, and the S.S. before he reaches the heart. Both men have to pass these stepping stones of evil before they meet the final evil, the King. Their journey is extremely similar to Dante's. Riccardo and Marlow both find themselves in a dark wood with the choice of either turning back to the safe, protected life or travel into the dark where there is only one trail to reality, the trail of evil. . . .
>
> Both of these men [Kurtz and the Doctor] were faced with a challenge from the ultimate darkness and had an immense fascination with abomination. They accepted the challenge and worked with what they hated and despised and, I believe, did what they knew to be morally wrong. They played God. They created their reality and ruled it. . . . They were challenging the silence in the skies to make them stop the horror they were creating. The Doctor wanted to be punished because, even though he would be damned, he would know the truth of God. Kurtz also asked to be punished. He wrote his pamphlet, "exterminate all the brutes!" This is a clear challenge screaming at everything. . . .
>
> For me, these two books shed a horrible light on man, one which I don't want to face but must. The most frightening thought is that these living Hells will probably continue to be created by man. . . . We . . . have created this kind of reality and are capable of doing it again and again. Marlow also acknowledges this: "The mind of man is capable of anything—because everything is in it, all the past as well as all the future."

Another student, who wrote about usury in the love relations in *The Merchant of Venice*, used a similar topic in the next quarter, tracing the use, abuse, and final explosion of the courtly love tradition in Ibsen's *A Doll House.* Since we began the first quarter with a casual and rambling discussion of a speech by Solzhenitsyn and ended the second quarter with a more sophisticated analysis of it, one student decided to discover Solzhenitsyn the novelist in *One Day in the Life of Ivan Denisovich* and show in his paper how the models of Hegel, Marx, and Lenin become inverted in that account. In preparation, this student read Bettelheim's *The Informed Heart* to show how in a coercive antiutopia the human being devises defensive structures in order to maintain the ego in an environment that threatens to swallow it.

The Honors Program

Matteo Ricci College presents a challenge but also a frustration for the teacher, who deals with a group of students who have known each other for several years and who are still very much under the influence of peer pressure. This does not apply to the Honors Program, in which a group of students spend two years together. The program is the heritage teacher's dream come true, without the problems of stasis that ideal situations are usually subject to. That stasis does not happen is due largely to the continuous self-critical evaluation of students and teachers. The core of Honors is a systematic, in-depth exploration of the development of Western culture from classical antiquity to the present. During their freshman and sophomore years, twenty to twenty-five students have seminars together in philosophy, literature, and history for four hours a week each. The program also includes four seminars in the development of science and one each in art and music. For the literature teacher this means that by the spring quarter of the second year, the students will have had five seminar courses in the tradition of literature.

Learning about tradition in Honors is not merely cumulative and not confined to reverence for the past. Through dialogue and through the development of increasingly sophisticated written expression, the student hones the critical spirit, learns what self-education means, and ultimately becomes deeply concerned with humanistic values and goals. Of course the great diversity of ideas, beginning especially with the breakdown of the medieval world picture, can and sometimes does become disconcerting to the intelligent student, who discovers that truths are not simple and who yet has a need to give shape to his or her experience. The student eventually copes with such existential anxieties by synthesizing to her or his satisfaction the plurality of possibilities in a personally meaningful "necessary fiction."

The study of literature in the Honors Program is consonant with T. S. Eliot's (1960) concept of tradition as involving "a perception, not only of the pastness of the past, but of its presence . . . . The existing monuments form an ideal order among themselves, which is modified by the introduction of the new (the really new) work of art among them. . . . The difference between the present and the past is that the conscious present is an awareness of the past in a way and to an extent which the past's awareness of itself cannot show" (pp. 49-52). Thus, as the student begins the study of literature, the Homeric epics and the Greek tragedies and comedies appear at first as self-contained expressions or as reflections of philosophy or history. But with the teacher's guidance, those early statements very soon lose their rigidity and vibrate for the creative reader as living expressions. I teach students to revere and submit empathetically to the text's historical uniqueness, but I also urge them to engage in a constructive rebellion against the seeming exclusiveness of the ancient images.

Diachronic perception of literature dominates the first year of study while synchronic perception dominates the second year, but this "dominance" is a matter of emphasis. It is here that the phenomenon of repetition compulsion in the form and content of literature comes to the fore. For example, we study Petronius's *Satyricon* as an ironic response to the *Odyssey* and the *Aeneid* and as diametrically opposed to the dignity of ordinary people in the contemporaneous New Testament; we relate both to Eliot's "The Waste Land" where the promise of the New Testament has remained unfulfilled and Petronius's landscape blends with the "Unreal City, under the brown fog of a winter dawn." The student is encouraged to see that the chronological study of literature allows us occasionally to detour or even to "tesser," that is, to complete a link across time and space before getting there by the regular route.[1] The student realizes that poets write because there is poetry and, as the student's skills in creative reading develop, realizes that "whatever

---

[1] This useful neologism is found in Madeleine L'Engle's metaphysical science fiction fantasy for children *A Wrinkle in Time*. In *The Anxiety of Influence*, Harold Bloom uses the word *tessera* (token, a password, a small piece of marble for a mosaic) in his discussion of completion and antithesis.

flames upon the night / Man's own resinous heart has fed." In the sixth quarter, the literary tradition seems to arrange itself around every work we happen to look at and is contained even in such fragmented and painful works as Borowski's *This Way for the Gas, Ladies and Gentlemen* or Handke's *A Sorrow beyond Dreams.*

Communications Activities

The Honors Program emphasizes the development of oral and written communication skills in all disciplines. In the seminar the student is guided to contribute relevantly, to listen carefully, and to engage in dialogue with the class. Lecturing is kept to a minimum. I resort to it spontaneously only when the discussion has reached an impasse that can be resolved through specific knowledge or evidence. First-year students tend to think that seminar discussion means "guessing what teacher thinks," but the growing realization that insights into a text *evolve* during a discussion affirms for the student in the second year that the discovery of meaning is a communal experience.

Besides seminar discussions, two ways of fostering this experience are readers theatre and paper conference groups. Readers theatre allows students to explore literature with their emotions and not just with their intellect. On a smaller scale, group interaction is also furthered in the paper conference group, though there are sometimes competitive tensions between group members. At the beginning of each quarter, the director divides the class into groups of four or five and determines the due dates for papers in each discipline. I meet with each group member to discuss the literature paper topic. The student writes the paper, duplicates it for me and for each member of the group, writes critiques of the other papers, and duplicates the critiques also. The student, therefore, writes not only for the teacher but also for the group. If a student, for example, chooses the topic "The Pity of War in the *Aeneid* and in the Poetry of Wilfred Owen," relevant poems must be included in the paper or appended and the readers given pertinent facts about the poets and their work.

The critiques are very important in developing writing, editing, and critical skills. Clichés such as "Your prose flows smoothly" are a temptation but the students learn to avoid them. Many a student has overcome writing problems by analyzing the writing of a peer. The critic looks far more objectively at another's text, and then becomes able to transfer skills and correct weaknesses. Having read and critiqued each other's papers, the students meet with me as a group for the two-hour paper conference where each paper is given twenty to thirty minutes of attention. These conferences are usually constructive because the students follow the same procedure in philosophy and history and are therefore much more aware of each other's progress than I am. Comments such as "This time you focused much better than in your history paper" or "You still have not quite solved the problem of transitions between contrasting ideas" are the rule. At the end I summarize and give my impressions, but the students do most of the evaluating, though they do not grade the papers.

I have not held paper conferences in the sixth quarter, for it seemed to me that by then everyone has become conscious of what is involved in writing a good paper. Instead I have urged students to write longer, integrative papers to synthesize their experience in literature over the two years and have received very mature efforts. Each topic has to be well-grounded theoretically and supported with carefully selected examples from classical or biblical antiquity to contemporary literature. Paper topics have included "The Metaphor of Hunter and Hunted" (from Euripides's *Hippolytus* to the film *The Deer Hunter*) and "The White Goddess and Female Individuation: A Search for Woman's Muse" (from Apuleius's Cupid and Psyche to Sylvia Plath). Some students chose to emphasize theoretical problems such as narrative distance, the phenomenology of space, or the problem of saying the unsayable. In each case the writer was conscious of synchronic and diachronic dimensions in a literary work.

As it does for Matteo Ricci students, the ideal synthesis, while much more complex in Honors, combines feeling and thinking. For instance, one outstanding paper explored the relationship between consciousness, repression, and pain in Western literature. The student, who was not an English major, grounded his exploration in the philosophies of Sartre, Nietzsche, and Marcel and explored ten works including the Book of Isaiah, Dante's *Divine Comedy*, and Lessing's *The Summer Before Dark*. He concluded that only these three works include the possibility of some kind of salvation as the questers turn "back to the people from which they have been temporarily alienated."

Conclusion

The elective, the required course, or the choice of a program with required courses all can awaken in the student the values and relevance of tradition. If the reader looks back over the topics of student papers, it is noticeable that all the topics relate tradition to knowledge of self. I had not intended such a convergence when I planned this essay. It just happened, but it reveals what the study of tradition is all about. The past is stories that can be told. As the empathetic reader connects with the form of each story, there resonates with infinite variations the message: I am, you are; you are, I am.

References

Adorno, Theodor. "Erziehung nach Auschwitz." *Stichworte: kritische Modelle II.* Frankfurt: Suhrkamp, 1970.

Cassirer, Ernst. *An Essay on Man.* New Haven: Yale University Press, 1944, 1965.

Eliot, T.S. "Tradition and the Individual Talent." In *The Sacred Wood,* pp. 49-52. New York: Barnes and Noble, 1960.

21 Student-Centered Teaching and Industrial Management Theory

Elizabeth Cowan
Texas A&M University

A number of years ago, two valued friends made statements that have directed my reading, thinking, and research ever since. The contents of this chapter can be traced to these two experiences. First:

> I remember sitting with Mina Shaughnessy one spring day in 1974 on a lawn in Princeton, New Jersey, and hearing her say, "You know, Elizabeth, it is impossible to know the disciplines of rhetoric and composition without knowing many other disciplines, too— areas such as linguistics, sociology, motivational theory, group dynamics. . . . We have to begin making the connections that cause us to see the whole."

Second:

> It is the summer of '75. Alan Hollingsworth is addressing a group of English department chairpersons at a seminar in Flagstaff, Arizona. He tells us that it isn't enough now just to know our own specialties well. A chairperson who wants to create a depart- ment that grows instead of shrinks in the 1970s and 1980s will branch out into many other disciplines. He suggests we start with industrial management; and his fascinating and scholarly talk that day introduces us to new words like *metagrumblers* and *eupsychian management* and to new names like Leikert, Argyris, McGregor, and Maslow.

This chapter was the stimulus for me to make some of the con- nections Mina and Alan were talking about. When I began to think seriously about student-centered teaching, many pieces began to fit together to make a whole. I saw that student-centered teaching in the classroom was like patient-centered care in hospitals which, in turn, was like the Scanlon Plan in business which was also like. . . . And the list went on. I began to look for the assumptions that all these had in common. I hoped, thereby, to show that student- centered teaching, rather than being an isolated educational phenomenon, is actually just one more manifestation of a particular philosophy about human relations already pervasive in business, industry, human services, and health care. Management theory proved the place to start.

Two Management Styles

A brief look at the history of industrial management theory provides the background for discussing student-centered teaching. In this historical review, two main theories emerge: Scientific Management and Participatory Management. Each reflects a particular set of assumptions about human relations and, in a larger sense, represents a particular way of seeing the world.

Scientific Management began in the early 1900s with the work of Frederick Taylor. The theory argued for a method of managing business that was based on scientifically determining both the flow of work and the limitation of responsibility for each worker. Scientific Management held that "management processes should be specified, that tasks should be measured and programmed, that responsibility should be 'commensurate' with authority" (this and following quotes are from Leavitt, 1964, pp. 327-339). Its tools were "job descriptions, work standards, individual incentive schemes, organizational charts, work-flow diagrams, and the other things that went with them."

The theory, however, had little regard for the employee. In 1911 Taylor wrote about workers in a steel mill this way in *Scientific Management:*

> Now one of the very first requirements for a man who is fit to handle pig iron . . . is that he shall be so stupid and so phlegmatic that he more nearly resembles . . . the ox than any other type. . . . he must consequently be trained by a man more intelligent than himself.

The mechanization of industry at the expense of the people working in it brought attacks from social reformers who felt Taylor was dehumanizing men and women (there was even a Congressional hearing about his methods) and from the workers themselves, whose rebellion took the form of "slow-downs, sabotage, pegged production." So, in spite of the fact that Scientific Management did bring increases in production for a time, some of the "unforeseen costs" of the theory began to appear. Leavitt reports that "under the influence of Taylorism organizations had indeed grown and prospered, but the human costs were becoming increasingly apparent. Human resistance became a major problem."

At the Western Electric Company in the late 1920s, a new theory of management researched by the Harvard Business School began to emerge as a viable method of improving production and showing concern for the employees at the same time. Leavitt describes an experiment set up to investigate one production variable, plant lighting, but which ultimately showed the effects of far less easily measured factors. The hypothesis in the experiment was that production would increase as lighting increased above the workers. Production did go up, but it went up regardless of whether the lights were bright or dim. The search for an explanation finally led to the social and psychological needs of the workers. Leavitt reports it this way:

> It turns out that the increased productivity was caused not by lighting, but by *attention*. These workers were now in a smaller, separate room. The environment was less formal. And a lot of other social and psychological factors were now operating that were much more difficult to measure and grasp than lighting. But ephemeral and intangible or not, they seemed to be closely and causally related to production.

What finally emerged from this and other studies was a group of theories that came to be called the *human relations approach*. In these theories the main focus moved from "rational models which ignored people's emotions to models which took into account the workers' feelings, attitudes, beliefs, perceptions, ideas, and sentiments." And as time went on, these general human relations approaches began to form the nucleus of specific management theories developed by revisionist thinkers in management. Of these new theories, Participatory Management was to have the most impact on American businesses and industries. As contrasted to Scientific Management, Participatory Management theory held that involvement in and enthusiam for the *group* would work almost as a substitute for authority. The theory argued also that it was extremely important for workers to be allowed to participate in the running of their jobs because people always tend to "support what they help to create." Various forms of Participatory Management began to appear, and many companies were actually transformed by the new management theory. (For a fascinating and amusing account of one such company, see McGregor, 1960, pp. 116–117.) Some aspect of the Participatory Management style is in operation today in most large American and many foreign corporations.

Theory X and Theory Y

Douglas McGregor, professor of industrial management at the Massachusetts Institute of Technology, identified two opposing sets of assumptions that inform Scientific Management and Participatory Management. In *The Human Side of Enterprise*, McGregor described his now famous Theory X and Theory Y. In his view the assumptions behind Scientific Management, or Theory X, led to a traditional view of direction and control and to ineffective group relations. Theory Y's set of assumptions, illustrated in Participatory Management, brought about effective group relationships and were characterized by an integration of the individual's and the organization's goals, McGregor argued. Here are the two sets of assumptions and the characteristics of groups holding such philosophies, as quoted or adapted from the work of McGregor (see pp. 33-35, 41-43, 47-48, 54, 232-241).

Theory X: The Traditional View of Direction and Control

Assumptions

1. The average human being has an inherent dislike of work and will avoid it if possible.

2. Because of this, most people must be coerced, controlled, directed, threatened with punishment to get them to put forth adequate effort toward the achievement of organizational objectives.

3. The average human being prefers to be directed, wishes to avoid responsibility, has relatively little ambition, wants security above all.

Characteristics of groups under Theory X

1. The atmosphere is likely to reflect either indifference and boredom (people whispering to each other or carrying on side conversations, individuals who are obviously not involved, etc.) or tension (undercurrents of hostility and antagonism, stiffness, and undue formality).

2. A few people tend to dominate discussions.

3. From the things which are said, it is difficult to understand what the group task is or what its objectives are. These may have been stated by the leader initially, but there is no evidence that the group either understands or accepts them.

4. People do not really listen to each other. One gets the impression that there is much talking for effect.

5. Disagreements are generally not dealt with effectively. They may be completely repressed by a leader who fears conflict.

6. Actions are often taken prematurely, before the real issues are either examined or resolved.

7. Action decisions tend to be unclear; no one really knows who is going to do what.

8. The leadership always clearly remains with the person up front.

9. Criticism may be present, but it is embarrassing and tension-producing. Criticism of ideas tends to be destructive.

10. Personal feelings are hidden rather than being out in the open.

11. The group tends to avoid any decisions about its own "maintenance."

About Theory X McGregor has this to say:

> The "carrot and stick" theory of motivation which goes along with Theory X works reasonably well under certain circumstances. . . . [It] is inadequate, [however], to motivate because the human needs on which this approach relies are relatively unimportant motivators of behavior in our society today. . . . People, deprived of opportunities to satisfy at work the needs which are now important to them, behave exactly as we might predict—with indolence, passivity, unwillingness to accept responsibility, resistance to change. . . . Because Theory X's assumptions are so unnecessarily limiting, it prevents our seeing the possibilities inherent in other managerial strategies. . . . However, so long as the assumptions of Theory X continue to influence managerial strategy, we will fail to discover, let alone utilize, the potentialities of the average human being. . . . It appears to be something of a tribute to the adaptability of human beings that [Theory X] procedures work at all.

Theory Y: The Integration of Individual and Organizational Goals

Assumptions

1. The expenditure of physical and mental effort in work is as natural as play or rest.

2. External control and the threat of punishment are not the only means for bringing about efforts toward organizational objectives. People will exercise self-direction and self-control in the service of objectives to which they are committed.

3. Commitment to objectives is a function of the rewards associated with their achievement.

4. The average human being learns, under proper conditions, not only to accept but to seek responsibility.

5. The capacity to exercise a relatively high degree of imagination, ingenuity, and creativity in the solution of organizational problems is widely, not narrowly, distributed in the population.

6. Under the conditions of modern industrial life, the intellectual potentialities of the average human being are only partially utilized.

Characteristics of groups under Theory Y

1. The atmosphere is informal, comfortable, and relaxed. It is a working atmosphere in which people are involved and interested. There are no signs of boredom.

2. There is a lot of discussion in which virtually everyone participates, but the talk remains pertinent to the tasks of the group. If the discussion gets off the subject, someone will bring it back in short order.

3. The tasks or objectives of the group are well understood and accepted by the members.

4. The members listen to each other. The discussion does not jump from one idea to another unrelated one. People do not appear to be afraid of appearing foolish by putting forth a creative thought even if it seems fairly extreme.

5. There is disagreement. The group is comfortable with this and shows no signs of desire to avoid conflict or to maintain superficial cordiality.

6. Most decisions are reached by a clear consensus.

7. Criticism is frequent, frank, and relatively comfortable. There is little evidence of personal attack, either open or hidden. Criticism has a constructive flavor.

8. People are free in expressing their feelings as well as their ideas.

9. When action is taken, clear assignments are made and accepted.

10. The leader of the group does not dominate it.

11. The group is self-conscious about its own operation. Frequently it will stop to examine how well it is doing or to discover what may be interfering with its operation.

McGregor remarks on Theory Y this way:

> There is substantial evidence for the statement that the potentialities of the average human being are far above those which we typically realize in industry today. If our assumptions are like those of Theory X, we will not even recognize the existence of these potentialities, and there will be no reason to devote time, effort, or money to discovering how to realize them. If, however, we accept assumptions like those of Theory Y, we will be challenged to innovate, to discover new ways of organizing and directing human effort, even though we recognize that the perfect organization, like the perfect vacuum, is practically out of reach.

Theory Y as Classroom Pedagogy

Theory Y describes the basic philosophy, attitude, and expectations of both Participatory Management and student-centered teaching. The manifestations of Theory Y in a college classroom are as follows. The class atmosphere is informal, and there is much discussion. The course objectives are clearly understood and accepted by the students. Both teacher and students listen to each other. There is room for disagreement; students and teacher alike are free in expressing their feelings as well as their ideas. Criticism is constructive and is frequent, frank, and relatively comfortable. There is little evidence of personal attack. The teacher, while clearly directing the class, is not authoritarian. Emphasis is on the process of learning; grades, while a significant part of the course, are not used as threats, weapons, or anger releases. The criteria for grading are clearly set out by the teacher before evaluation occurs. Students are encouraged to know they can do the work. The teacher believes that everybody wants to learn at some level of her or his being. The focus of the classroom is clearly on its purpose: learning the subject matter of the course. Students are praised as well as constructively criticized. There is enormous variety in the class; no two days are ever completely alike. Students are excited about learning; they experience joy as well as frustration and tension. Everyone in the room is engaged in a mutually beneficial task: learning whatever the course and teacher are there to teach.

This description is, of course, ideal. In my own classes—and I suspect in most Theory Y environments—some modification exists. My first preference always is to come from a Theory Y context. At times, however, I use the traditional church and military model of "authority from the top," when this seems appropriate. I also use persuasion as a means of directing the class and will even "sell" my ideas. However, I think I do my best teaching, and my best controlling, when I direct the class on the basis of the "authority of my knowledge," to quote McGregor's phrase. This is the control we teachers have as a result of placing our professional knowledge and skill at our students' disposal. The atmosphere in such a classroom is similar to the atmosphere when a person is taking tennis lessons: there's no upset or embarrassment because you can't already perform the skill or because you do it badly when you begin, and there is every reason to learn how to do it because someone is there totally at your disposal who wants to teach you how.

I suppose my management style is closest to what Morse and Lorsch (1973) describe as the Contingency Theory. This theory holds that the fit between the task, the organization, and the people requires a management style appropriate to and contingent upon what has to be done and the people who are doing it. The assumptions behind the Contingency Theory are something like the following (see Morse and Lorsch, 1973, pp. 401, 410).

1. Human beings bring varying patterns of needs and motives into the work organization, but one central need is to achieve a sense of competence.

2. The sense of competence motive, while it exists in all human beings, may be fulfilled in different ways by different people depending on how this need interacts with the strengths of the individuals' other needs—such as those for power, independence, structure, achievement, and affiliation.

3. Competence motivation is most likely to be fulfilled when there is a fit between task and organization.

4. Sense of competence continues to motivate even when a competence goal is achieved; once one goal is reached, a new, higher one is set.

I always intend that my students leave class with that sense of competence having been achieved. I want to enable them, to make them powerful when they read and write. At times I have students who have never been in anything except a Theory X environment, who are immature, or who think they are willing to settle with just getting by. In cases like these, I may have to start with Theory X, but my goal is always to assist students in experiencing the involvement and joyful satisfaction that come from achieving competence in the subject matter of the course and from expanding in a Theory Y atmosphere.

Course Content in a Student-Centered Classroom

What about the content in a student-centered classroom? A set of assumptions neither provides nor describes next semester's curriculum. If the student-centered approach leads to discovery, as Barrett Mandel says it does in the introduction to this book, what do students discover about? If it leads, as Barrett says, to confidence, what do students feel confidence in? There has to be some specific direction in the course, some "playing field" for students to achieve this sense of competence and success. That's where process comes in. I, personally, am not willing to wait for unguided, undirected "natural growth" to occur in my classes, mainly because I get paid to teach some specific subjects: writing and literature. I do believe natural growth occurs and that I can help to accelerate that growth. I also believe that as the instructor I have a direct responsibility for setting up a specific course of study that will foster growth and sense of power. I aim, therefore, for guided discovery and focused confidence.

A typical dictionary definition of *process* is a "systematic series of actions directed to some end; a continuous action, operation, or series of changes taking place in a definite manner; the action of going forward." Being a process teacher thus means that I decide what end I intend to achieve in the class and take the responsibility for setting up a systematic series of actions directed toward achieving that end. Although I set up a process curriculum in both my literature and my writing classes, I will use the latter to illustrate the systematic planning and correlating of subject matter with organic growth in the students that occurs in a process-oriented curriculum. I choose a freshman writing course for discussion for at least three reasons: English teachers, by and large, have more success in their literature classes than they do in their writing classes and, hence, probably have a less critical need for a process model in literature; writing breaks down naturally into stages which can be illustrated clearly in a process curriculum; and my area of research is the teaching of writing.

The Process Model: Teaching Writing in Sequence

Students are taught in sequence the three basic stages a writer goes through in producing a piece of work: creating (getting an idea), shaping (organizing, arranging, finding form for that idea), and completing (revising, correcting, editing, polishing the final version of the idea). Although these stages certainly overlap and are actually recursive, they nonetheless can be seen as the basic steps that writers follow. The process curriculum clearly distinguishes each stage and is organized to teach the stages individually before the student is expected to be simultaneously proficient in all three.

Such a curriculum begins with two or three weeks' emphasis on creating—on learning ways to discover ideas on any subject. Specific invention heuristics are practiced in class, and students experience the act of finding something valuable to say on a topic. The course never begins with instructions such as "Decide on a thesis sentence," "Narrow a topic," or "Learn these editing skills before you write anything." Instead, with specific, repeatable activities, students learn what it feels like to go after something to say and be successful at the hunt. These invention activities, unlike free writing and pre-writing, are not designed to loosen up the students or make them feel comfortable with the act of writing, although such benefits do usually occur. Rather, these creating activities are designed as the necessary and important first step toward a specific expository writing assingment.

In my own class, I teach a number of different creating techniques. Here is a description (from Cowan and Cowan, 1980) of one of the techniques, Cubing, as it appears in the handout that I give to students:

> Cubing is a technique for swiftly considering a subject from 6 points of view. The emphasis is on *swiftly* and *6*.
>
> Often writers can't get going on a subject because they are locked into a single way of looking at the topic. That's when *Cubing* works well. *Cubing* lets you have a single point of view for only 3 to 5 minutes; then you move on to the next point of view. When you have finished *cubing*, you have spent 18 to 30 minutes looking at the subject from varying perspectives.
>
> Do each of the 6 steps in order, spending no more than 3 to 5 minutes on each.
>
> 1. *Describe it.* Look at the subject closely and describe what you see. Colors, shapes, sizes, and so forth.

2. *Compare it.* What is it similar to? Different from?
3. *Associate it.* What does it make you think of? Times, places, people?
4. *Analyze it.* Tell how it is made. If you don't know, make it up.
5. *Apply it.* Tell what you can do with it, how it can be used.
6. *Argue for or against it.* Take a stand.

When you have finished all six, read what you have written. If one angle or perspective strikes you as particularly promising, you probably have come up with a focus for your essay. There will very likely be at least one thing you really enjoyed writing during the *Cubing* activity, something you felt some interest in or even excitement about.

The next few weeks of the course are devoted to the shaping stage of the writing process. Here the students learn (1) the difference between public and private writing; (2) the essential role of the reader; (3) the importance of knowing the purpose for the piece of writing; (4) the concept of thesis and organizing idea; (5) the concept of promise and delivery—letting the reader know what is going to be discussed and then faithfully discussing that and only that; (6) ways to develop an idea; (7) techniques for critiquing writing in order to learn how to do a better second draft.

Much of this content is commonly taught in freshman English. Unfortunately, however, many courses begin with shaping rules long before there is anything to shape. This inversion almost always results in canned subject matter (usually presented in three paragraphs sandwiched between an introduction and a conclusion) that makes no real attempt at communication. The essay is merely something written down to complete the assignment and get a grade. However, when the shaping stage is done in its proper place in the sequence, after the student has found something to say, it can powerfully serve the writer and the reader.

Here is a sample (from Cowan and Cowan, 1980) of the kind of information I give my own students when we move into the shaping stage of the writing process:

The Truth about All Audiences

1. Readers do not like to be bored, and they do like to be stimulated.
2. Readers have a hierarchy of things they need to be happy, and one of the highest is the need to feel achievement and accomplishment.
3. Readers want to get something out of what they read.
4. Readers resent being told something they already know, unless the writer brings something new or different to the subject.

5. Readers are busy people; they will not tolerate a writer who wastes their time.

6. Readers are often reluctant to read; they would rather be watching television or playing tennis.

7. Readers need to have ideas, opinions, information *explained;* they demand expansion and development of points so that they can "see" what the writer means.

8. Readers like order and hate chaos if it lasts very long; they need to be able to sense where the writer is going.

Finally, the course content turns to the completing stage of the writing process, where editing, proofreading, polishing, revising for style, and so on take place. By this time the students have learned to create ideas on any topic, to shape these ideas into a piece of public communication directed toward some real (or invented) specific audience. Now at this point in the process, they can concern themselves with such things as errors, revisions, codes of correctness. Putting these concerns earlier is inappropriate because students will not be diligent about perfecting something which they didn't even care about saying in the first place. By separating completing activities from creating and shaping, the instructor not only follows the old "divide and conquer" maxim, but she or he also sets up a situation for students in which each stage is much more likely to be learned because each is a specific action in "a systematic series . . . directed toward some end."

In my own classes, I introduce the completing stage by giving information (from Cowan and Cowan, 1980) like this to the students:

Why Completing is Necessary

1. Completing removes the last source of confusion. Things written in haste sometimes confuse a reader because the message is actually blocked by errors, gaps in organization, or inadequate development. The completing stage gives the writer a final chance to make the message totally clear.

2. Completing is a way of making the reader more receptive to your message. People do have certain expectations of a paper—they want it to be neat, to make sense, to be readable, and to have correct spelling and punctuation. Because that's so, some people see only the error, the smudge, the misspelled word, and fail to see anything else. You may not think it fair, but many people do equate mistakes with sloppy thinking. Completing gives you a chance to make the writing blemish-free and helps focus the reader's attention where you want it.

3. Completing is a way of making life easier for yourself. There are certain things that we all do because they are proper and appropriate; wiping our hands if they are dirty before we reach

out for a handshake; not talking out loud at a wedding; dressing up to go to a fancy restaurant. These customs or established ways of doing things are violated only at the person's peril who breaks the rules. If you don't observe the code, you produce a hassle. There are codes in writing: margins, titles, spacing, etc. It's just plain smart to check to see that you have kept all the rules. As a friend says, "Ride the horse in the direction it's going." Don't turn in work that is certain to produce a hassle.

4. Completing lets you say what you mean in a way you can be proud of. There is nothing like the good feeling a writer gets by saying something important in just the way it should be said. And it's impossible to check on this earlier when the thoughts first come rolling in. It's only after the words are "cold" that you can turn writing into its best form. Completing gives you a final chance to make the writing something you can be proud of.

After students have moved consciously through this distinct three-stage sequence eight to ten times during the term, they may find the stages melting into each other, telescoping, or even happening simultaneously. Writing is in the end a very individual affair, with the stages often occurring in unique ways for each person. Until students have had this practice, however, they often don't know how to get started, can't think of anything to say, and feel overwhelmed. They start worrying too early about whether the teacher will be pleased, long before there's anything to be pleased about. When everything is expected at once, when there is no sequence to the content of the course to make writing seem doable and manageable to the inexperienced writer (and almost all students *are* inexperienced writers), it's little wonder that students hate and fear freshman English before the first day of class.

The Process Model: Teaching Writing in a Situational Context

Situational context is another central part of a process approach to the teaching of writing. The process approach is not compatible with writing done in a vacuum—even if that vacuum is a classroom—because such writing elicits no personal involvement from the student and does not teach writing as an act of communication. Therefore, every writing assignment is placed in a context which determines the purpose and the audience for that piece of writing. Several outstanding authors have discussed the importance of situational context in recent books, and no one does so more dramatically than Ong (1977):

> To sense more fully the writer's problem with his so-called audience, let us envision a class of students asked to write on the

subject to which schoolteachers, jaded by summer, return compulsively every autumn: "How I Spent My Summer Vacation." The teacher makes the easy assumption, inviting and plausible but false, that the chief problem of a boy or a girl in writing is finding a subject actually part of his or her real life. In-close subject matter is supposed to solve the problem of invention. Of course it does not. The problem is not simply what to say but also whom to say it to. Say? The student is not talking. He is writing. No one is listening. There is no feedback. Where does he find his "audience"? He has to make his readers up, fictionalize them.

If the student knew what he was up against better than the teacher giving the assignment seemingly does, he might ask, "Who wants to know?" The answer is not easy. Grandmother? He never tells grandmother. His father or mother? There's a lot he would not want to tell them, that's sure. His classmates? Imagine the reception if he suggested they sit down and listen quietly while he told them how he spent his summer vacation. The teacher? There is no conceivable setting in which he could imagine telling his teacher how he spent his summer vacation other than in writing this paper, so that writing for the teacher does not solve his problems but only restates them. In fact, most young people do not tell anybody how they spent their summer vacation, much less write down how they spent it. The subject may be in-close; the use it is put to remains unfamiliar, strained, bizarre. (pp. 58-60)

Hirsch (1977) argues for the importance of situational context this way:

> The chief distinction between oral and written speech, when the two are considered from a functional point of view, is the absence, in writing, of a definite situational context. . . . Written speech . . . most normally secures its meaning in some future time, in varied and unpredictable situations, and for the understanding of a varied and unpredictable audience. . . . To speak or write is to project meaning as *understood* meaning, and this requires an implicit imaging of one's audience—a crucial point in composition teaching.
>
> [In writing] the absence of actual persons, speaking in actual contexts, requires the creation of implied persons speaking in implied contexts. This eccentricity of written speech creates problems which cannot be solved by the ablest of native speakers without practice and instruction. This is why one needs to be *taught* composition in one's own language. (pp. 28, 30, 31)

The problem—the need for situational contexts—is clear; what does the solution—the actual classroom assignment—look like? I first make up the situational contexts for the students' assignments and later assist them in making up their own. Of course what is important is not the actual contexts themselves but the underlying concept that they represent: writing is done by a specific person for a specific purpose and for a specific person or persons. Here is an example (from Cowan and Cowan, 1980) of the type of situational context I give my students early in the term:

> The elementary schools in your area are starting a new program this spring: Super Saturdays. Various volunteers in the community will work with the children in subjects such as science, history, arts and crafts, writing, and music. The idea of these Super Saturdays (there will be two a month for three months) is that the children can learn new things in an informal, active environment. The science group, for instance, meets in the park. The children signing up for arts and crafts will gather at a store that sells original paintings, drawings, and crafts. You love the whole idea and have agreed to be a volunteer for the _____ group. For the first Saturday, you are going to explain one aspect of your subject that you think will really interest the children. (One of your friends in history is going to explain the effect of the discovery of the cotton gin one Saturday and the meaning of democracy another. The person in arts and crafts says that he will begin by explaining to the children what weaving is, how and where it began, and the types of looms people use in weaving. The volunteer in science has several subjects in mind: why the sky is blue, why clouds have different shapes, what makes rain.)
>
> You are preparing for your first meeting with the children. Your group will be 10-12 years old. You want to write out what you plan to discuss. The essay will be the guide for your first Super Saturday discussion. Prepare the essay that you will later turn into a talk with the children. Use the form of explanation essay that you learned in school.

Sequence and situational context are just two of the components of a good process curriculum in a writing class. Nonetheless, they illustrate the essence of such a course: each activity, each part of the subject matter, is presented deliberately at the time and place it appears, as part of a series of actions that will cause the students to go forward in a definite manner to the desired end of writing well. The process teacher never takes anything for granted, never puts something into the syllabus, without thinking about its appropriateness for the time and place it is appearing and is always willing to take the responsibility for how much, how soon, and how often something is taught.

The responsibility is stiff. Such a content can't be handled by relying on one's past or on one's own teachers as models or even on one's beliefs that such and such are good for the students. In a process curriculum, the contents of the course must always contribute to the "act of going forward." Being a process teacher, then, means that I decide the class objective, based on the authority of my knowledge, not the authority of my place, and I work to set up a class environment and course content that will encourage my students to reach that objective.

Student-Centered Teaching as Context; Process Curriculum as Content

Finally, the two, student-centered teaching and process curriculum, come together. The first is actually a context for the second. Student-centered teaching, like Participatory Management, is a particular set of assumptions, a philosophy about human relations and working environments. Process curriculum is a specific series of actions informed by that philosophy and directed toward a determined end. The two complement each other, although the first, student-centered teaching, accommodates many other forms of course content, in addition to a process curriculum. The mutual influence of a Theory Y-based, student-centered philosophy and a process curriculum can be seen in the details of how I work.

I teach in a workshop atmosphere. When class begins, the students and I exchange "journals," pieces of paper on which we have written our reactions to the last class. We also begin each class with "foregrounds," one-sentence statements of what is foremost on our minds at that moment. I make sure, too, that the class always knows what sequence we are moving through at any given point and why.

We have situational contexts for every writing assignment. The students must indicate their thesis or organizing idea, audience, and purpose for every piece of writing they do, and the entire class gives a response, noting especially whether they can see any possible value or contribution to the reader in the proposed idea. When a paper is finished, everything done prior to the finished draft— all the creating, all the shaping—is attached so that I can see the entire process, from the first glimmer of an idea to the polished, completed final copy. All students are required to read their papers to at least one other person before giving them to me, and some students read their papers aloud in class.

The course syllabus provides time to respond to ungraded versions of all papers and time for revisions before final copies are due for a grade. I make sure that students know in advance what the criteria will be for their grades. I grade on a continuum that is cumulative.

The first paper, for instance, will be graded on three criteria: the presence of a writer's voice, the potential value of the subject for the reader, and the appropriateness of the writing to the purpose and audience for which it was intended. By the end of the term, all papers are graded for their success in all three stages of the writing process, creating, shaping, and completing. Even though the things on which I base my evaluation accumulate as the term progresses, I am never, at any one time, grading for more than three "new" aspects of good writing. I type a full-page evaluation of each student's paper and do not put any marks at all on the paper itself. This evaluation is attached to the first page of the student's writing. I put the grade on an index card and paperclip it to the back of the essay so that the grade and the evaluation are separate in location and, I hope, in their effect on the student. In class I ask the students to write a reaction to my evaluation and my grading as soon as they read them so that we can finish up with that paper and move ahead to the next.

I begin my course believing that all students can learn to write and can be relatively happy doing so. Writing never ceases to be hard work, both for them and for me. But what we do in class does bring competence and achievement. I teach for power in life, for the ability to write under any circumstance in the real world. I believe, with Jerome Bruner, that all students can learn anything, given enough time. Not having enough time is one of those things Carl Rogers so aptly calls "institutional press." The end of the term does win in some cases: a student just will not have had enough time to practice sufficiently in order to become a fairly consistent good writer. I let such a student know at the end of the term just how much and how well he or she has accomplished the objective of the course. I don't grade on effort; I grade on quality and achievement. By the end of the course, there has been enough teaching, practice, and exchange for most students to be at a decent level. When some aren't, I don't pretend they are. But I do acknowledge and discuss with these students the power of institutional press; I also take responsibility in some cases for not having found the approach that would have unlocked the writing process more quickly for a particular student. Even when every student does not become a superior writer by the end of the term, we all leave the course knowing that each of us has made a contribution to the other. The atmosphere in a student-centered classroom absolutely causes that to be the case.

References

Cowan, Gregory, and Cowan, Elizabeth. *Writing.* New York: Wiley, 1980.

Hirsch, E. D., Jr. *The Philosophy of Composition.* Chicago: University of Chicago Press, 1977.

Leavitt, Harold J. *Managerial Psychology.* Chicago: University of Chicago Press, 1964.

McGregor, Douglas. *The Human Side of Enterprise.* New York: McGraw-Hill, 1960.

Morse, John J., and Lorsch, Jay W. "Beyond Theory Y." In *Readings in Managerial Psychology,* edited by Harold J. Leavitt and Louis R. Pondy. Chicago: University of Chicago Press, 1973.

Ong, Walter, S. J. *Interfaces of the Word.* Ithaca, N.Y.: Cornell University Press, 1977.

Contributors

Hamida Bosmajian received her doctorate from the University of Connecticut and is Associate Professor of English at Seattle University. She is the author of *Metaphors of Evil: Contemporary German Literature and the Study of Nazism*, and is co-editor of *The Rhetoric of the Civil Rights Movement* and *This Great Argument: The Rights of Women*.

Ouida H. Clapp, Director of Language Arts for the public schools of Buffalo, New York, has taught English at both the junior and senior high levels. She has been recognized for her contributions as an educator by the New York State English Council which awarded her its Instructional Supervisor's Award of Excellence in 1975, and also by the Freedoms Foundation at Valley Forge awarding her its Classroom Teachers Medal in 1963.

Elizabeth Cowan received her Ph.D. in English from the University of Tennessee and is currently Coordinator of Graduate Emphasis in Rhetoric and Composition at Texas A & M University. She has taught at both the high school and junior high levels, is the author of several books and monographs, and has published numerous articles in various scholarly journals.

Philip Cusick is Professor in the Department of Administration and Higher Education at Michigan State University. He currently serves as editor of *Secondary Education Today*, the quarterly journal of the Michigan Association of Secondary School Principals. His publications include *Inside High School: The Student's World* and numerous articles in a variety of scholarly journals.

Eldonna L. Evertts, Professor of Education at the University of Illinois, received her Ph.D. at Indiana University, concentrating on the learning of language and the language arts at the elementary school level and its relationship to reading and composition. Currently, she is teaching courses in research in the language arts, linguistics for teachers, composition, and issues and trends in children's literature in the Department of Elementary and Early Childhood Education.

George L. Groman is Chairman of Humanities at LaGuardia Community College, City University of New York, and also a Professor of English. In addition to his academic duties, he serves as Director of the Office of Cultural Affairs. Publications include *Political Literature of the Progressive Era* and *The City Today*, as well as many articles on scholarly and pedagogical issues.

Richard E. Hodges is currently Director and Professor in the School of Education at the University of Puget Sound. He has been both a teacher and principal at the elementary school level and has spoken on the teaching of language arts at a number of professional meetings.

Ronald LaConte is Professor in the School of Education Curriculum and Instruction at the University of Connecticut and has taught at the secondary level. His publications include numerous articles in a variety of scholarly journals as well as *Challenges and Change in the Teaching of English* and *Teaching Tomorrow Today*.

Sara W. Lundsteen is Professor of English at North Texas State University and has taught language arts at both the elementary and middle school levels. Her publications include *Children Learn to Communicate, Ideas Into Practice*, and the forthcoming *Guiding Young Children's Learning*. She has contributed nearly 100 articles and reviews to such scholarly journals as *Elementary School Journal, Elementary English*, and *California Journal of Educational Research*.

Barrett J. Mandel is Associate Professor of English at Rutgers University and Director of the Cook College/Douglass College Writing Center. Under the aegis of the National Council of Teachers of English, he has published a book as well as several articles in *CE, CCCC, EJ* in the areas of transactional criticism, pedagogy, and the writing process.

Theodore Manolakes, Professor of Elementary Education at the University of Illinois, received his doctorate from Teachers College, Columbia University. He has taught in the public schools of New York and served on the faculty of Hunter College. While at Illinois, he has served as Director of Student Teaching and chair of the Department of Elementary Education. His recent work has focused on alternative curricular and program elements of the schools in the United States and Great Britain.

Paula S. Martinez is an Assistant Professor teaching language arts and reading courses at Wheaton College, Wheaton, Illinois. Previously, she served as a language arts consultant for a Texas Regional Service Center in the Dallas area, a classroom teacher for primary and middle school, an assistant principal for grades K through 6, and a junior college instructor of reading/writing courses.

Betty O. Mason is presently Assistant Professor and Director of Early Field Experiences at North Texas State University and has had previous experience as a primary school teacher. Her publications include *The Story of Joseph, I Go to School*, and several articles in professional journals.

Elisabeth McPherson has spent the past twenty-two years teaching at the junior college level and is currently writing and consulting on the teaching of composition. She has served as chair of the Conference on College Composition and Communication and of the SLATE Steering Committee.

Louis T. Milic is Professor of English at Cleveland State University. He was one of the first to develop computer-assisted stylistics in his *Quantitative Approach to the Style of Jonathan Swift.* Other publications include *Style and Stylistics: An Analytical Bibliography, Stylistics on Style,* and *The English Language: Form and Use.*

Walter T. Petty is presently Professor of Educational Studies at State University of New York. He is a member of the NCTE Committee on Teaching Written Composition in Elementary Schools and co-author of *Developing Children's Language, Experiences in Language,* and other books for teachers and children.

Lucille Shandloff is presently Senior Research Associate with Ellis Associates, Inc., an educational consulting firm. She was previously Associate Dean for English Studies at Prince George's Community College. She has a masters degree in literature and a doctorate in Administration of Higher Education and has published in professional journals in both fields and consulted in a variety of educational settings.

Barbara Stanford received her doctorate in Secondary Education from the University of Colorado and has taught at the high school and college level. Publications include over fifteen titles in the field of education, including *Black Literature for High School Students* and *Theory and Practice in the Teaching of Literature by Afro-Americans,* as well as numerous articles in a variety of scholarly journals. She is currently a freelance writer.

Gene Stanford is Director of the Child Life Department, Children's Hospital of Buffalo, New York. He was previously an English teacher at Horton Watkins High School in Ladue, Missouri, and Associate Professor of Education at Utica College of Syracuse University. He has served as chair of NCTE's Committee on Classroom Practices in Teaching English, and is the author or co-author of over twenty books in the field of education and language arts.

Russel G. Stauffer, Professor Emeritus, University of Delaware, is a lecturer and consultant on the teaching of reading throughout America and abroad. He was the founder and director of the Reading-Study Center at the University of Delaware and is author or co-author of numerous books on reading and the language arts.

Karl K. Taylor is Chairman of Adult Basic Education and Professor of English at Illinois Central College in East Peoria, Illinois. He is currently working on the relationship between thinking and writing under a grant from the Spencer Foundation.

Donna Townsend is Program Director for English Language Arts at the Texas Education Agency, Austin, and has taught English at both the high school and college levels. Publications include *English Language Arts Curriculum Framework K-12* and *English Language Arts and Career Education* as well as articles and book reviews in *English Journal* and *Ohio English Bulletin.*

Edmond Volpe, President of The College of Staten Island, is author of *A Reader's Guide to William Faulkner* and a number of articles on American Literature and higher education. Previously, he was Professor of English at The City College of New York and served as chair of the Department of English.

Dorothy J. Watson is Associate Professor of Education at the University of Missouri—Columbia. Previously, she was a classroom teacher and a reading teacher in the Kansas City, Missouri, public schools and has worked in inservice teacher education programs across the United States. She is currently working with Teachers Applying Whole Language (TAWL) to analyze and describe a first-grade language arts program built on a whole language model of reading and a process curriculum model.